ST RICHARD'S HOSPITAL AND THE NHS

An Oral History

ST RICHARD'S HOSPITAL AND THE NHS

An Oral History

Chris Howard Bailey

Phillimore

1998

Published by
PHILLIMORE & CO. LTD.
Shopwyke Manor Barn, Chichester, West Sussex

ISBN 1 86077 068 1

Printed and bound in Great Britain by
BOOKCRAFT LTD.
Midsomer Norton, Avon

CONTENTS

Dedicated to the Memory of

William Forbes Petrie Gammie, DL, MA, BM, BCh, FRCS
(1926-1996)

PREFACE

A hospital is a community in its own right, a microcosm of wider society, and people are the key ingredient in both its character and its success as a caring institution.

This book traces the social history of St Richard's Hospital from 1939 to 1994 through the oral testimony of people who served on the hospital staff. Spoken in their words, the text portrays the conditions of work, advances in technology, changing roles of doctors and nurses, and the increasing expectation of patients. Its insights capture the humour, adversity, disappointments, successes and triumphs over the years.

The book is dedicated to Bill Gammie who, together with Paddy Whiteside, initiated and inspired this work a year before Bill's death in 1996. During his 28 years at St Richard's, Bill contributed not only great surgical expertise but also the leadership and vision that helped the hospital to survive and flourish.

In addition to the people and personalities who have made up the hospital and built its reputation for innovation and friendliness, the professional excellence of the service has been nurtured and developed through a focus on postgraduate education. The Chichester Medical Education Centre, known locally as CMEC, has provided top class educational facilities which act as a hub of learning within the hospital and, indeed, the local medical community. The hospital therefore owes much to those who conceived, funded and developed this centre.

A significant proportion of the funding for CMEC was provided by the Dinwoodie Trust which continues to encourage improvements in the facilities for postgraduate medical education by offering independent trustees elsewhere in the country support for the construction of new centres or extensions to existing ones.

Like all projects, success is a reflection of good teamwork but two people stand out in the production of this oral history. Maureen Ward has worked tirelessly to co-ordinate everything from interviews to transcriptions and photographs; and Chris Howard Bailey, a social historian, whose recent work has been on naval history, has given voice to those within a hospital who would not normally be heard. The insight that results is one of which, I believe, Bill Gammie would have been proud and, despite great pressure of work, she managed to meet the deadline that enabled publication on the 50th Anniversary of the NHS.

ROBERT LAPRAIK
Chief Executive
St Richard's Hospital, 1997

St Richard, the patron saint of healing

INTRODUCTION

The 50th anniversary of the introduction of the National Health Service (NHS) in Great Britain is celebrated in July of this year, 1998. The history of that Service, as all other public institutions, mirrors the political, economic, social and cultural influences of its time. To chart the history of the NHS, therefore, is a complex matter and one which could be tackled on many fronts. Hence, it seemed timely, as an acknowledgement of the tremendous value the Service has been to the general health and well-being of the nation, to examine the history of one district general hospital, St Richard's in Chichester. This might provide, as a microcosm, a useful insight into what has been happening in one area of the National Health Service over the last fifty years.

St Richard's itself has undergone its own metamorphosis, as will be evident, from an Emergency Medical Services hospital, originally designed for the elderly and disabled, to one that has consistently been at the forefront of many medical developments, especially in the field of medical education. Indeed, it has recently (December 1996) opened a new state-of-the-art hospital wing, which will rival many in the country and possibly will be the envy of numerous others. I decided, therefore, to approach this topic using oral history, the testimony of eye-witnesses, as the most appropriate prime methodology for commemorating the work of a great number of individuals who strive under often very difficult circumstances to provide healthcare for all people. The past, of course, is never the past itself; rather, it is a narrative, a series of discourses traced through various transformations into recollections of what was and what is, consequently, now. This account, therefore, is a narrative, on all levels, by people attempting to give meaning to their work and life in a local hospital.

The Organisation and Re-Organisation of the NHS

Much has been written about the history of the NHS[1]; suffice it here, therefore, to give a brief overview. The government established in 1939, as mentioned, Emergency Medical Services in an effort to co-ordinate, under a Minister of Health, the treatment of war casualties. This established a central co-ordinated administration for hospital care in Great Britain for the first time. The success of this first 'national hospital service' indicated that such a system could work effectively. In 1941, Ernest Brown, the then Minister of Health, commissioned an investigation into the state of all the country's hospitals and how they could best serve the needs of the nation. In 1942, Sir William Beveridge published a Report, which addressed all the basic welfare needs of the nation and was to form the basis of the post-war National Health Service.[2] Beveridge felt, in part, that adequate healthcare for all was necessary for any improvement in the nation's general quality of life. In 1943, the Coalition government accepted the need for comprehensive healthcare and began negotiating with all interested parties. This was eventually, under the then Minister of Health Aneurin Bevan, to result in the 1946 *National Health Service Bill*,[3] which essentially proposed the nationalisation, under an appointed Regional Hospital Board, of all hospitals. Local responsibility, however, was to be delegated to Hospital Management Committees. After many detailed negotiations, especially with the British Medical Association which did not wish to see power vested in the hospital service, nor to risk losing the right to care for private patients, the National Health Service came into being on 5 July 1948.

The greatest achievement of the Act was to make healthcare available to all free of charge on the basis of need. Prior to the Act's introduction, healthcare was only easily available to those who were insured or could afford private healthcare. The NHS provision of services, however, into a tripartite division of hospital, local authority and executive council services did not work as well as had been hoped. This was primarily because the various interest groups of the three divisions had not been able to work out an agreeable compromise between their particular interests, values and beliefs concerning healthcare planning and delivery. Hospital-based values and attitudes dominated healthcare and there had not been an effective agreed liaison set-up between hospitals generally and those staff who were working in the community. Standards of care, therefore, were not universal.

Table 1: The Organisation of the NHS, 1948-1974

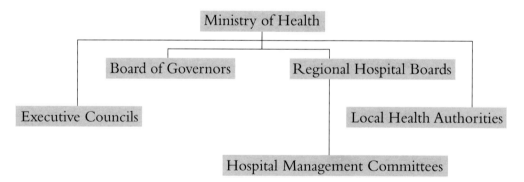

In part this was understandable. The NHS had developed dramatically over its quarter century of life to become, as services expanded, a complex organisation. By 1974, it employed over 900,000 people and was spending over £3,000 million pounds a year.[4] This growth emphasised the need for more structured and effective management. There had to be a way of utilising, in the best possible manner, the limited resources available for healthcare at a time when more and more people were expecting and demanding increased services. The ideas of Beveridge and his colleagues in the 1940s that there was a finite number of people whose illnesses could be controlled (indeed, healthcare costs reduced) with a set number of resources was no longer the case, and, of course, never had been. Medical knowledge had expanded; technology and drug treatments had expanded. More could potentially be achieved for increasing numbers of people. The question became, however, not how do we go about providing healthcare for all, but how could a nation continue to afford healthcare for all? It became apparent that the situation had to be evaluated seriously and available resources allocated in as fair a way as possible. A number of reports were commissioned,[5] and the government concluded that more effective management of the available resources had to be somewhat stringently introduced.

All the major decision-making bodies of the NHS were disbanded, therefore, by 1974, and replaced with new more unified ones, which more closely linked hospitals and their communities. This required a great deal of preparation, organisation and planning both prior to and during the establishment of new regional and area health authorities. Despite extensive plans, however, there was administrative disruption and the ensuing initial disorder produced some disquiet and insecurity, which took some time to dissipate.

Table 2: The Organisation of the NHS (in England), 1974-1982

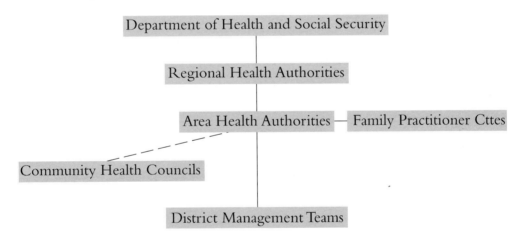

By 1976, the then Secretary of State, Barbara Castle, felt it necessary to establish a Royal Commission on the NHS to examine the most effective possible management of its resources.[6] A new Conservative government under Margaret Thatcher came into power in 1979 and had to deal with the results of this Royal Commission, which had taken three years to produce. Essentially, it praised many aspects of the Service, but it indicated that it had too many layers of authority and too many consequent administrators, which often slowed down the decision-making process and wasted a lot of money.[7] The new government, advocating monetarist theories, quite quickly proposed a new structural change. It advocated, in part, more delegated authority so that decisions were made nearer to patients, and that District Health Authorities be established, thereby removing the Area layer of authority.

On 1 April 1982, the second reorganisation of the NHS was implemented and then completed by the end of 1983. Each region was left to arrange its own reorganisation. During this time, there were many discussions concerning the underlying principles for free healthcare for all, particularly in terms of the viability of the privatisation of services. The cost of national health care soared astronomically, especially as advanced technical treatments became available, and the new government determinedly sought ways to off-set some of its costs.

Privatisation was encouraged, as was the contracting-out of services. Cut-backs and a new emphasis on 'value for money' and 'cost-effectiveness' became the order of the day. Accordingly, Mr. Roy Griffiths, the Deputy Chairman and Managing Director of Sainsbury's, was asked by Norman Fowler, the then Secretary of State, to set up an inquiry into the NHS.[8] The Griffiths Report noted that there seemed a lack of drive at every level of management in the NHS, in part because no one person was accountable for actions. Griffiths advocated appointing a general manager at unit, district and regional levels who would be tasked with improving the efficiency of the Service and offering a more dynamic leadership approach.

Table 3: The Organisation of the NHS (in England) 1982-1990

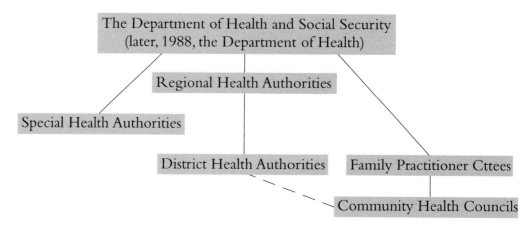

In June 1984, Griffiths' proposals were implemented. Doubts were expressed that this might lead to more autocratic leadership and undermine the impact of some groups, especially the nurses. Some also disagreed with Griffiths' criticism of consensual management. Nevertheless, a phased programme of implementation was planned and general managers were expected to be in place by the end of 1985. The Report also advocated that doctors should play a more involved role in management and should exercise more control over their budgets. The Report initially only covered England, but these recommendations were later implemented in Scotland, N. Ireland and Wales over a longer time-scale.

One of the general manager's first tasks was to develop a management structure. As there were different general managers in different hospitals, then there was a natural diversity of structures. Some worked better than others did. The impact, therefore, of the Griffiths Report was mixed both on national and regional levels.[9] Initiatives and directives from central government were immense and every general manager spent a lot of time responding to these directives rather than experimenting with new management procedures. The emphasis throughout was to keep within budget. Financial control became paramount. Essentially, hospitals were to become efficient businesses; and managers were to apply viable business methods to the health service. These were all shaped by strong political forces, which often constrained managers who also found it difficult working with disparate hospital groups. They found this to be especially so with some doctors as the nature of their relationship was dramatically changed by the new structures. Doctors saw themselves as essential service providers who were used to having control over their work; they did not respond initially as a group terribly well to losing any of that control. The general managers, on the other hand, who had been specifically tasked with increasing efficiency, had been thrust into this role at a time when the cost of healthcare was continuing to escalate. This necessitated them generally having to make some very hard choices about budgets and personnel matters. The emphasis was on accountability and fiscal responsibility.

In the late 1980s, in a series of White Papers, the Government advocated further reforms of the NHS.[10] These proposals essentially adopted the Griffiths reforms and advocated, in part, that local authorities become purchasers which enabled and co-ordinated the provision of services, providing some itself. These reforms were quickly passed into law in June 1990. Providers (Trusts) were held accountable through contracts with purchasers (District Health Authorities and GP Fundholders) who were able to use their buying power to achieve greater efficiency and responsiveness of services. GP Fundholders were given a budget that enabled them to buy from Trusts elective treatment, mainly non-urgent surgery and some other services, for example physiotherapy. This undoubtedly shifted some of the power base away from hospital consultants and encouraged hospitals to meet the quality standards expressed by GPs.

Table 4: The Structure of the NHS in the early 1990s

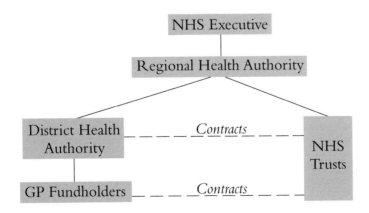

Hospitals, on the other hand, which had been directly managed by District Health Authorities, gradually assumed Trust status, which St Richard's did in 1994. This meant that they were independent entities with their own Chairman and Board of Directors who were accountable for strategy and financial performance. Trusts owned their assets, land and buildings, which they could sell in order to raise capital. At this point, also, all hospital staff became employees of the Trust, including consultants whose contracts had previously been held by the Regional Health Authorities.

By 1994, then, the National Health Service had changed quite radically from its first inception. Indeed, the vision of its original architects had been realised in many ways, but the full extent of what they had set in progress had not. The kind of world they had envisioned had altered so monumentally that whilst their basic tenets could still be adopted by many, their realisation had to be seriously considered. New drugs and advancing techniques fuelled increasing expectations over what could be possible, but the cost of that possibility was also escalating. Effective management of resources and the need to balance wisely between potential and reality are likely, therefore, to be of paramount concern in the healthcare of the nation long into the next millennium.

The Evolution of St Richard's

The surges of changes and counter changes that were taking place in the NHS generally were, of course, affecting hospitals, doctors, nurses, support personnel, and all those who had ever needed medical attention. St Richard's Hospital in Chichester was no exception. Chichester had had a long tradition of providing care for the sick and elderly extending back to the 12th century, when the leper Hospital of St James and Mary Magdalen was founded to the north east of the city at Westhampnett at the end of (Ho)Spitals Field Lane.[11] Another hospital in the heart of the city, St Mary's Hospital, St Martin's Square, was founded in 1253 and was said to be the oldest existing hospital building in Europe. A further hospital, Bartholomew's Hospital, Broyle Road, to the north of the city, was founded in 1626 by William Cawley. A public dispensary was established in cottages on the site of the Royal West Sussex Hospital, also in Broyle Road. The Hospital in Broyle Road was named the West Sussex, East Hampshire and Chichester Infirmary. It was opened in 1826 and extensions were added in 1840 and 1870. The Infirmary was renovated and reconstructed in 1910-13 and opened by King George V, who named it the Royal West Sussex Hospital as a memorial to King Edward VII. These hospitals were all supported by voluntary contributions. The Royal West Sussex Hospital continued to provide acute medical and surgical care on a voluntary basis until the National Health Service took it over along with nearly all the voluntary hospitals in July 1948.[12]

The West Sussex County Council decided to build St Richard's Hospital in 1937 as a long-stay hospital for the elderly and handicapped.[13] The Hospital was opened in August 1939. On the outbreak of war in September 1939, the Ministry of Health designated St Richard's as a general hospital under the Emergency Medical Services [EMS]. In 1940, 10 EMS hutted wards of 40 beds each were completed, bringing the total bed complement to 594. Mr. Douglas Martin was appointed Surgeon Superintendent on 1 August 1939, and immediately he found himself adapting the hospital to meet the requirements of a general hospital, including the provision of an operating theatre, not included in the original plans. The process of adaptation has continued over the last 50 years to meet the changing needs of medical and surgical care. A phased development of a new hospital on the site was started in 1969, only to be cancelled after completion of phases I to IV of an VIII-phase development. Over 15 years later, revised plans to proceed with the development were accepted. The new hospital was formally opened by the Duchess of Gloucester on 13 June 1997. What follows is a record of how a hospital, built to plans prepared by architects who never envisaged the speed of change in medical and nursing care, has managed to adapt the limited facilities to meet these changes and remain in the forefront of medical progress. It is a story that, to some extent, has been repeated throughout the country. Most of these adaptations, however, have applied to existing voluntary hospitals, rather than a County Council hospital which found itself outdated from the day it opened. Furthermore, it subsequently has been hamstrung by the apparent modernity of the buildings, which were constructed without consideration for the functional need of the occupants, patients, nurses and doctors.

The scene is presented in three time frames, 1939-1948, 1948-1974, and 1974-1994. These periods represent the broad changes in the organisation of the National Health Service over the years, as we have seen, from the direct ownership and management of the County Council, through successive reorganisations within the National Health Service management to the achievement of self management Trust status in 1994. Accepting that this outline has been chronological, it is felt that the problems faced by St Richard's over the last 50 years forms not only part of the local history of Chichester, but also part of the history of the National Health Service itself. It would have been too easy for the staff over the years to sit back and be dictated to from regional authorities, as happened in the case of other former county council institutions. This was never good enough for the medical staff of St Richard's, who, bolstered by the nursing and support staff, have fought over the years to maintain a centre of excellence. This they have done against all the odds, considering the degree of under funding they have experienced over several decades.

The Community of St Richard's

At the beginning of the National Health Service, St Richard's had three consultants and 21 other medical staff and by 1994 it had 69 consultants and 105 junior staff offering 26 specialities.[14] The enormous expansion in medical staff at St Richard's was instrumental in the major development of the hospital. With them came an increasingly professional nursing and support staff. All, of course, were influenced by the fluxes of organisational change, the changing values and mores of their time, economic exigencies and technological developments. As the NHS was established, grew and changed, so, too, did the hospital and its staff. The emphasis in the healthcare system shifted from being seen as a service which was designed to provide basic, essential healthcare for all, to one which was accountable and subject to the constraints of market forces, and, often, political ideology. Tangentially, doctors as managers were replaced by professional managers, often recruited from business or the military services. Emphasis was placed, therefore, on effective administrative, financial and medical management. This was happening gradually against a backdrop of fluctuation and constant change, at one moment expanding and then retracting; and at another centralising and then decentralising. Matching this tornado swirl of ever-present variation were developments in technological possibilities, not only in medical diagnosis and treatment, but also in the general environment of a working hospital. How the individuals coped with these challenges is, of course, the subject of this book.

As an oral history, an eye-witness account of the past, I have made every effort to balance the voices of the narrators. In many ways, this is an orchestration on my part as I have selected excerpts of long interviews and juxtaposed them in such a way as to present an historical interpretation. Inevitably, that interpretation is mine. I have made every effort, however, to be true to the narrators' own perceptions of their past as they have reflected on and articulated them to me. Twenty-six people from a broad range of jobs across different generations were interviewed over a period of two years. Three, May Burrows, Theatre Sister, Bill Gammie, Consultant Surgeon and Donald Russell, Electrical Services Manager, have died since I interviewed them. Miss Rice, Matron, died shortly after agreeing to be interviewed, but unfortunately before I could actually interview her. In many ways, though, this book is testimony to their life's work. For what we learn from the narratives, in part, is that no matter how difficult and frustrating the changes were that occurred, the staff of St Richard's always put the care of the patients, as far as they most conscientiously could, above organisational or political imperatives. They may now find themselves in a business, but it is the business of 'fixin' people up' and taking care of them, and this they do very well. This spirit of care prevails throughout the hospital. The challenge of the dichotomy between business and care, however, is, undoubtedly, to get the balance right. Perhaps, though, it is essential first for all to acknowledge that there is a balance to achieve.

If there is a voice missing in this account, therefore, it is that of the patients. It is as well to remember, it seems, that we are all likely to be, if we have not been already, patients at some time or another, and what constitutes hospital care is of fundamental concern to us all. We as readers are, consequently, the patients, and if we learn one thing alone from the interviews, it is that no matter how much technology takes over procedures of all kinds or market forces influence potential care, there is still an art to surgery and healing and that is not quantifiable.

Acknowledgements

This project has involved a great many people throughout the community, and I would like to thank them all for their generous support. Most especially to Bill Gammie and Paddy Whiteside who first asked me to develop a history of St Richard's. Paddy has long been engaged in charting the history of the hospitals in Chichester and, along with Bill, has guided me through the intricacies and history of the medical profession. Robert Lapraik, Chief Executive of the hospital, who must deserve a great deal of credit for the spirit of humanity and teamwork that prevails at St Richard's. His patience and wisdom must see him through a great many difficulties, which would perhaps deter others. Certainly, it helped him believe in this project actually coming to fruition! Maureen Ward, who has been instrumental in coordinating the myriad of details necessary for such a venture. Val Billing, Curator of Oral History and Sound Recording at the Royal Naval Museum, for working in her own time on the intricate art of transforming the oral testimony into a written one, and for her personal and constant encouragement when she knew I was fully stretched with other responsibilities. Jane Newman and Sandra Ford for their help with the transcriptions; Pauline Watkins, the Chief Executive's Secretary for all her assistance; Sandy Randle for her help with the photographs; Helen Stobie for her meticulous auditing of the oral history tapes; Wendy Cheshire for her insights. The staff at the West Sussex Record Office. The staff at the Medical Education Centre and Dunhill Library. Jim Bailey for carefully reading and offering comments on the manuscript. Gill Howard for allowing me to use her computer and supporting me throughout the project. Campbell McMurray, Director of the Royal Naval Museum, for supporting my work on this project and allowing me a mental distraction from my other responsibilities. A special thank you to my family, particularly my daughter, Cora, for enduring my long absences. Lastly, and most especially, I must thank the interviewees for graciously allowing me into their lives and without whom this book would not have been possible.

CHRIS HOWARD BAILEY
Chichester, 1998

Notes

1   See especially, for example: Christopher Ham, *Health Policy in Britain: The Politics and Organisation of the National Health Service* (Macmillan, 1994); Ruth Levitt and Andrew Wall, *The Reorganised National Health Service* (Croom Helm, 1984); Peter Spurgeon (ed.), *The New Face of the NHS* (Longman, 1993).

2   Parliament, *Social Insurance and Allied Services*, Report by Sir William Beveridge (HMSO, London, 1942, Cmnd. 6404).

3   HMSO, London, 1946 (Cmnd.6761).

4   Office of Health Economics, *The NHS Reorganisation*, 1974, p.6.

5   These included: Ministry of Health and Scottish Home and Health Department, *Report of the Committee on Senior Nursing Staff Structure* (Salmon Report) (HMSO, 1966); Ministry of Health, *First Report of the Joint Working Party on the Organisation of Medical Work in Hospitals* (Cogwheel 1) (HMSO, 1967); Ministry of Health, *The Administrative Structure of the Medical and Related Services in England and Wales* (HMSO, 1968); *Report of the Committee on Local Authority and Allied Personal Social Services*, Cmnd. 3703 (Seebohm Report) (HMSO, 1968); DHSS, *The Functions of the District General Hospital* (HMSO, 1969); DHSS, *The Future Structure of the NHS* (DHSS, 1971); DHSS, *Second Report of the Joint Working Party on the Organisation of Medical Work in Hospitals* (Cogwheel 11) (HMSO, 1972).

6   *Royal Commission on the National Health Service*, Cmnd. 7615 (HMSO, 1979).

7   Levitt and Wall, p.24.

8   *The NHS Management Inquiry* was published in the form of a letter sent to the Secretary of State, October 1983.

9   See Christopher Ham, *Health Policy in Britain: The Politics and Organisation of the National Health Service*, 3rd edition (Macmillan, 1992), p.34.

10 Secretary of State for Social Services and others, *Promoting Better Health* (HMSO, 1987); Secretary of State for Social Services and others, *Working for Patients* (HMSO, 1989); Secretary of State for Social Services and others, *Caring for People* (HMSO, 1989).

11 Jack N. Mickerson, MD, FRCP, 'The City of Chichester and its Contribution to British Medicine', unpublished paper, West Sussex Public Record Office, Acc.No. 8692.

12 William F.P. Gammie, DL, MA, BM, BCh, FRCS, 'The Hospitals of Chichester', unpublished paper, and private correspondence, nd; John 'Paddy' Whiteside, MD, FRCP, 'The History of Chichester's Hospitals', unpublished paper, nd.

13 For a detailed account of the history of Health Services in West Sussex, see: Peter Thatcher, *Now Another Pharaoh* (WSCC, 1988).

14 Medical Staffing Centre, St Richard's Hospital.

THE INTERVIEWEES

Robin Agnew
Served as Senior House Officer and later
Medical Registrar, 1953-1956

David Allen
Consultant General Surgeon since 1991,
but also served as Houseman, 1979-1980

Dennis Barratt
Laboratory Technician, 1948-1991

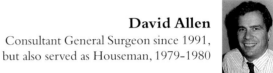

Judy Barratt
Laboratory Technician, 1952-1959

Christopher Bateman
Consultant Haematologist and later Medical Director
of the Royal West Sussex Trust, 1973-1996, and
Chairman of the Trustees of Chichester Medical
Education Centre, 1990-1996

Clive Bratt
House Surgeon and later Casualty and
Admission Officer, 1954-1956

May Burrows
Telephonist, Secretary to Crom Polson, State
Registered Nurse, then Theatre Sister, and later
Nursing Officer in Charge of Theatre, 1948-1982

Sylvia Dadswell
Staff Nurse and later Ward Sister,
1939-1941, and 1953-1978

Maureen Davis-Poynter
Member of the Regional Hospital Board and
Chairman of St Richard's House Committee,
early 1960s

Bill Gammie
Consultant General Surgeon, 1964-1991

Trevor Hayes
Catering assistant and later Catering Manager,
1967-present

George Jarratt
Deputy Medical Superintendent, 1943-1947

Zaida Jarratt
Wife of George and host to many social events at St
Richard's during his tenure

Heather Jeremy
Member of the WRVS who volunteered in the
Tea Bar, 1969-1995

Robert Lapraik
Chief Executive, 1992-present

Eric Lock
Member and later President,
Friends of Chichester Hospitals, 1973-1997

Jean Monks
Nurse and later Ward Sister, 1947-1983

Crom Polson
Hospital Administrator, 1948-1971

Lyn Robertshaw
Director of Operations and Nursing, 1991-present

Shirley Roberts
Principal Nursing Officer and later Director of Nursing
Services, 1972-1990

Alfred 'Bud' Robinson
Consultant Paediatrician, 1965-1996

Donald Russell
Hospital Engineer and later Electrical Services Manager,
1973-1995

Pat Saunders
Driver and later Transport Manager, 1942-1992

Marjorie Semmens
House Physician and later Consultant Paediatrician,
1955-1992

Eric Skilton
Office Administrator, 1941-1945, and 1948-1956

Paddy Whiteside
Consultant Physician and Cardiologist, 1946-1978;
later returned as a Cardiac Investigator, 1978-1985

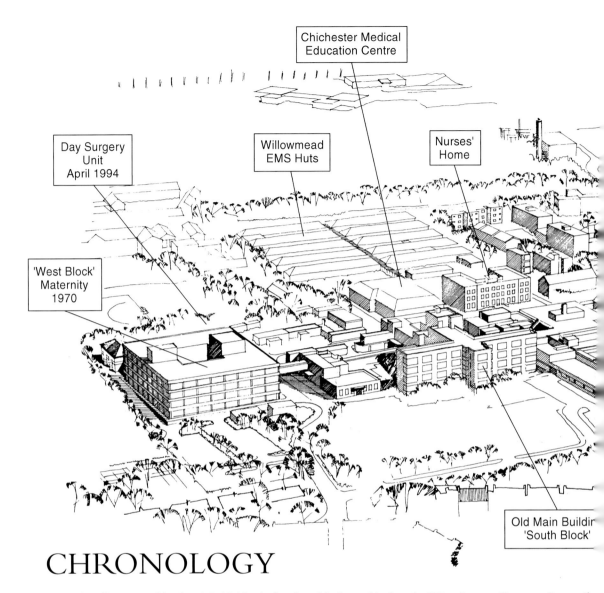

Chichester Medical Education Centre

Day Surgery Unit April 1994

Willowmead EMS Huts

Nurses' Home

'West Block' Maternity 1970

Old Main Buildir 'South Block'

CHRONOLOGY

1938-9 St Richard's Hospital built with 194 beds for the elderly and infirm by West Sussex County Council.

1939 Government declared it an Emergency Medical Service General Hospital.

Mr. Douglas Martin appointed Surgeon Superintendent.

1940 Ten EMS hutted wards completed with 400 beds. Full-time staff at the hospital were: Mr. Douglas Martin and Mr. E. P. 'Nobby' Clarke (surgeons), (Mr. George Jarratt took Mr. Clarke's place from 1943 to 1947 when Mr. Clarke was called-up.)

1946 Dr. John 'Paddy' Whiteside was appointed resident Medical Officer.

1957 Mr. Roger Miles appointed Surgeon to Royal West Sussex Hospital, Broyle Road.

1961 Twin theatre block completed to replace original theatre.

1963 Mr. Douglas Martin died. Mr. Bill Gammie appointed to succeed him on 1 February 1964, having acted as a locum since 5 November 1963.

Between 1963 and 1988 three surgeons covered all emergency general surgery at RWSH and SRH on a 1/3 rota.

1966 Postgraduate Medical Education Centre opened.

1968 Start made to transform SRH into a modern District General Hospital.

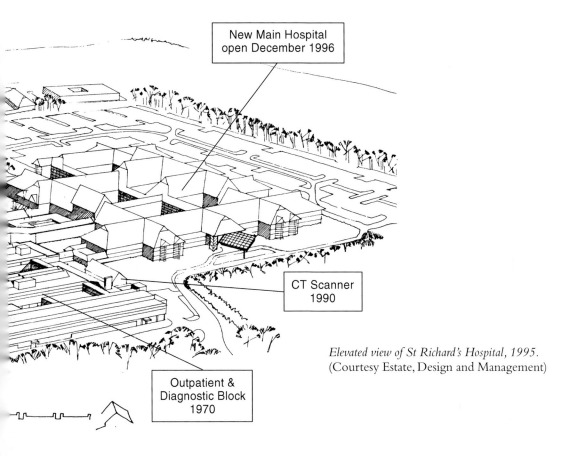

New Main Hospital
open December 1996

CT Scanner
1990

Outpatient &
Diagnostic Block
1970

Elevated view of St Richard's Hospital, 1995.
(Courtesy Estate, Design and Management)

1970 New Accident and Emergency Dept., Outpatient Dept., X-ray Dept., two additional operating
theatre suites and residential accommodation completed.

1970 60 maternity, 39 gynaecology, 33 surgical beds and residential accommodation completed.

1971 Further twin theatres with recovery room added with Theatre Sterile Supply and Central Sterile
Supply Units.

The theatre at RWSH remained open until 1973 and the one at Bognor War Memorial Hospital
until 1977.

1973 Royal West Sussex Hospital closed as a fully functioning hospital. It was sold in 1995.

1975 Barnfield House: Medical Handicap Unit completed.

1975 Donald Wilson House: Young Disabled Unit completed.

1977 Pathology, Mortuary, ITU/CCU, Recovery and Short Stay Ward, Medical Physics and
Photography, staff changing area, and extension to Boiler House completed.

1976 Intensive Care Unit opened.

1994 SRH achieves Trust status.

1994 Day Surgery Unit opened.

1996 SRH awarded Charter Mark.

1996 New SRH wing opened to patients.

I
———

1939–1948

THE CHALLENGE

St Richard's Before the NHS

THE YEARS 1939-48 provided the greatest challenge for St Richard's. The County Council had had long experience in managing the care of a diverse number of medical institutions and types of patients. It looked after the mentally ill at the West Sussex Mental Hospital, Graylingwell, with its 1,074 beds; it cared for patients with tuberculosis at Aldingbourne Sanatorium; and it provided maternity care at Zachary Merton Maternity home at Rustington. The Urban and Rural District Councils ran the isolation hospitals at Chichester, Bognor Regis and part of Swandean, and the concept for St Richard's was that it should replace the 'infirmary' wards in the public assistance institutions.

The start of war in 1939 precipitated the opening of St Richard's, which at that time was still a shell of a building not properly fitted out. It had been built with large airy wards facing south with nursing stations and a day room in the spine. Toilet and bathing facilities were minimal, it being considered that few patients would be ambulant. There was no operating theatre, no radiology, outpatients or casualty department and the pathology department was located in County Hall. The early staff, like Sylvia Dadswell, the first nurse at St Richard's, had to cope with moving into a new unfinished hospital in wartime whilst simultaneously getting the necessary equipment and supplies together. They were extremely short-staffed, for obvious reasons, and they had great difficulty managing to keep the hospital going and coping with the great influx of patients, many of whom were war casualties or prisoners of war. The addition of 400 EMS beds in the hutted wards at St Richard's to the 194 beds in the main block placed a heavy burden on the limited medical staff of two full-time surgeons and one junior doctor, joined by a physician, Dr. John 'Paddy' Whiteside, in 1946. There was one junior medical member of staff. This small team dealt with the pressures of suddenly finding the Hospital in the front line during the war years, acting as a back up to the Portsmouth hospitals during the D-Day landings. Nevertheless, under the authoritative but determined and, in retrospect, paternal leadership of Douglas Martin, they coped under extreme circumstances with very basic tools for survival both in the conditions they worked under and the treatments and technologies they had available to them. These did not radically change until the introduction of the National Health Service in 1948. Perhaps what helped, to some extent, in the staff's ability to cope under adversity was the fact that there was a war and that they had strict social and moral codes which bound them together. These most clearly defined who they were and what role they were expected to play. These moral and social expectations were only regularly questioned in the carefully scripted Christmas pantomime they looked forward to each year.

'Just a shell'

THE ENVIRONMENT

6 When St Richard's was built, it was just a shell. There were no beds, no staff. I was the first nurse there for about forty-eight hours. There was an Assistant Matron, and no beds, nothing. The hospital was just an empty building. We had to do everything. We made beds, you know, you can imagine. We just started to get the place organised 9 *(Sylvia Dadswell, Ward Sister)*

Sylvia Dadswell (née Halfacrée) was the first nurse to arrive at St Richard's shortly before it opened. She and some of the other early workers such as Eric Skilton the office boy, Pat Saunders the Van boy, and George Jarratt the Deputy Superintendent, spent the arduous war years trying to get the hospital to work while at the same time coping with the influx of new patients, many of whom were casualties of the war. They had a very difficult time improvising with whatever they could. Even getting food and adequate heating was troublesome. When D-Day came, they were prepared to take as many injured as they could, and the staff from that time remember caring for our own war wounded as well as prisoners of war.

Paddy Whiteside

St Richard's was greatly resented by the Royal West Sussex Hospital, which was founded in 1784 as the Chichester Dispensary, and later was fully re-built in 1825 by John Forbes, who became Sir John Forbes and the Queen's physician. Then in 1913 it became the Royal West Sussex. It had always been high-class, well looked after by the GPs, surgeons and physicians and attended by the aristocracy and the wealthy people in the town. The social event of the year was always the Royal West Sussex Hospital dance, which was attended by everyone, particularly by the Officers of the Royal Sussex Regiment. And there was a certain amount of resentment.

When St Richard's Hospital was built by the County Council it was initially to be a hospital for the disabled and poor people but, with the war coming and on Government orders, it was made into a general hospital. There was a certain amount of friction, but fortunately not on the medical side, but with certain people it was nick-named *Dirty Dick's*. There was no problem about all the doctors of both hospitals attending patients in the other hospital. A hospital like St Richard's was a

Aerial view of St Richard's Hospital, 1939. [Courtesy: Eric Skilton]

county hospital, and was financed by the West Sussex County Council. The Royal West Sussex Hospital was a voluntary hospital and was run entirely on charity contributions and also the patients were asked to pay what they could afford for their hospital treatment.

Clive Bratt

The Royal West was the old hospital, and St Richard's was the new hospital. And because it was thought to be a geriatric hospital, even when I came into practice, people said, 'Can't I go to the Royal West; I don't want to go to St Richard's, that's where you die.' So there was quite a resistance and quite a lot of rivalry between the two hospitals.

Eric Skilton

St Richard's was a single building, which had been designed to have a hospital block containing 200 beds. The object was that they would also build another block, which would be a surgical block, but, of course, with the outbreak of war it was rushed open and there was just the one block. When I joined it in 1941, even at my young age, there was a stigma about this hospital being a council hospital. The Royal West Sussex was the élite hospital and everybody was dubious about St Richard's. Only the poor would go there.

Hospital Superintendent's House, c.1939. [Courtesy: Eric Skilton]

George Jarratt

St Richard's was a beautiful modern hospital, and it was the nicest planned hospital I saw for many, many years. We had the four floors, one, two, three, four. I don't know what the block is called now, but that was the hospital, which had attached to it 10 EMS huts, one to ten, numbered one to ten. There wasn't anything else apart from the two houses, our little Lodge, and Douglas Martin's house, which was far away on the Graylingwell side, behind the Nurses' Home.

Sylvia Dadswell

When St Richard's was built, it was just a shell. There were no beds, no staff. I was the first nurse there for about forty-eight hours. There was an Assistant Matron, and no beds, nothing. The hospital was just an empty building. We had to do everything. We made beds, you know, you can imagine. We just started to get the place organised. In the beginning there was only me and I think some domestic staff, cleaners and general workers. Then other nurses arrived quite shortly afterwards. I can remember that one or two of them were London School nurses who were evacuated. I can't remember their names really. Then things sort of snowballed slowly. At first, of course, the wards were empty; there were no beds. It was a lovely building, but the windows were bricked in for blast protection and just the top fanlight allowed in air. All the rest was full of bricks and the outside was built in with wood. Rough un-planed wood. You had to be careful, if you knocked your elbow against it you took the skin off. Mr. Martin said to me, 'This is built as a Medical Unit, but I'm a surgeon and they've promised me that there are enough bricks in these windows to build my Surgical

Unit.' Because he really was a surgeon, not a physician. I mean he was a medical superintendent but he really was a surgeon. And very quickly they got beds. The equipment was sort of stood around in piles. There were bedsteads. There was one room, a storeroom as big as this lounge, full of blankets from the floor to the ceiling. I can smell them now. We had to sort them all out. I remember they were in piles and they all sort of fell down and we were mountaineering over the blankets. They were nice, proper, woolly blankets. They didn't last long, but they were there. We got beds made up with all sorts of porters and people, you know, just got beds made up. Surgical patients on Ward 1—men. Surgical women on Ward 2, medical women on Ward 3, and children—Halstead was children and medical women. And Baxendale was medical male—Ward 4 that was in those days. And that was the hospital; that's all there was.

Then later they built the huts. That must have been, I suppose, a year later. Temporary huts to be built for the duration of the war or ten years as a maximum— they're still there. And we made the theatre in Ward 1. We put in an extra sink. There was no changing room for the surgeons or anything like that. No anaesthetic room. We had a little office sort of place outside, but we had a pile of drums and a curtain in the front, and that was the surgeon's dressing room. That's where they got dressed. They did all sorts of emergency things in the theatre, with precious little equipment. Yes, the equipment we didn't have is more to the point.

We had to get more beds, though. There was never enough beds. They were always sort of saying—well I must admit this—'This is an emergency!' So we just used to have extra beds put up. Originally, I think each ward was supposed to be for 24 beds, or even 18, and two wards per floor, I'm not sure. But, of course, that didn't work. There was a row of beds, and I think that was divided into three sort of bays, and I think the partitions have been taken out now. But, you know, if a patient came in needing to be put to bed somewhere you just had to find a bed.

St Richard's Hospital, main entrance, 1939. [Courtesy: Eric Skilton]

Then, of course, the war started. I suppose it was several months before we started having casualties. There were not enough beds; there were no furnishings; there was no equipment; there was no cruet in the nurses' dining room. In fact, I don't know that there were chairs originally in the nurses' dining room. It was all brand new. I was a Ward Sister for a little while in one of the huts. I delivered the first baby that was at St Richard's. This woman came in—because the war was on things were not organised properly in the outside world, you know; there were terrific sort of emergencies going on all the time—and this lady came in to St Richard's in the advanced stages of labour, and I don't think she'd booked up anywhere to go and have this baby, and Mr. Martin said, 'Well, find a side ward—you've done your midder [midwife's course], haven't you?' I said, 'Yes', and he said, 'Well, find a side ward and get on with it.' So we did. We just found an empty bed in an empty side ward and delivered this baby. It was about her fourth baby so there was no drama, no problems.

Pat Saunders

My working career in the hospital started off, really, in March 1942, when I went to Central Laundry, which was the Hospital Laundry that was run by West Sussex County Council. We sort of serviced the local hospitals. We also took in nursing homes, maternity homes and institutions, which were more or less nursing homes. St Richard's had gardeners. They were all hand dug in those days; no mechanical means to help out whatsoever. They used to supply potatoes, cabbages, leeks, all that sort of thing, as required by the kitchen. They had Land Army girls there in those days, actually. They had lady porters as well. The ladies had taken the men's place.

Sylvia Dadswell

The food became quite a problem. There was one night nurse who used to have to go and do the supper for the day staff, you know, and, of course, food was rationed and short, and we were hungry a lot of the time, I remember. Anyway, she went down to do the night nurses' supper and she found a big tin of tomatoes and she thought, 'Oh good, tomato soup, make tomato soup for the night staff'. Well, that caused a big problem because it was the tomatoes and bacon for breakfast for the day staff, and we'd eaten their tomatoes. The food was a problem! Later on, when we had soldiers, or men anyway, down on Martin Ward, we had the kids up on Halstead. You know what kids are like in hospitals, they don't eat. So we used to serve their dinners and then rush downstairs with any food we'd got left to help feed the soldiers. And they used to ring up and say, 'Have you got any spuds, or have you got anything?' So it was quite difficult to maintain any kind of proper diet, or adequate diet, for young soldiers.

Eric Skilton

Of course, it was the war years. We knew—going on a little bit—we knew that D-Day was coming, for instance, because the people we had in the hospital at that time were mainly people from Portsmouth, air-raid victims that had been brought over and put in St Richard's. But suddenly all these people were moved out and I don't know if they went inland somewhere. But the hospital was completely empty apart from the odd couple of cases of someone seriously ill, dangerously ill. But the hospital was empty. And we had these 10 hutted wards as well, attached to the hospital. About a week before D-Day, as I say, we knew something was happening because we had, I think it was called the Middlesex Hospital in London, their staff, some of their staff and doctors were transferred down.

George Jarratt

We got casualties from the Army, from Normandy. They came by ambulances and coaches. We also used to get Americans as well and Canadians. We had Canadians before the invasion because they were stationed near Chichester and in Chichester. We had prisoners of war. They came a month or two after the invasion. We had a signal. We used to get regular signals from the RAF, from their airfields, to say, 'Will you take so many patients? I'm sending an ambulance with so many patients.' 'Right', we'd say. And they would arrive. We'd know they were coming sometimes because some of the planes were limping home, firing Verey lights and things as they were trying to land. And we knew we'd get some work that night. But we did have a signal one day to say could we take, I've forgotten how many, but it must have been about forty or fifty German prisoners of war. As usual, we said, 'Yes, right oh, we'll take them.' Then Douglas [Martin] and I looked at each other and we said, 'We haven't got a guard.' So we got in touch with the barracks, and they weren't very pleased to have to find a guard. But eventually, I think it was just before the prisoners arrived, we saw rather a motley crew arriving. All sorts of patchy uniforms and what not, with rifles and bayonets. I should think there must have been a dozen, perhaps more, marching up, or trying to march up, past our house, which was the old Lodge, and up to two of the huts where we were going to put the prisoners of war. And they arrived. The next morning I was doing a ward round and I went to the first hut and at the door was rifle and bayonet propped up, and at the end of this ward was this guard who was playing chess with one of the prisoners of war. The prisoners of war were Ukrainians and people who had been conscripted by the Germans and they were jolly pleased to be out of the war. So we had no problems at all from them, as opposed to one or two Luftwaffe pilots who were captured. If they were wounded and we had them, they were almost admitted at the same time as the intelligence officers from one or other of the RAF stations. And they were very soon moved away as soon as possible. As, of course, were the air crew casualties; they were moved to the hospitals. And we had regular sessions in outpatients with RAF sick who were sent by their Medical Officers.

The blackout, of course, was the blackout. We blacked the theatre … I don't know how it was blacked out but it was blacked out. And there we were. We operated—Arthur Ord, a Portsmouth orthopaedic surgeon, incidentally, talking about the blackout, he'd operate all night at Portsmouth sometimes and then came to us. He had an MG which he used to drive very quickly between Portsmouth and Chichester. There

St Richard's Hospital, front entrance, January 1947. [Courtesy: George Jarratt]

wasn't the motorway but there wasn't much on the road because nobody had cars. We obviously hadn't cars; we had bicycles. We used to cycle. Douglas used to cycle, Douglas Martin. Douglas had a car which was up on bricks and he didn't use it during the war.

Sylvia Dadswell

Of course, the hospital got very full and there were all sorts of complications because frequently the lights went out. When they bombed Portsmouth, it seemed to affect St Richard's lighting. And we had a light like this in the middle of the ward and almost, you couldn't see. And it became even more complicated because, on the kids' ward when the lights went out, it also meant the laundry was out of action, which put paid to the nappies and things, you see. And so a lot of the time we were very short of linen. Quite difficult really. We had all manner of different things in the ward. On one occasion I came back—I must have been on night duty at this time—I came back into the ward, having left it with three civilians, and when I came on duty that night it was full of soldiers. There seemed to be hundreds of them. They all had their guns and their gas-masks and their kit bags and their boots and their great coats, and none of them were ill, so they were all milling about in this ward. They were what were described as walking wounded, I suppose. They had things like bunions and hammer toes and all sorts of things. They were sort of officially off sick but none of them— there was nobody really desperately ill.

I was alone on the ward this evening. I was horrified when I saw them. I thought, God what do I do with this lot? Of course, I was young and I got all sorts of wolf whistles, and, 'Where have you been all my life?' And, 'Oh look, isn't she lovely.' All this sort of thing. So I said there must be an officer in charge of this lot. So I said, 'Who's the officer?' So somebody said, 'Bill'. So Bill came along; he must have been all of nineteen, gorgeous young man. And I said, 'Now look will you tell your men, order them all to find an empty bed and get in to it, and put all their impedimenta under the bed, and I'll go and put the kettle on.' And when I came back—it worked like a charm—when I came back they were all sort of sat to attention in their beds with everything stowed underneath. It was wonderful. Yes, but it's surprising what putting the kettle on will do.

As far as I can remember we all had a cup of tea, yes. Then on another occasion, in the middle of the night they brought me all the children from Gosport Memorial Hospital. I think they must have been from Portsmouth. Because there was bombing in Portsmouth, they got the kids out and they brought them to St Richard's in the middle of the night, and we had no lights. And that was chaos because they just arrived in ambulances. And people arrived, and some of the parents arrived to see if I'd got their little Willie. And I didn't know little Willie from Adam. And I had no notes or diagnosis or names or anything, just kids. And that was quite a thing. And that was on one of the occasions when we also had no nappies. [laughs]

How did we cope? Well, it was quite difficult at times. But it all worked, you know. But they seemed to do an awful lot of transferring people from A to B all the time. The ward you left when you went to bed in the morning probably wouldn't be there … It could be something quite different when you went back on duty at eight o'clock, you know. On one night I was on one of the hutted wards, I was a Ward Sister at this point, and I was doing night duty, and when I came on duty the ward was full of Germans, German airmen. And that was something quite different really. They'd only come in during that day and of course they were very distressed. And I had no German, so you couldn't talk to them or anything. And there seemed to be a hell of a lot of them. And of course you have soldiers at each window with his rifle and that sort of thing. And lots of policemen all milling about and everything. I only remember them being there two or three days. That's what I say, they seemed to move people. There seemed to be an awful lot of shifting from A to B and where they went I wouldn't know. But that was quite an experience. I can remember some of those boys very vividly. One was a nice young boy, he had a very badly smashed knees. And holding in his hand tight was a photograph of a girl with a baby.

'You name it; we done it'

THE WORK

❝ You name it; we done it. In those days the dressings and so forth were sterilised. We never had a Sterile Department at St Richard's in those days. No, I had to take them to the autoclave at the Central Laundry. They were taken around there about eight-thirty in the morning and collected round about eleven-thirty in the morning again. The nurses packed the tins and drums, which we put the dressings and so on in, and they were collected by the porters, and I collected them from the loading bay and delivered them to the laundry and collected them again later. ❞ (*Pat Saunders, Driver*)

One of the difficulties of getting a new, unfinished, hospital started in wartime was finding the staff and equipment to resource it. A very small nucleus of medical staff was drafted in from various parts of the country and was supported by an equally reduced number of nursing staff and support personnel. They all worked extremely long hours under arduous conditions trying to build up the hospital, maintain routine medical care and provide emergency medical services for war-time victims. They had to use whatever was available to them and if they could not find something suitable then they had to improvise. George Jarratt recalls his arrival at St Richard's as Deputy Superintendent, and Sylvia Dadswell, Ward Sister, remembers some of the difficult circumstances she and her colleagues worked under. While Eric Skilton, office boy and later to become a hospital secretary, outlines all the odd (and unusual!) jobs he was asked to undertake; and Pat Saunders, Driver and later to become Transport Manager, reflects on the unusual improvisations the hospital had to make in order to meet even basic hygiene and health requirements. Paddy Whiteside, one of the hospital's earliest physicians, additionally remembers the kind of workload he survived shortly after the war ended and how this was alleviated gradually as the hospital secured more staff in the lead up to the introduction of a National Health Service.

George Jarratt

[How did I find my job at St Richard's?] I was approached by my Chief in Barnet, who had been Douglas Martin's Chief when Douglas was the Deputy Medical Superintendent at the Wellhouse Hospital, Barnet. He said that Douglas was looking for a new Deputy, was I interested. And, of course, I said, 'Yes'. Zaida, my wife, and

I then made a trip to Chichester and met Douglas and fortunately he asked me to join him. This happened on 5 June in 1943. Things were pretty hectic, especially as we were surrounded by three main airfields, Ford, Thorney Island, and Tangmere. We had a lot of work to do with air crew casualties. Douglas and Arthur Ord, the other surgeon, spent a lot of time treating these patients, who were then moved on, as soon as possible, to RAF hospitals. Every morning Douglas or I had to contact the Central Office of the Air crew Casualty Department of the RAF, which was commanded by Air Vice Marshal Geoffrey Keynes, on whose firm I had been a student when I was at Bart's [St Bartholomew's Hospital, London]. Geoffrey Keynes himself would travel down and see any very difficult cases, which he did on several occasions.

As we were an Emergency Medical Service Hospital, we also had frequent visits from Rear Admiral Sir Gordon Gordon-Taylor, a famous surgeon, who was inspecting the EMS Hospitals. He used to arrive in a staff car with a Rear Admiral's pennant flying. He was always charming and seemed to enjoy his cup of tea, which we had in the theatre changing room. This was really the Sister's office on Ward 1, on the ground floor, next to what we had, in those days, as our operating theatre, which was really only a side ward on Ward 1. You must remember that the hospital was incomplete when the war started and we just carried on with what was there.

Sylvia Dadswell

When I started my training, I was paid two pounds and four shillings a month, for one year. Then at the end of the first year we were paid two pounds and eight shillings a month. We had a shilling a week raise. Then the next year we got two pounds and eight shillings a month, and out of this we had to pay our examination fees, which cost us ten pounds. And at the end, when we'd finished our training, we were given that ten pounds back. But it would have been rather nice to have had it a bit earlier, you know [laughs]. We had all sorts of dodges about the money, though.

When I was at Chichester I was trained then, but we were hard up. We were badly paid.

I lived in Chapman House. The first Matron was Miss Chapman. She was nice—so Chapman House—yes, it was nice. And during, I don't know if it was once a week, once a fortnight, we used to have to go up on to the roof of Chapman House, all night, and watch for the doodlebugs, the fire things. You see we had to just stay awake and watch for them. We used to sit there and watch Portsmouth burning. I remember I did some knitting, and I seem to remember I made a rug, because you were supposed to stay awake,

On obtaining the qualifications " State Registered Nurse " or " State Enrolled Assistant Nurse," students may be offered appointments as Staff Nurses or Enrolled Assistant Nurses, at the salaries shewn below :—

FEMALES (Resident).

STAFF NURSES.	STATE ENROLLED ASSISTANT NURSES
£140 per annum rising to £200 per annum.	£120 per annum rising to £170 per annum.

(In addition, residential emoluments are provided free of charge).

MALES (Non-Resident).

STAFF NURSES.	STATE ENROLLED ASSISTANT NURSES
100/- per week, rising to 120/- per week.	92/- per week, rising to 112/- per week.

(Meals can be obtained whilst on duty at appropriate charges).

November, 1947

Nurse salaries, 1947.

and it was all night. As far as I remember we were alone as well. I think there was only one of us. God knows what we were expected to do if we did see a fire … [laughs]

We were short of food, but then so was the whole of England. No there were no rules and regulations. And Mr. Martin said, 'Let's talk about the uniform.' So between us we designed the nurses' uniform. Because to begin with you just had a white overall you know, because there was nothing really. And I designed the nurses' uniform and it was a violet, very fine stripe, with buttons all the way up, so that we could roll our sleeves up with no bother. We had stand-up collars, which made our necks stiff. Well, we only had little tiny collars and very nice caps. Then we had a violet petersham belt. And, of course, the trained nurses were allowed to have a nice buckle. And it was a very smart uniform. I was very proud of it. And we had square bibbed aprons with no straps. Well, they had their Hospital Badge and their General Nursing Council badge to keep their pinny [pinafore] up. The uniform was very smart. You know, we were quite proud of our uniform.

We had sheets and blankets, no duvets. No, no, no. And after a few years it was decided that the blankets—you couldn't boil these blankets you see—so they got those folk weave things, you know, cottony things. And they were more serviceable, I suppose, really. In the beginning we had screens. I don't remember curtains round the beds like there are now, but in the beginning there were screens. And they were lined with fawny sort of stuff, you know. But they were not very satisfactory. They were never where you wanted them. And the wheels used to come off, and yes it was more difficult really to maintain the place.

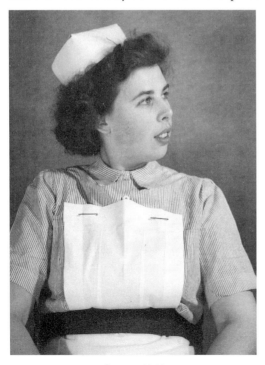

May Burrows in uniform, c.1948.

Later I trained as a Midwife. It took a year and it was six months in the hospital, in the maternity home, you know, and six months out on the District. Nursing, delivering babies in their own homes, with a qualified midwife then. That was an education. If you've dealt with the District Midwifery you could cope with anything. You've just no idea how some people live. I went into one house; it was across two ploughed fields. And I used to tank around this on a bicycle with my little black bag on the back, and the tiny little bicycle lamp, you know. And I had to walk across a field, and then across a second field, right out in the sticks. You wouldn't think that. And she was in a very, very poor home. And she was in the middle of a double bed and all sunk in the middle. And there was a candle on the mantelpiece. And I said, 'Goodness me, is this all the light there is?' And she said, 'Oh no, I've got another candle.' Oh yes! And, of course, she kept disappearing. Well, we both finished up in the bed together; there was no two ways about it. But I loved midwifery. I think it's great. Each new baby is a miracle, every one.

Eric Skilton

As the office boy—and, of course, being young in years, I did all sorts of things. I was doing duties on the telephone switchboard. I was, by the way, paid ten shillings a week plus one and tuppence bonus for the use of my bicycle. Because I used to take all the laboratory specimens down to the County Hall Laboratory. The laboratory was at County Hall, at the top of the building in County Hall. County Hall was West Street in Chichester, where it is to this day. The back of Wren House. And at the top of the building was the Council Medical Laboratory. I had to take down all the blood samples for the day and then the other things that had been removed in the theatre [laughs] down in my little saddle bag. So I'm cycling one day with all these specimens, and I'm going round Chichester. Of course, I also used to deliver mail to the local doctors. And I'm going round Chichester Cross and I came off me bike and all these specimens came out in the street. I had an amputated breast at the time in this jar; anyway, it was all formalin, and I put it all back in this jar. And I picked up my letters and I went round and delivered them. Well, the thing was one of these letters, obviously, I must have not picked up, and someone picked it up and put it in the post for Dr. Dick in West Street. And two or three days later I was summoned before Mr. Martin who was then called the Medical Superintendent in St Richard's, and he said, 'I have a complaint from Dr. Dick; he's received a letter with no stamp on', he said. 'And you were supposed to deliver it.' And he said, 'I'm asking you now to give me the five-pence for the overcharge.' And that was that.

But the thing about St Richard's then was that you never knew what you were going to do next. As I say, I got involved in fire watching. I eventually drove the van at 16 years of age. We had one little Morris Cowley van there, which I drove eventually. I took over the driving of this at sixteen. So I drove the van and I did all these little odd jobs.

The routine at the Hospital then was that there was a lot of respect. You daren't call anybody by Christian names. I used to go up to the wards. I had a job of filling the inkwells in the Sisters' office and changing their blotting paper. You had to knock on doors to enter and knock on doors to go in the ward. And get Sister's permission to go in the ward. And if you passed Mr. Martin in the corridor you'd say, 'Good morning, sir.' He'd be walking down the corridor and he'd just nod or grunt, you know. That was the sort of situation then. But everybody was very kind when it came to helping out or there was an emergency on.

I was the only office boy. Everybody knew me. They fussed over me a bit because I was the only youngster. And, of course, the fact that my mother was out at work all day. They took such a keen interest that Mrs. Fellows, who was Mr. Martin's secretary then, insisted I'd go up with the doctors and the senior staff to their dining room, which was separated from the nurses' dining room, go up there for a meal every day. And they took a complete interest in my well-being as such and fussed over me. And I used to volunteer for everything. If it was a question of doing night duty on the telephone switchboard, then I would do it. I lived over St Richard's more than I did at home. [laughs]

I delivered things from ward to ward, from laboratory to laboratory. They'd just ring down to the office. Ordinary telephone situation there. And I used to troop over to the huts. I used to write letters, too, funnily enough, for some of the wounded. Because we had some very interesting cases. Within a few days the situation got better. Because obviously they were getting into France and they were then establishing field hospitals. But, as I say, in that early part they came in soaking wet. And we had everything. We had every regiment under the sun you could imagine. We had French girls who were married to Germans and who had been shooting at our chaps. We had white Russians, as they called them, who had been working on defences. A lot of those went to Graylingwell. A lot of the foreigners were pushed off to Graylingwell. And the casualties then were brought in … Some of them came in from, say, Littlehampton and we had the old coaches, Southdown coaches, with all the seats taken out. And they'd have slings in the roof on which they used to hang stretchers. And then stretchers on the floor of the coach. And that's how they used to come in.

We had them all up the corridor at St Richard's. And remember that we didn't have a proper operating theatre. We only had this four-bedded ward which was converted into an operating theatre. And they then decided, in the hallway of the outpatients, the old outpatients, in the hallway they put a theatre table. And then all the way up the corridor they laid these stretchers head to head. And the medical officers would go round and grade them according to their degree of injury. And those that weren't too bad were sent further inland. They would go to a place like Basingstoke and be transferred the same day. And only the very serious were kept in. But the work that Mr. Martin and Dr. Clark did then must have been marvellous, because they were on the go all day. And if you can imagine the situation now where a doctor or a consultant has so many beds, they'd have a whole ward of 30 beds. And then Mr. Clark would have the maternity unit which was in one of these huts to look after. I don't know how they did it. Most amazing.

I used to help lift as well, you know, stretchers and patients. That went on for not more than about three weeks when it gradually eased off. Because they were, by then, establishing field hospitals and the chaps weren't coming in soaking wet through. I'm not sure of the actual year but probably another eighteen months later, probably in 1942-1943 period, the Americans started coming in. We had a whole ward, the top ward, which we used to call ward four in those days. We only had ward one, ward two, three and four, they didn't have names like they do now, Baxendale and that. And the whole of ward four was full of Americans with trench feet, due to wearing their boots for several days, you know, in snow and ice. And it was like a form of gangrene, I believe. And painful, you know if you knocked their beds they used to shout out.

And I used to write a few letters for them. You know postcards to their wives. But they were wonderfully looked after. The minute they arrived they'd got a pack of everything; toothpaste, chewing gum, all in a little pack—soap and what have you. And, of course, we then had a Canadian Medical Officer move in and the Canadian Wing established. And, of course, they were all very popular then with the nurses and the girls then because they had all the stockings and cigarettes and things.

We established one of the huts as an entertainment hut in those days. And, of course, the majority of the other huts were used for the elderly people, some from Portsmouth who'd been moved out because of air raids. We used to go up and fire watch on the top of the roof of St Richard's and we could see them bombing Portsmouth. Where the Medical Centre is now there was just a field with a huge air raid shelter underground which we were supposed to go to if anything came our way. And, of course, we had our own produce. And a lot of our stuff, even our milk, came from Graylingwell. They had a big farm at Graylingwell. And we had our own Land Army girl, who used to grow the vegetables all round, where they could, in St Richard's. So we were pretty self-contained. We had a kitchen and the foods went up as they did today on a trolley, a heated trolley. Each ward had a kitchen then, and I think they did the breakfasts in the kitchen then, because one of the jobs I then went up to as I gradually got promoted, sort of thing, I did the diet sheet for the day. And patients would submit little diet sheets with their requirements on and I would transfer all that lot to a big diet sheet, which went up to the cook. We didn't have a Catering Officer in those days. We had one storeman in the stores, in the provision store, and the cook

Willowmead—the hutted wards.

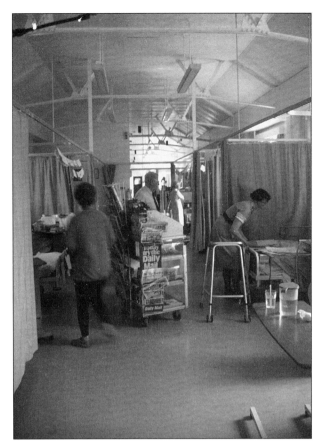
Morning in Willowmead—the hutted wards.

and her assistants. And, of course, we were on rations like everybody else. We had a chart. I used to work it out, a quarter of an ounce of tea and so on, one tin of chocolate biscuits a month, shared. It went to one ward and then to another ward and so on.

My job later as hospital secretary, with the Steward then was to go around and collect all the information we could on, what we called a Kalamazoo system, and record these documents. And then we started getting German prisoners in who were placed in one of the hutted wards. They were frightened of us; we were frightened of them. [laughs] One very old soldier, who obviously was too old to do any active service, he'd sit in the middle of the huts at St Richard's, with his rifle, tin hat on and the fixed bayonet. The Germans weren't allowed to have a knife and fork; they could only have a spoon for their meals. And we took everything off of them, except they were allowed to keep a personal photograph. But the British being very thorough in everything, we had these special envelopes which, although other things were put in them, the prisoners' watches and their rings and all this were put in to this envelope and details were put on the front. And we did have a little chap who was made a Lance Corporal in the Signal Corps who was of Jewish German origin and he spoke German fluently and he used to interpret and tell them what we were doing. We'd then place the stuff in the envelope and I myself, personally, would then light the sealing wax and seal the back of these. And these went off to somewhere I believe, the Ministry of Defence or somewhere, till after the war. And then they were handed back probably, to the individual.

Pat Saunders

I was the Van boy at the Central Laundry in Broyle Road. It was a hospital laundry, plus, as it belonged to the County Council, it was also dealing with the institutions at Midhurst and East Preston, and others. I did mainly loading and unloading, because in those days there was only one driver, one van driver. The laundry used to have an ordinary boiler in those days, which was fed by coal, and being war time, people used to store most of the fuel out in the yard. The fuel took up most of the yard, so it was pretty tight turning around in the yard to reverse up to load and unload the laundry van. We brought white sheets from the various hospitals. Mostly women worked in the laundry. There weren't many men about.

Once the laundry was sorted out, it was put into various machines like sheets in one, towels in another and clothing in another. It was from various hospitals. It was separated afterwards to be taken back again to the various hospitals. They used to dry it through hydro-hose [hydro-extractor] and air dryers. The big blankets and so forth went through another processor, a large container which you walked in and placed them up on racks and they dried off for two or three days, maybe not as long as that. It was hot air, you see, from the steam. Then they went through colanders, large colanders where the width would take a whole sheet. You used to have two girls feeding it in, two girls taking it out and folding it up at the same time; so they had to work pretty smart to get it out and folded up in time to take the next one. Then the laundry was loaded back into baskets for us to take away. When we collected it we collected it in bags and we took it back in bags, so there was no actual handling of the laundry ourselves. Just collecting and delivering.

When I became a driver, we were attached to the Portering Department where everybody sort of done everything, not just one job; whatever it was you done it: delivering meals, laundry, general work within the hospital, and so on, but, as I say, the main job was driving. Everything was done by hand with an old truck either you pulled or pushed. Various loads were heavy and sometimes it took two or three to move that particular load, like delivering the laundry round the wards, etc., and the hutted wards. That was quite a thing in those days. I also delivered some of the food. I mean, it wasn't a very good thing at all. Your early morning breakfast was delivered on an open truck, and that was put in an oven as soon as you got there and warmed up for the old patients, you know, that sort of thing. But the main meal, during the day, that sort of had an insulated box that you delivered in those days and again that was pushed over on a truck and transferred on to a specialised trolley, which the box fitted on. And you pulled that into the ward, and that was insulated so that was quite warm. Then I'd deliver milk afterwards, round wards, collecting the empties. You name it we done it.

In those days the dressings and so forth were sterilised. We never had a Sterile Department at St Richard's in those days. No, I had to take them to the autoclave at the Central Laundry. They were taken around there about eight-thirty in the morning and collected round about eleven-thirty in the morning again. The nurses packed the tins and drums, which we put the dressings and so on in, and they were collected by the porters, and I collected them from the loading bay and delivered them to the laundry and collected them again later. These were war-time measures. We didn't have sterile drums or couldn't afford them in those days. We used ordinary biscuit tins, which we used to seal before they came back out again. Part of my job was to seal them up and bring them back to the hospital. They were then delivered back round to wards again and we would repeat that Monday to Friday.

Paddy Whiteside

I had joined the staff of St Richard's in 1946 on demobilisation from the R.A.F. There were very poor facilities there then because it was a new hospital. We had two surgeons, Douglas Martin, the Surgeon Superintendent and E.P. 'Nobby' Clark, his Deputy, who had not yet passed his surgical qualification (Fellow of the Royal College of Surgeons). The two surgeons had 96 surgical beds and 12 obstetric beds and only the make-do theatre. They covered accidents and general surgery apart from chest and brain surgery, but including gynaecology and obstetrics, orthopaedic, paediatric and geriatric. They had no junior staff to help.

It was not until the National Health Service came in in 1948 that we got an increase in our equipment, and the appointment of junior staff, such as house-physicians, house-surgeons and registrars to help us. We were then part and parcel of running the hospital, taking part in the administration with the other doctors. The County Council avoided spending money on a hospital shortly to be taken over by the state, and, of course, equipment was rationed and very difficult to obtain.

As the lone physician, I had a similar load to carry but I had an able junior doctor, John Winkler, to help. We covered 72 acute medical beds, 21 children and 210 geriatric beds, and took alternative evenings and weekends on duty, although the physician was always on call. Both surgeons and physicians had outpatients once or twice a week. Relief came with the NHS, when two physicians at the Royal West Sussex Hospital (which we all referred to as 'Broyle Road') came to help, and junior staff were appointed.

The conditions were good, but everything was rationed, including food, and this applied even to the hospitals. People who had been excused military service during the

In the operating theatre, c.1948.

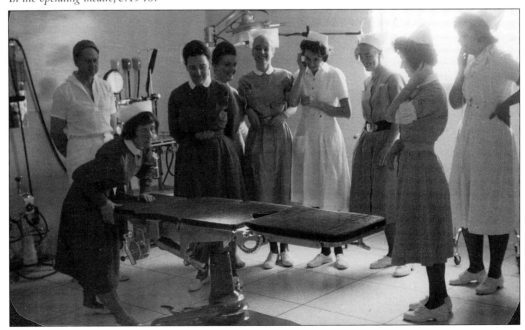

war because of essential jobs were then called up, including some of the medical staff in both our Chichester hospitals. Equipment was extremely difficult to get and we had previously, during the war, sterilised all our dressings in the Chichester Laundry in biscuit tins. And it was only after 1948 that we got proper drums for sterilisation. I lived in the Hospital. I was a resident physician. My pay, and the pay in all West Sussex jobs, was extremely low. It was thought to be a pleasure to work in Chichester. I got paid as a Consultant, £700 a year, and my Senior Surgeon and Superintendent got paid £1,100 a year, but of course we were resident and we got all our resident facilities and food free.

A surgeon does mainly work in the theatre—wards and theatre, operating—and the physician takes on medical illnesses such as gastric ulcers, diseases of the colon, heart diseases, pneumonias, all the medical disorders that patients get. And we had to deal with this very large number of beds with just a physician and an assistant doctor. We had a full complement of nurses. But that only came later, because at the beginning of the war there was a great shortage of nurses and during [the war] these could not be replaced. But we did start a School of Nursing and very quickly trained up as many as we could at St Richard's. That was started in 1940 by the Matron. But during the Normandy invasion we had to have nurses sent down to help us from the teaching hospitals in London who were not that heavily pushed at the time, and whose hospitals may well have been partially destroyed by bombing. During wartime, we admitted mainly war casualties, and there had been a very large intake of casualties during the actual Normandy invasion, and the bombing of Southampton and Portsmouth. We also admitted patients from the local airfields at Tangmere and Thorney Island. We did take a number of civilians, usually very ill patients, on to one ward of floor three. Sexes were not segregated and the military were usually given priority.

My daily routine would be to go round all the patients under my charge, which was two full floors of medical patients, together with all new admissions who had to be examined and diagnosed, and do simple procedures like aspirating chests and simple diagnostic tests, like doing an electrocardiogram on the patient. I would do a morning round which would take me some three to four hours. I would not be able to do every morning my whole number of patients. I would do one floor one day, the other floor the next day, but I would always see any new patient admitted to any ward under my care. The afternoon and evening was spent completing this work, and we were working certainly 15 or 18 hours a day, even at that time and after the war. It was only after the National Health Service came in that we got a sufficient increase in physicians, increase in housemen and registrars to make the work much easier. We worked very, very long hours. There were no fixed hours; you finished when your job was finished and that was often quite late in the evening.

George Jarratt

After the War ended, we had less to do. We hadn't air crew casualties. We didn't have any air raid casualties. Not that we had many in Chichester anyway, or service sick. But the RAF and the Army were still present in and around Chichester during that time so we would have cases, medical and surgical cases from the RAF stations. But then, you see, we still had our ordinary, normal work from the population of West Sussex. In Chichester, that bit of the population that didn't go to the Royal West Sussex. There wasn't any lead up into the National Health Service in 1947, except that the BMA and company were dead against the formation of the National Health Service. And when I was in Hong Kong we regularly got plebiscite forms to complete, saying we didn't want to join. Or if we didn't want to join we could say so. In fact, I think the one that came out was after the Health Service in fact had been accepted. But no, we weren't terribly keen at the time. I must say that experience since has perhaps changed quite a bit. Although I think there're a lot of problems which could have been better dealt with.

Paddy Whiteside

The National Health Service came in in 1948. We never took part in any of the central planning. The country was divided up into regions and there was a possibility that Chichester would be associated with Brighton or associated with Portsmouth or remain as it did, an independent member of the South West Metropolitan Region. It had to come [The National Health Service]. It was partly financial, but it was mainly the provision of medical services to the country as a whole, poor or rich—no division on those grounds.

It did not affect our work, virtually not at all. We joined up with the Royal West Sussex Hospital as two equal partners. What I had failed to say was that we were also called out into the district by general practitioners and this might mean the whole of your weekend was visiting patients, but this could now be shared between the physicians at both of the hospitals. The same applied to casualties. Each hospital was on alternate days, but there was no such thing as cars, and the casualty officer at one hospital had to cycle over to the other hospital to see the accident or other problem that had been brought to the hospital.

Gradually, I got more junior staff. I got a good deal of help from the two physicians, Dr. H. Seward Morley and Dr. Guy Emerson, who were at the Royal West Sussex Hospital. They previously were working in general practice, which they gave up and became hospital doctors, both eventually consultants. And they gave me a good deal of help at the St Richard's Hospital which had at least twice as many beds—medical beds, than there had been at the Royal West. In addition, of course, junior staff were appointed, other speciality units developed, such as paediatrics. We got a geriatric physician, we got a visiting neurologist, a visiting dermatologist; all of these would take work off my shoulders.

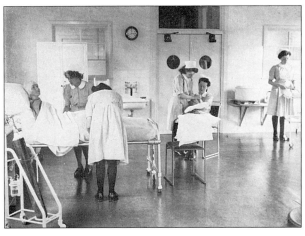
Nurse training, 1947.

'The improvising that went on'

THE TREATMENTS AND TECHNOLOGY

❛ The improvising that went on in the theatre during the war is incredible really. I don't remember too much about the blood in St Richard's. I do remember a blood transfusion when I was training, and they had the patient, the recipient here, and the donor was on another trolley just there, and they took blood from there to there. ❜ *(Sylvia Dadswell, Ward Sister)*

For the most part, changes in treatment and technology did not alter radically at St Richard's during this time. Much of the restrictions that the country was experiencing as a whole were so for the hospital. The office management, for example, relied on the hand-written, and legible, work of the office staff, as Eric Skilton recalls. Advances in medical technology were slowly introduced to a staff skilled and adept in the art of improvising. When new technologies or drug treatments were introduced, as George Jarratt remembers, it was as much to do with individual initiative as it was organisational innovation.

Eric Skilton

In the office, we used just ordinary typewriters for letters and forms. Mostly, though, everything was hand-written. The wages book was hand-written. In there you'll see: 'The office boy, ten shillings a week, and one and two-pence bonus for use of bicycle'. I also used to write the death register, all by hand.

George Jarratt

On the wards and in the theatre: Mr. Douglas Martin and I used to meet at nine o'clock every morning in his office, when we went through the night reports and then decided what to do. We'd do our ward rounds and if any things had happened requiring any surgical treatment he or I would give, in the day-to-day things, we'd give anaesthetics for each other, and do the operations.

Paddy Whiteside

The technology when I first went was very poor indeed. Our total X-ray Department consisted of one portable X-ray machine. We had, originally, no electrocardiogram. Pathology was a visiting technician coming from County Hall in the morning and doing very simple tests only. We had a theatre adapted from a hospital ward, and old sterilisation. We sterilised swabs in a biscuit tin and the instruments were boiled up in the sluice, where all the bedpans were rinsed, carried to the theatre and used. There was only one set of everything in the hospital and if something was dropped the instrument had to be boiled up and the operation would stop until that had taken place.

The very first operation in the hospital in 1939 was a Caesarean section, and the gynaecologist who came in, Miss Shippam, had to bring her own instruments and her operating table to do the operation. The table remained 'borrowed' for some time before it could be replaced. This was typical of the shortages that we had in those days. The operations were done in a small four-bedded ward that had been converted into a theatre, and the Sister's office was converted into the room where patients were anaesthetised before going into the theatre. We used Nitrous Oxide gas or ether; chloroform occasionally, but chloroform had been largely replaced or wholly replaced by ether.

George Jarratt

We had Bard–Parker scalpels and blades, and I think that was about the only disposable thing we had really. I'm trying to think where we did the sterilisation; I think it was done in the theatre probably. We'd nothing fancy. There was no proper surgical theatre suite at all; that came later.

The anaesthetist in those days was Brian Sandiford, who really was top notch. He was a first-class anaesthetist, who later was also on at the Portsmouth Royal Hospital. I remember during the war when we were having a lot of activity there. But we had some of the people who were the chief people in the anaesthetic side of the Emergency Medical Service, and they were extremely impressed by Brian's instruments and all his gadgets for anaesthetics which were really in advance of a lot of other people. Apart from anything else Brian was adept at giving local anaesthetics. He used to give splanchinc blocks and intercostal blocks, as well as doing the general anaesthetic side of things.

I do remember, when Geoffrey Keynes was operating on a very badly wounded RAF pilot, he said, 'Of course this chap has got to have penicillin straightaway.' And I said, 'Well we haven't got penicillin.' And this was in the very early days of penicillin, and he said, 'Well, you will get it from now on.' And we were one of the very first hospitals to have penicillin, which used to be given intramuscularly by a little gadget we fixed up. It had a cross of pieces of copper on which was mounted a piece of Meccano which held the needle in place, and this was dripped in permanently. Something like 30,000 units were given in a few hours, which, I suppose, is a small dose in present-day terms. Anyway, we got penicillin very early on, long before it was in general use. But this was for the air crew casualties.

Paddy Whiteside

The basic way of finding out what was wrong with the heart at that time was history, and examination of the heart with the stethoscope. If it was a heart case,

I would refer it to the teaching hospital, St George's Hospital, in London. If it was a chest or abdominal disorder, or a bowel disorder I would treat it myself down here, or ask one of the local surgeons to operate.

Sylvia Dadswell

The improvising that went on in the theatre during the war is incredible really. I don't remember too much about the blood in St Richard's. I do remember a blood transfusion when I was training, and they had the patient, the recipient here, and the donor was on another trolley just there, and they took blood from there to there. They just transferred it. And another thing I remember once is that they had blood and they collected it in a bottle and they stirred it with a glass rod so that it wasn't allowed to coagulate, you know. So that was vastly different, vastly different. They had to boil the instruments. There was no proper autoclave system. There was a little tiny thing, and it was in a room upstairs … The top of the first flight, you go to the kitchen along there. Well, at the top of the stairs, over there, is a little room but in there was a drum, an autoclave thing. And it was about the size of my table, and I used to put these drums in there every morning. And then there was a little graph which showed the temperature it had reached, and it was on a paper thing, and I used to have to chop that off each morning and take it down and put it on Douglas Martin's desk, to prove what it was. It wasn't as big as my settee, the whole machine. Incredible really. But I believe, in the very beginning, the dressings and things—it must have been before that autoclave thing was ever there. You see a Medical Unit wouldn't need all this sterilising equipment. So I think that was added as an after-thought. And the stuff used to be put in biscuit tins and taken over to the laundry somewhere, and sterilised somehow or other.

When I was training we had stock bottles of things. We had Aspirins and we had Veganin. And it seemed that if somebody said they'd got a headache you'd give them a pill; you didn't have to get it signed on a Blue Form or anything, and it was more lax in those days. Morphia we used to give, and, of course, that had to be very carefully signed. I mean, post-operatives, grains a quarter of morphia, times five. So you could give one the night of their operation and then perhaps three tomorrow, and save the last dose for the night of the second night. And that was all you were allowed to do. And then they

Halstead Ward staff with the children, Christmas 1940. [Courtesy: Sylvia Dadswell]

had a couple of Panadols or something like that, you see. No, I think in a way the drugs have tightened up. Well, they've certainly tightened up since the days when we were allowed to issue a little dose of cough mixture or a mixture for a stomach ache or something like that. But I mean now you'd be shot. My husband had a hernia repaired by Douglas Martin, in St Richard's, and he was in Martin Ward for three weeks. And that was it, you know, after about eighteen days they got him up. But he was in bed for three weeks. He says it's the best time he's ever had in his life.

May Burrows

To repair a hernia when we first went to theatre, they used to cut a long strip of fascia out of the thigh and actually sew it into the hernia to repair it. The man would end up with a great big long incision on his leg, just under the skin, but with a long row of stitching all up his leg. They used the fascia to repair the hernia. It was a long scar on his leg. Then the theatre sister taking the case used to have to prepare this fascia for the surgeon, while he went on to do a bit more surgery. To get the wound ready you used to have to scrape it all clean and actually stitch it on to a special fascia graft needle, or, if you actually damaged this graft, you used to have to cut it down so it was all neat and tidy and then stitch it on—scrape all the fat off of it, and if you broke it heaven help you!!

'Ready for duty', 1940 (left to right: *Nurses Peshett, Beasley, Anderson, Arnell, Godwin, Gorton*). [*Courtesy: Eric Skilton*]

Sylvia Dadswell

As for midwifery, well, you can't change midwifery very much can you? [laughs] They did decide during my time that it's probably kinder to dim the lights, so that the baby isn't born into a bright light. But in fact we used to do that. There's nothing new about that, we used to dim the lights. Apart from that you, you know, what is there to alter really? They have epidural injections and things now, but we used to have gas and air, and the Queen Charlotte's apparatus, which is a little suitcase, which had two little cylinders. And that was talked about by Dr. John Elam, who was our anaesthetist at Barnet, and he started that. That was very new then. Our patients, our new mothers, they were in bed for nine days, and then they were allowed to get up. All being well, if their stitches had healed, or whatever; if there had been any complications then, on the twelfth day, they went home, having seen the doctor, you know, to make sure all was well.

'The pubs had no beer'

THE PEOPLE AND THEIR SOCIAL LIFE

❝ The pubs had no beer, and of course there were no trains. I had a month's holiday and I wasn't allowed to go away, so I stayed on the ward, because what do you do in Chichester if you're not allowed … And I couldn't … My home was in Oxford. But there were no trains and they did sort of say you shouldn't really leave. ❞ (*Sylvia Dadswell, Ward Sister*)

A hospital is a community of people, and how well that community works together depends much on the people, their attitudes and the social cohesion they have managed to knit together. These, of course, are all influenced by the mores, and social and cultural conditions of the time. At St Richard's the dominant figures of the period were the Superintendent and the Matron, the father and mother figures who both wielded almost despotic power during a time of tremendous uncertainty. Most recall it as a benign paternalism, supported and reinforced by protocol and social rituals which were strictly followed. The improvisation that was evident in their working lives was also apparent in their social lives. The intense hardships of the time are glossed over with the memory of how they made an effort to minimise them through a communal fight against adversity.

Sylvia Dadswell

Mr. Martin was wonderful. Yes, he was wonderful. He was a very kind, caring man. I loved Mr. Martin; he was a real gentleman. I knew his wife quite well and she was a charmer as well. We were shattered, shattered, when he had a coronary and died at the age of fifty-three. Couldn't believe it. I came on duty and there was a hush about the place. And I said, 'What's the matter with everybody?' And they said, 'Haven't you heard? Mr. Martin.' 'What's the matter with Mr. Martin?' And they said, 'He's dead.' 'Couldn't be.' You know. I knew Mr. Martin, or I've known him since I was eighteen.

We always seem to be alone, that's the thing with nurses; you're always the only one, you know. And I was put on the men's surgical ward. I suppose I was eighteen and a half, very raw, I didn't know anything, very ignorant. And Martin Ward was men's surgical and we had a young man brought in that day, and he was fine; he was

Douglas Martin, Superintendent, and Mrs. F. Fellows, his Secretary, with staff, c.1946. [Courtesy: Eric Skilton]

full of fun, but he'd had a bad pain. During the night, in the small hours, he suddenly started shouting. He was in a terrible state with a dreadful pain, rolling round the bed, this young man, terrible. And I couldn't find the Night Sister; I rang everywhere and I couldn't find the Night Sister. And he was really in a dreadful state. And in the end, in the middle of the night I rang Mr. Martin, an unheard of thing. You just don't ever,

Nurse Sylvia Dadswell with Staff Nurse Martin at Chapman House Nurses' Home, 1940. [Courtesy: Sylvia Dadswell]

but I did, because I didn't know what else to do. And he came in his pyjamas with a dressing gown on, across a bit of a field. He lived on the premises but away a bit. And he came instantly in his pyjamas, and I said, 'I'm so sorry, but I don't know what to do for this man ...' I met him at the door, and do you know when we got to this man he was sound asleep, but his bed was like a battlefield. And the perspiration was stood on his face, you could see. So I said, 'Oh, I'm terribly sorry, but I didn't know what else to do; it was a very, terrible pain.' And he said, 'No, you did the right thing, and that's renal colic.' And he said, 'Now you'll never forget that; that's renal stones.' And he said, 'You did the right thing.' But he wrote him up for some … It would be morphia in those days, it would be pethidine now. But he said, 'Oh yes, now you'll never forget that; that's renal colic, and the pain is absolutely intense.' And once its moved you see the pain's gone; and the man was asleep from pure exhaustion. And a lot of doctors probably would have said, 'Well, get the Night Sister or something.' You know, but he didn't, he came and he was very good, too.

George Jarratt

In fact, talking of staffing, we had Douglas and myself and usually two residents. Sometimes when we were very lucky we had three. They stayed as long as we could keep them, usually, if they were suitable, and most of them were. I can remember very well people like Ruth Giles, whose husband was a Pathologist in the Army. She qualified in Manchester, and she was extremely efficient and good. Winston Palmer, who was older than most of us because he'd taken up medicine later in life and later on went in to General Practice in Worthing. John Winkler, who was a very good young physician, although only holding a relatively junior post, and there's Tony Hammerton who, because he was diabetic, was exempt from military service and was with us for quite a time. All these people were there and worked jolly hard, because in fact we had 600 beds in those days, which were later reduced to 400, when I went back to do a locum's job there, for a week, in 1949. 400 beds. And by then what had been the administration by one man, who was called the Steward, and an elderly man, who was his deputy, who was really retired and was a local J.P.

Matron in my day had a secretary, and the General Office had two or three girls and that was the sum total. I must admit though that I think things were a little simpler in those days. One couldn't do anything very fancy. Our surgical work was almost certainly basic in every respect.

Sylvia Dadswell

There were no Christian names. Doctors were Sir and Matron was Matron. And at that time we had a Matron who was like a beanpole. Victoria Chapman was her name. But I suppose there was that amount of respect. The Hospital consisted then of a Matron, a Nurses' Home Sister. And then the four wards had a Sister on each ward and then the huts had like what we call a Staff Nurse today. They didn't have Sisters on the huts then until later. As I say we were using one hut as a maternity unit. The maternity unit hadn't been built. But people like, as I say, your

Nobby Clark with nursing staff, 1945. [Courtesy: Eric Skilton]

radiographer was Mr. Devereau, your pharmacist was Mr. Hodder and everybody was Mr. this and Miss that. And then, of course, everything was so distinct in regards uniforms. If you went up to the nurses' dining room, you'd see, you know … You'd call them the third year nurse, the state enrolled you called nurse, and then the Sisters at their little dining tables you'd call Sister.

The open end of your pillow on your bed, the open end, had to face away from the door. All the counterpanes were lined up in a row. Military patients who were out sitting in a chair on the doctor's round had to what they call, sit to attention, on his round. And as I say I daren't go into any ward without going to the Sister's office knocking on the door and then waiting for her to say 'Enter', and then ask her, 'Can I go into the ward and see so and so?' She was the Queen Bee of the wards. And by Jove when you think the visiting was only one afternoon a week on the wards. And she was very strict with the service men. There wasn't so much on smoking then because the men used to get free issue of cigarettes in those days. So there wasn't any problem on that score. But their cigarettes had to be put out, as I say, military patients were expected to sit up to attention if they were actually in their chair by the side of the bed. And all doctors were 'Sir'. It was a very strict, regimented set up. One accepted that as the norm. Mr. Martin was the King Bee of the whole set up.

Zaida Jarratt

We lived in the hospital at the Lodge, which was a little house with dining room, sitting room. We had a kitchen. We had central heating. We had a boiler in the kitchen. We had—outside in the back garden—we had an Anderson shelter, which we never used but behind which we grew tomatoes. I don't know whether I should say this but a lot of the out-of-date blood was used to help them to grow. To us it was quite exciting living in the Lodge because it was our first home, really. I remember going out and doing my first shopping. I bought provisions, I suppose, for the week, which probably cost under a pound in those days.

Anyway, eventually Anne was on the way. My mother wanted to come down, or I wanted my mother to come down and help me, but I had to have special permission for her to come down to Chichester because it was just before the invasion. The streets were sort of lined with these TLC's I think they were. Tank Landing Crafts, and things like that. Then she was given permission to come, which she did. And I had our daughter, Anne, in the Twyford Nursing Home. We had no transport so we had sort of people who used their cars to take us and I was taken to Twyford by one of these cars. And then I had Anne. I can remember hearing gunfire while I was waiting for her to come. I was in for a fortnight say, and I know when I came home, the deputy steward who must have had a lovely garden, had brought so many flowers that the house was full of flowers, which was absolutely super. I didn't do very much but look after the children, really. I used to join in the social side of it a bit. But that was about all. George was sort of in and out. He used to come home for lunch. [laughs] I remember Anne had a little tricycle; she used to sit on it watching the

George Jarratt's daughter playing outside The Lodge, summer 1945. [Courtesy: George Jarratt]

people going up and down to the hospital. We had a little garden, not much. It was just a sort of hedge and a lawn. And she used to see people going up and she used to say, 'My daddy makes people better'. [laughs]

George Jarratt

The most worrying time, I think, when I was there, was when we were getting the V-1 bombs coming over. We'd hear them coming over. Anne then was tiny, in the first year or so. And we used to grab her and take her to somewhere safe in the house and hope the flying bombs would go over.

Zaida Jarratt

Once they were overhead you sort of heaved a sigh of relief, because even if the engine stopped then they would go on somewhere else.

George Jarratt

Some poor old soul would get them somewhere else. We had some damage in Chichester from these things, but not a lot.

St Richard's cricket team, c.1946. (Crom Polson is in the front row extreme right.) [Courtesy: Crom Polson]

Sylvia Dadswell

We used to organise parties and stuff like that, you know. But it was difficult, really. There was not a lot of money, and there wasn't a lot of food so you couldn't. Of course, the pubs had no beer, and of course there were no trains. I had a month's holiday and I wasn't allowed to go away, so I stayed on the ward, because what do you do in Chichester if you're not allowed … And I couldn't … My home was in Oxford. But there were no trains and they did sort of say you shouldn't really leave.

Christmas was fun, though. I was on a children's ward one Christmas and we had all this wood. You see the windows up as far and the fanlights was this rough wood, so we got a roll of paper, you know, like wallpaper. I think they used to put it on the sheet, you know, the kind of stuff they have in surgeries now, they put you on a paper sheet. Well, we had rolls of this stuff and we cut up Christmas cards, and pictures of every description, we had a complete frieze, right round the kids' ward. It went on for weeks. And there was a pub that used to collect presents.

I've often thought, though, don't bother to send a toy to a child in hospital. Remember the poor kids that are in their own homes who don't have a lot. The decorations on the wards was wonderful. Halstead, on one occasion, we had an orderly who was an artist and we turned the whole place into an old-fashioned pub. We had built a sort of fireplace. We got the carpenter staff, you know, it's surprising what you can do if you talk to them nicely. And this orderly painted paper plates with a willow pattern on. The whole place was all sort of decorated like a pub. This was during the

The Christmas Pantomime, 1946. [Courtesy: Eric Skilton]

'Nursemaid's Knee'—Christmas Pantomime, 1946. (Paddy Whiteside is third from right, George Jarratt fourth from right, Douglas Martin, fifth from right.) [Courtesy: Paddy Whiteside]

war, yes, this was during the war, when you couldn't buy things, so things had to get made, you know. Christmas in hospital is great fun, great fun. You get rid of most of the patients, especially the difficult ones. [laughs] And the whole thing becomes … It's good fun.

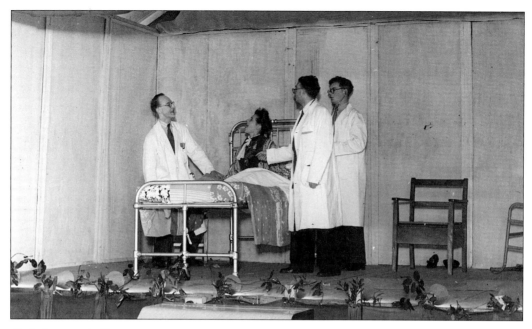

'Bedside manner', Christmas Pantomime, 1946. [Courtesy: Paddy Whiteside]

Eric Skilton

Usually at Christmas, Graylingwell was interesting. Graylingwell had … they used to get quite good symphony concerts up there and well known pianists used to perform up there because they had the room and the big hall. And if we had any mobile patients that could get up there we'd take them up. But otherwise there wasn't an awful lot that went on, sort of daily, as regards entertainment.

George Jarratt

We had to work hard, the work was there and it had to be done. We had a very happy atmosphere, though, in the hospital, because of Douglas and the Matron who ran things very well. The rest of the staff were always very helpful. We had actually in 1945 and 1946, at Christmas time, we had, did, two pantomimes, for which I'm afraid I was responsible both for the script and also for trying to direct these amateur actors. But we had a very jolly time. There was one male nurse who had been severely wounded in the head during the First World War when he was a warrant officer in the Royal Army Medical Corps. And he was a jack-of-all-trades and used to do all sorts of things, plasters and goodness knows what. He used to have very bad times sometimes with his head injury and Douglas and I used to try and cope with this. We used to give him a lot of paraldehyde at one time. Anyway, I've got some pictures of him as the good fairy in *Sleeping Beauty*, which is rather funny. In fact, in one of them I was in some sort of a laundry trolley, which was used to make a pram; I was in that as the babe. And two of the porters were the Ugly Sisters.

II
————

1948–1974

A RAPIDLY PROGRESSING SCENE

St Richard's and the Promise of the NHS

BETWEEN 1948 AND 1974, the administration of St Richard's passed from the County Council to the Chichester Hospital Management Committee with headquarters at 174 Broyle Road. St Richard's found itself the poor relation of the former voluntary hospital, Royal West Sussex, Broyle Road and intense rivalries existed throughout this period, St Richard's being referred to as 'Dirty Dicks' by the staff at Royal West Sussex. The leadership of Douglas Martin, at St Richard's, supported by E.P. 'Nobby' Clark and Paddy Whiteside, and followed by Bill Gammie from 1963, saw a steady improvement in the relationship between the staff of the two hospitals and the services provided at St Richard's. Part of the administration block was converted to a casualty and outpatient department, with a small X-ray department. The pathology department was moved from County Hall to one of the Emergency Medical Service huts. Two huts were converted for use as an obstetric department and one into a physiotherapy department. A paediatric ward was provided from part of one of the medical wards, and Paddy Whiteside converted a day ward into a coronary care unit. Not until 1961 was a twin operation theatre suite completed to replace the temporary theatre in the ward day room. Further plans for upgrading the wards and huts were pursued as funds allowed. There was no question of standing still as the medical staff were determined to keep the hospital in the forefront of medical advances. This rapidly progressing scene called for facilities for postgraduate medical education; thanks to the vision of Jack Mickerson, encouraged by Paddy Whiteside, one of the first four postgraduate medical centres in the region was built at St Richard's from voluntary donations, and later there were additions like the Goldsmith Undergraduate Centre for medical students in training. The subsequent development of this Centre, first opened in 1965, into the splendid Chichester Medical Education Centre of today forms part of our story. Finally, this period saw the start of an VIII-phase development plan for St Richard's, producing a new outpatient and casualty department, short stay, intensive and coronary care wards, two new theatres with a Central Sterile Supply Department and Theatre Sterile Supply Unit, and a new X-ray and pathology department, as well as the unexpected bonus of a maternity block.

`Money was always a problem`

THE ENVIRONMENT

❛Money was always a problem, so I campaigned to have these elaborate teas, which were served at committee meetings, with cakes, meringues, sandwiches, scones, and so on, reduced. I also made full visits to the hospital's kitchens, because, of course, all the food was strictly controlled.❜

(Maureen Davis-Poynter,
Chairman of St Richard's House Committee in the early '60s.)

In 1948, St Richard's was still in a state of 'in-betweens', gradually emerging from the restrictions of the war and rebuilding with the limited resources available to them. Paddy Whiteside, Crom Polson, Eric Skilton and Jean Monks recall 'making-do,' and the gradual introduction of improved facilities. This slowly changed during the 1950s and 1960s as more amenities were built, but these were still, as Jean Monks further recalls, facilities which by today's standards were quite primitive. Efforts were made to improve these facilities: both the buildings and the systems, which operated within them. Maureen Davis-Poynter remembers serving on the Hospital's House Committee as a Labour Councillor, for example, in the early 1960s and pushing through reforms for the quality of patients' food. The lack of resources, however, was a constant problem, so much so that even routine maintenance was left undone. There were, however, local, regional and national efforts to improve and develop these services. Shirley Roberts recalls the tinkering that occurred with nursing structures when the position of Matron was eliminated and replaced with the administrative post of Chief Nursing Officer in the late 1960s. Throughout the later 1960s and early 1970s there were developments in services, all of which required for implementation meetings and decisions and the difficult management of radical change. One major and significant development of buildings and services was the opening of the Chichester Medical Education Centre in 1966, one of the country hospital's leading post-graduate medical education centres in the country. Paddy Whiteside and Bill Gammie discuss its origin and early development. As structures were modified, there was a parallel demand for more and better services. The expectations of patients and doctors alike were increasing and they demanded some real attention, as Bill Gammie comments.

Paddy Whiteside

The Royal West Sussex Hospital and St Richard's Hospital worked to a degree in competition, but there was a requirement for all the beds provided by each of the hospitals. In addition to the patients in the Royal West paying what they could afford, there was also a local branch of the 'Hospital Saving Association', a voluntary patient subscription, where subscribers paid weekly or monthly to a fund, which would also pay towards the hospital care. That all ended in August 1948, when both hospitals became part of the National Health Service, financed centrally by the government. All staff became interchangeable and we were fortunate in that the medical staff, particularly, co-operated fully with each other.

The Royal West Sussex Hospital and its famous wisteria, c.1948.

The voluntary hospitals, as they were called in those days, took patients, generally, sent into hospital by their own GP, who was quite likely to be a staff member of his hospital. The senior staffing of the hospital was by a number of GPs, many of whom had done their higher degrees in medicine and surgery, but not all. With the introduction of the National Health Service, the GPs were compelled to decide whether they would carry on in general practice only, or give up general practice and become a hospital doctor.

There was a certain amount of friction between the old hospital and the new. Nobody at the Royal West Sussex Hospital welcomed the County Council building a hospital in Chichester. But while there was friction amongst some people, this was not so amongst the medical staff as a whole. The medical staff formed a Joint Medical Staff Committee and they actually had their first meeting on the day the National Health Service came into being, 5 July 1948. We had a senior GP as our Chairman to avoid any friction. Fortunately there was none and this was largely thanks to the diplomacy and common sense of the Senior Physician at the Royal West, Dr. Seward Morley and our Surgeon Superintendent at St Richard's, Dr. Douglas Martin.

Eric Skilton

When I came back in 1948, there was a young girl doing my job, who unfortunately had to leave because that was the regulation then. All servicemen had to be given back their job on returning after demobilisation. I'd come back to take up my occupation. I noticed the staff had been increased. There were more nurses. We had more resident doctors then. Outpatients was flourishing. The operating theatre remained the same. And there was still a certain amount of rationing on because one of the jobs I took on was dealing out soap coupons. They used to come to the office for soap coupons and things of that nature.

Crom Polson

When I started at the Hospital in 1948 the medical and surgical staff had not been fully appointed as far as the Regional Hospital Board was concerned. Douglas G. Martin was Surgeon Superintendent. He had a deputy, Nobby Clarke, E.P. Clarke, Nobby to everybody there. They were both resident and at times they thought nothing of a 24-hour day. Paddy Whiteside was the Physician, and his right-hand man at that time was a character called Jimmy James, a very good servant of the Hospital. We then were fortunate in getting Reg Weeks as the Casualty Officer and we thought now we really were going places. At that time, the operations were carried out in a converted ward in Ward I. There were so many operations done there with the anaesthetist in a little side ward, in the corridor, which was enclosed, and there was never any scare about cross-infection or any upset with the wards and patients. They certainly worked their heads off in that area. We later developed the new theatre and frankly the surgical staff didn't know they were born having been transferred from that, almost a cubbyhole, to a really new theatre. We were fortunate at that time to have a very good Matron, Miss Chapman. She was an elegant lady, firm, but compassionate and her presence around the Hospital was noticeable. She visited the wards, she knew all her nurses, she knew their failings and their good points and I am certain that of the cases I know personally, whenever one of her nurses was in trouble she was an absolute backbone for that nurse. Her shoulder was very large and they could rely on her. Miss Chapman will always be known as a Matron and she was symbolic with everything that people thought of as Matrons.

Jean Monks

We always had a Hospital Administrator in the sense that he was in charge of the money side of things, because they used to pay us actually in the Hospital with money when we got paid. And Mr. Polson was the head of the clerical side, like the medical records and the pay, and also the ordering of the drugs and dressings and instruments, theatre stuff and things like that. Dougie Martin's house was at the top of the drive and he was so proud that he was able to graft mistletoe onto apple trees and this was the first thing he showed you when you went to his house, how the mistletoe had grown.

Crom Polson

When I went to the interview I was met by Mr. Douglas Martin who seemed very pleased that I'd been appointed. When I took my post I must say that he greeted me with open arms. The Hospital itself had undergone a few changes. The erstwhile steward had left and the Matron had been off ill and one thing and another they were in a state of, well, 'in betweens'. The first thing I had to do was to look around the Hospital and see the staff situation and I remember firstly the assistant to the steward had also taken up an appointment in Lancashire, so I appointed Bob McFarlane to be my Deputy. The office staff had a Wages Section of two people; there were seven members in the general staff; I think there were three in the Medical Records and Matron had a secretary and I think they were the sum total to run the whole Hospital and I don't think any of them were under-employed. I always think of Eric Skilton who, apart from his job in the office, was responsible for the pensions of all the people, patients in Willowmead or as it was called then, the hutted wards. There were ten wards and he kept them and their pension books in order. He really was a tower of strength and a great intermediary between the patients and the Hospital. The medical records were very, very sparse on the ground in those days. Mrs. Fellows was the boss lady and she was considered as DG's [Douglas Martin's] secretary as well. We were later joined by Miss Walden who never stopped working and she always did everything at a trot. John English was later brought in to build up the medical records section and he did quite a good job of it.

At one of our monthly meetings of the House Committee the question of the hutted wards arose and D.G. Martin thought it would be a good idea if we altered the name, have a collective name instead of hutted wards and they hit on the idea of Willowmead, which was immediately accepted. Great discussion then occurred as to whether the huts themselves should be named after trees or flowers or what have you, and it was decided trees, and the men then put forward their views and that's how it came to be names! Now having completed the naming, Paddy Whiteside had a lot of patients across there and it was decided that this place was not actually as cold as the Arctic but it seemed to be because it rained so often, and whoever went across from the main Hospital to the wards, Willowmead, either got soaked or frozen. And the huts themselves were individual huts, ten of them, and we had a discussion one day as to the possibility of enclosing those huts and making them one composite unit. So we got George Drake who was the backbone of the carpentry staff; he was the only one, to give us a sketch of an idea, a price, and within a day we had the basic scheme. With the help of his fellow craftsmen he did that job single-handed and enclosed the whole ten wards, and it made it a palace compared with what it was previously.

The only good thing about the hutted wards came when we were allowed to use the shelters in between the huts as storage space for medical records, furniture and anything else that they could hold. There's no doubt that the enclosure of those wards was a wonderful idea. I remember George Drake when I approached him and told him that we were now going to proceed with this scheme, he put his hands on his hips and looked aghast. He pointed to his toolbag and he said, 'Do you know sir, the tools in that bag are exactly the same as that carpenter in Nazareth used. [laughs] And I've got to do this job!' He'd been hankering after a planing machine. He'd made his point, we provided him with a planing machine to get on with the job.

Pat Saunders

When I first went there we didn't have names to the main wards. They were floor one, two, three and four. But number one became Douglas Martin Ward, after the surgeon; number two was Stillman, who was the architect, G.C. Stillman, of the Hospital and the County Architect as well; and number three that became Halstead. Now that was a local man who had moved away years ago. He had a sort of an ironmongery business in those days in Chichester actually, before he moved away. But he left his money to St Richard's Hospital. And you might find the plaque still within the front entrance of the Hospital—for Halstead. And Baxendale Ward, that was number four ward, that was Mr. Baxendale, he was our Chairman just after the war, or during the war come to that. He was on the County Council. So I suppose they all went together.

In the hutted wards, there was no central heating as such. At that time the huts were fired by Tortoise stoves and during the day and night stokers had to trail in with their buckets of coal, stoke up the fire and disappear. If you were a light sleeper it was bad luck because this happened during the night as well. Those old coke stoves were a hell of a job really. It was under the porters, three special porters that used to take care of them on a twenty-four hour system. The fuel they used in those days was the old coke, being war time it used to be stock-piled out in the open. And it used to get wet. Coke was always a cheap commodity anyway. And these chaps they were inundated with fires going out all the time. They used to clinker up. They had a hell of a job. Not that they gave off a terrific heat anyway and, of course, with fires like that and stoves like that you had nothing but dust as well flying around the ward.

[The patients] they just kept in bed. They were mostly geriatric anyway and they were more or less a twenty-four hour bed job. They stayed under the blankets. The wards were very narrow in those days. Overcrowded. Well, I would not say actually overcrowded, there was enough room there but it was very narrow between the beds. You could just get the patient's locker in there. And just barely enough room to move around. There were a few chairs in the ward; those that could get up and sit up would.

We [the porters] didn't help them so much in those days. It was the nurses' job. But, yes we did get the job occasionally of going and collecting them and taking them up for X-rays and that sort of thing. Because the X-ray was in the main building and they were in the hutted ward. They were pushed over on trolleys or chairs if they could manage a chair. The maternity block was over there as well. That was just a half a ward in those days, I think it was about eight or nine beds. And any operations, Caesarean and that sort of thing, well, they had to be taken to the main theatre.

We had Oaklands Park House in College Lane that was used for nurses at St Richard's Hospital. They had a little bit of transport there. They mostly walked across the field to St Richard's and then back up at night as it was a lonely old lane, College Lane, and very scary, hardly any lights there in those days. The porters used to have the

Aerial view of St Richard's Hospital, c.1970. [Courtesy: May Burrows]

job of escorting those nurses who required it. Those that didn't have their boyfriends escorting them, that is. Then the Oaklands Park House nurses they transferred into the old Isolation Hospital in Spitalfield Lane.

Dennis Barratt

In the 1950s there was a main block, but in those days it was just 1, 2, 3, 4. The present car park was an allotment; there were playing fields, there was a drive in, just the same, the front door's the same. There was Willowmead, the hutted wards, there was no Medical Centre. There was a nurses' home. But when I was there the hutted wards were just A, B, C, D, E, A1, B1, C1, D1 and E1 you see. The main hospital wards were just 1, 2, 3 and 4. There was the doctor's flat. There was out-patients. There were administrative offices. There was no chapel.

In 1954, there were no changes in the fabric, the blast walls were still there, because we used to be surrounded by blast walls around those huts—huge thick brick walls. That's one thing when we came back they started to knock them down, because we couldn't see very well, because they cut a lot of light out, as blast walls ought to, you know, because they're up in front of the windows. Dr. Harrison, the Pathologist, got up a working party and we all went out there with hammers and chisels and started taking these bricks off and one of the administrators, when he got to hear about it, he came hurtling out. We got thrown off this wall [laughter]. It was the demolition of this wall in no uncertain terms. We weren't allowed to do this that and the other. So those blast walls remained for a long, long time and reduced the light

In 'the yard', preparing the float for Gala Day, c.1950s. [Courtesy: Paddy Whiteside]

quite a lot. They eventually went. They were thick brick walls about 18 inches thick, I suppose, and stood, well as high as the huts, the guttering of the huts. They were in sections covering all the windows all the way round. Anti-bomb blasts, post war relics really. It must have been quite depressing stuck in those huts as a patient, because they were around every window. I mean the sisters used to do their best hanging flowers in baskets or things like that, but they were still there.

May Burrows

In 1954, the actual theatre was on the ground floor. It was called 'one' in my day, and was a four-bedded ward turned into a theatre. The windows contained wooden frames with gauze attached to them, butter muslin, and at the weekend one of our jobs was to take those frames out of the windows, wash the butter muslin, scrub the frames and put it back up again. It was very primitive. All our instrument cupboards were in the theatre, you see, and there were the old drums we used to use, and they used to be autoclaved for us. And we had no proper theatre uniform as such; I mean, we used to go into the theatre with our nurses' uniform with a gown on the top. We had no special uniform. No we just used to have to put a gown on when we went into the theatre, that was our uniform you see. And the one thing I liked about the uniform, we didn't have any stiff collars to worry about, it was just a nice soft collar attached to a dress.

Eric Skilton

During the '50s there was an easier attitude and you weren't doing so much work. You were doing a set job, like I was doing admissions, discharges and burials, as you say. Somebody else was doing catering and somebody else was doing the wages and finance and then eventually the Finance Department was opened up separately. The finance moved up to, what we called, the old hospital in Chichester. A lot of the nurses lived in Oaklands Park in the House up there opposite Bishop Otter College. Lots of the nurses lived there. And a lot of nurses were billeted out. My wife was billeted out in private accommodation. The Nurses' Home was full up. Then going back to the Nurses' Home you weren't allowed to enter there at all as a male. You had to ring the bell and wait for the Home's house-keeping sister to come down and see what you wanted. Males weren't allowed into the Nurses' Home under any circumstances without being escorted in and out in those days.

Clive Bratt

Early on in the '50s we only had four full-time consultants, and two surgeons. One physician—general physician. One obstetric and gynae consultant, who was Miss Everell Shippam, of the Shippam family. And Donald Wilson was rheumatology. All the other specialities were covered by people coming in. Some share, such as the paediatrics that was covered by one of the general physicians at the Royal West who came over and did the paediatrics at St Richard's. Dermatology was covered by a

Dr. Colin Jones from Brighton, who did the Brighton hospitals, Worthing hospitals and St Richard's. Neurology, we had no neurological clinic except a Doctor William Gooddy from the National Hospital for Nervous Diseases, lived at Haslemere—and at one time rang Dr. Whiteside, the physician consultant, and said, 'You know, Paddy, I'd be happy to see any interesting cases you've got on a Sunday morning'. And so every alternate Sunday morning we had a neurological clinic with a man of great expertise. Anaesthetics was shared between the hospitals. In fact one anaesthetist did us and Worthing. So there were just the one, two, three, four full-time consultants, who were based on St Richard's. Except the rheumatologist, Donald Wilson worked elsewhere, but he considered St Richard's his base. And all the rest were part-time. All the other specialities were covered by part-time. And the house officers, there were two house surgeons, a junior house physician, a senior house physician, a surgical registrar, a medical registrar, an obstetric registrar and the casualty admission officer. That was the total of the house doctors.

Paddy Whiteside

The Residents lived in a special part of the Hospital which was the Residents' Quarters. The nurses had always the Nurses' Home, of course, but the Residents' Quarters was a flatlet above the administration of the Hospital. I don't think anyone lived there when they were married. But, of course, following the improvement that took place in the 1950s, late 1950s, married quarters were built, not just for the doctors, but for other staff in the Hospital.

Marjorie Semmens

At the time we were there were very few staff. We were all single. We lived above the area, which is now part of the Administrative Department, so I suppose there were probably only about eight residents running the whole hospital.

Robin Agnew

However, being up at night time seemed part of our way of life. My only problem was that I didn't have a proper bedroom to sleep in. The only space available was at the end of the corridor in the Doctor's Residency and they had rigged up a bed there with a telephone and a screen around it. I was told by the Admin. staff that I was on the waiting list for a bedroom, as soon as one would become available. Funnily enough I didn't seem to mind this all that much in those days because one didn't spend an awful lot of time in bed anyway.

Bill Gammie

I well recall first appearing in St Richard's in 1963 because it was a very different scene to what it is now. On arrival it was quite a tranquil institution. The main entrance was on the west side of the Hospital which is now hidden partly by the bridge going on to the new block—the Obstetric block—and there is a slight underpass at this moment, and that was all level ground. And there was a few cars parked opposite the main entrance. Beyond that there was a row of trees where the Obstetric Unit is—very tall trees—and beyond that the playing fields of Bishop Otter College.

There were very few staff cars to consider in those days, which is quite fascinating. And the consultants' car park was in the loading bay just round the back on the north side of the hospital corridor and there were about five consultant parking spaces. Mr. Clark, the senior surgeon, who had been Deputy Superintendent since the Hospital opened, had a little garage as also, I think, had Dr. Whiteside, who had been at the Hospital since 1946.

Going in the main entrance to the Hospital, on the left-hand side of the entrance you went to a small corridor with the administrative offices, where Crom Polson ruled overall. And then to the right-hand side there was the out-patients; and along that corridor, on the left, there was the X-ray department and at the end of the corridor the casualty department. One went up the main corridor to the main ward block and that was a four-storey block with on the first and second floors surgical beds and on the third and fourth floors the medical beds. And a little bit further up the corridor the two purpose-built operating theatres, which had only been constructed, as I recall it, in 1961. Prior to that the operating theatre had been in the day ward on the ground floor of Douglas Martin Ward and the anaesthetic room had been one of the offices just adjacent to the day-room. And that temporary operating theatre had been converted, or put up, in 1939-40. That particular day-room is still there. The instruments were sterilised one floor up and brought down. And it took nearly twenty years after the Hospital was first built to actually build a pair of purpose-built operating theatres. And this was really quite an achievement.

Jean Monks

Sometime in the '60s, the main and only theatre for the Hospital was in the Douglas Martin South Ward which is a four-bedded ward and they had the main theatre there, and we did all the operations there. The office of the ward had to be turned into a surgeon's changing room. The sterilising room for the theatre was down the corridor next to the linen room on ward one. And all the hot water and cleaning of the instruments had to be done upstairs. Just really at the top of the stairs which is now turned into a lavatory or something, I think. I mean it was very, very primitive.

Marjorie Semmens

The hospital itself was very much smaller in those days, in the '60s I mean, it only had the hutted area which was the geriatrics, and what's called South Block, the pink block, as active parts of the hospital, you see. Subsequently, Maternity came up. I mean I was there when the Maternity was built and we moved from the first hut into Maternity. And then the Children's Wards which had been in the South Block and over at the Royal West Sussex they got together, and that's how Howard Ward

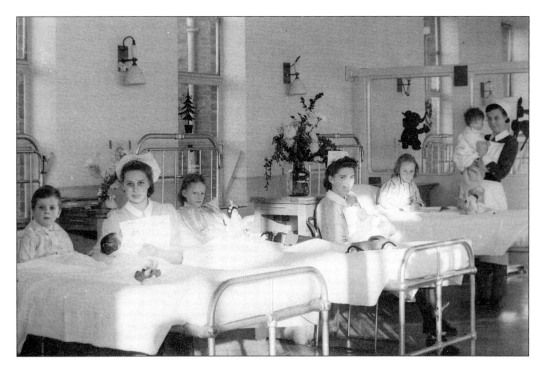

Ward 3, December 1948. (Nurse Betty O'Connell, left, Sister Norah Mattocks and Nurse Jean Monks, centre.)
[Courtesy: Jean Monks]

evolved. By the 1960s, paediatrics had developed. So if you were doing paediatrics as a job, the juniors, they had to use bicycles to get over to the Children's Ward to do ward rounds over there with the paediatrician when he came. Then they had to go back to St Richard's because there's been a call for something else. Many's the time [laughs] one hears of individuals going on a bicycle, which means coming round where there is now the dual-carriageway, which, of course, wasn't there then; round the theatre car park, there was only a single road there then, and going on the wrong side of the road to cut the corner to get up to the Royal West as quickly as possible.

Shirley Roberts

In 1963, we had two theatres at St Richard's, we had one theatre at Broyle Road and we had one theatre at Bognor. Now the theatre at Broyle Road was closed around 1971, when the work at the Royal West Sussex was transferred to St Richard's. The theatre at Bognor was closed in 1975 and from 1975 until the present time St Richard's has been endowed with only four operating theatres. It has never increased. [*Until the new wing was opened in December 1996.*] There were intensive efforts made by the surgeons over that 20-year period to increase the number of theatres available. We have existed on four theatres for all those years.

At the time I came there was Miss Shippam and Mr. Lynn Evans who were the gynaecologists at that time working at St Richard's. They were sharing, I mean. Before the transfer of work from Broyle Road around 1971 the gynaecologists were using the general surgical wards. The maternity block had not been built. So particularly the first floor surgical wards were at times somewhat dominated by gynaecological patients. It was always a slight source of friction, I think, between the general surgeons. Because you had, in fact, only 98 beds for use by the general surgeons, the gynaecologists and the orthopaedic surgeons. And there were no designated orthopaedic beds. It was really a free-for-all as to who had the beds. And it was inevitable that those that had the greatest emergency intake tended to occupy most of the beds. But despite that, somehow or other we managed to keep a reasonable turnover. I think it was partly helped by the fact that the hutted wards at St Richard's in the 1960s, of course, were labelled the geriatric wards. I don't think that term is regarded with much favour these days, but in fact there was a considerable back-up of beds in the war time huts built up in Willowmead.

In the 1960s, with house committees at Broyle Road and St Richard's, I soon found myself nominated the nursing representative on the House Committee which met once a month to discuss very mundane things like the catering in the hospital, the cleaning services and various other things. But it gave one a little insight into some of the problems of running a hospital. And it allowed one to meet a number of the local worthies who had an interest in the welfare of the institution. It didn't seem to have too much bearing on clinical activity but if one thought of it in the wider sense, of course, like any institution, the provision of these services is absolutely vital. And it was probably very relevant that there should be some medical input into their deliberations, because the well meaning members of the public had their own ideas as to how such an institution should be run but there was also the question of whether some of their views conflicted with current medical thought and opinion.

Maureen Davis-Poynter

I was Chairman of St Richard's House Committee and our duties were to visit the Hospital regularly and make reports to the Regional Hospital Board. Our meetings used to take place at the Royal West. There was this huge oblong table with about twenty people sitting round it. We would be served a very expensive tea by the Matron, who was Miss Rice then, and she would be dressed in full coiffure gear with starched cap and starched apron. Money was always a problem, so I campaigned to have these elaborate trays with cakes, meringues, sandwiches, scones, and so on reduced. I also made full visits to the hospital's kitchens because, of course, all the food was strictly controlled.

There was an allowance for each hospital and when I was going round the kitchens I noticed there was a large number of tins, large tins and packets which were mixes of various kinds. For instance, I knew the meringues we had at the Board meetings were not homemade meringues from real egg white. They were out of a packet or out of a tin and I did query the quality of this. Why couldn't the patients have fresh vegetables instead of, perhaps, dried beans or carrots? I was told the cost of producing fresh food was far too prohibitive and there was no cause for worry; all the required nutrients were in the packets.

Heather Jeremy

I started in the canteen in 1969, It was called Canteen then and somehow it became The Tea Bar. It's in the Outpatients Department; always has been; and was for outpatients, hospital visitors and staff. It was considerably smaller when I started. It only needed two people to serve and it was a little sort of narrow strip of ground as it were, with a counter and some cupboards and, as I say, I think there were so few customers in those days it just needed two of us. My other partner was then 80 years old, would you believe [laugh]. Splendid old girl and she lived to be 95, I gather. [laugh]

Shirley Roberts

The Salmon Report came out in 1966. [*Ministry of Health and Scottish Home and Health Department,* Report of the Committee on Senior Nursing Staff Structures, *HMSO, 1966.*] The Salmon structure created more of a management structure for nurses with the responsibility for specialist type of nursing, surgical, or medical, rather than have a Matron looking after everything, including domestic and catering and other things, which really weren't immediately involved with nursing. The nurses managed the nursing service and the structure was that you had a Principal Nursing Officer, with so many senior Nursing Officers looking after say, Medicine, Surgery, Theatres, Accident and Emergency, Outpatients. And then under them were a number of Nursing Officers who looked after, say, a group of wards, or a suite of theatres. It was a bit top heavy, really. The idea was, nationally, that they had so many pilot schemes, but because everybody liked the general philosophy behind it people started to introduce the Salmon structure to their Health Authorities, or Health Management Hospitals, as they were before the pilot scheme could come back with any comments. I think that was what happened in Chichester because Chichester began to establish the—what was known as the Salmon structure. They appointed Anne Whitney here as the Chief Nursing Officer and she came from the Isle of Wight. She was the Chief Nursing Officer to the Chichester Hospital Management Committee when I came. She had the responsibility for setting up the Salmon structure right across the board, because her responsibilities included Graylingwell, the Community, and the Acute Services, which was principally St Richard's Hospital, together with two hospitals in Bognor Regis then, the War Memorial and the Bognor Chest Hospital, and a cottage hospital at Midhurst. So it was quite a wide geographical area.

It was a management post, I then had to set up the structure, as it were, as according to the Salmon Report, which included, there were three Senior Nursing Officers, one to look after the Obstetric and Gynaecological nursing, that was somebody called Anne Buckler, one to look after the General Services, the Medicines, Surgery, Theatres, Accident and Emergency and so on and one to look after the Night Duty. I had to make those appointments and one had to, at that point, sort of absorb the people who were in post, which was quite a difficult time for them. There were more

(Opposite) A page from a publicity brochure, 1950.

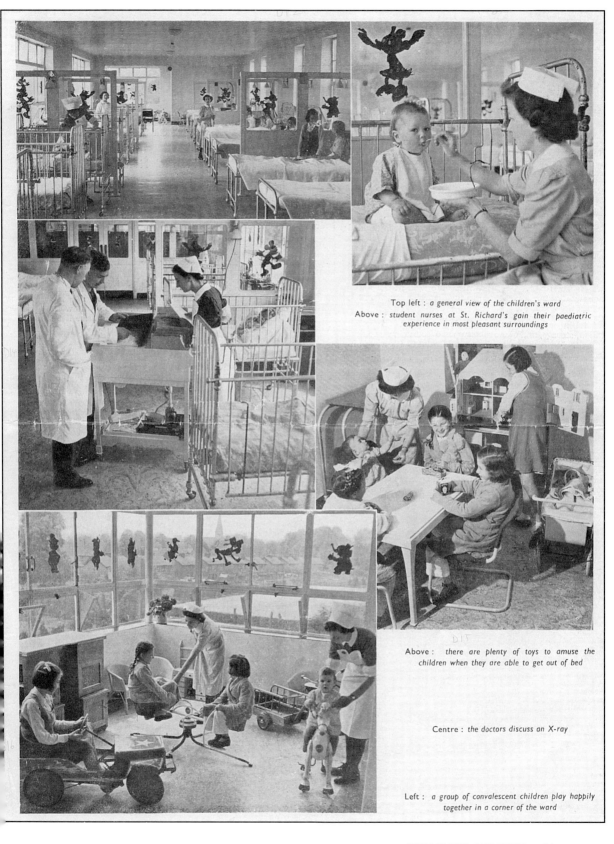

Top left : *a general view of the children's ward*

Above : *student nurses at St. Richard's gain their paediatric experience in most pleasant surroundings*

Above : *there are plenty of toys to amuse the children when they are able to get out of bed*

Centre : *the doctors discuss an X-ray*

Left : *a group of convalescent children play happily together in a corner of the ward* people than there were jobs at that point, because they were still slightly suffering from the linking together of the Royal West Sussex and St Richard's. So there were people there who had been Deputy Matrons of the Royal West; there were a lot of Royal West people.

Paddy Whiteside

During the '60s, it became popular to open, at the district hospitals, Medical Education Centres of our own, and not just to rely on the medical education offered by the big London hospitals. St Richard's was one of the early pioneers in this type of development. We officially opened the Chichester Medical Education Centre (CMEC) on 30 April 1966. Our best known physician, Sir George Pickering, who was the Professor of Medicine at Oxford, opened it. And at that opening we had a very interesting transatlantic link up with Philadelphia in the United States via the Telstar and a discussion on various problems with the Philadelphia physicians. We chose Philadelphia because, of course, the Quakers who opened up Philadelphia came from Sussex. The Centre is really due to the inspiration and drive of Dr. Jack Mickerson who was its first Chairman. He was my junior physician appointed next after myself. He managed to get a lot of money in, which allowed us to get a first-class development.

The Medical Centre was to be modernised continuously over the years since we first started it in temporary buildings, and it's really now one of the best in Britain, fortunately. I mean various societies would meet there, not just societies from Chichester but from Britain itself. It dealt with all aspects of medicine, medical education, but it was used, of course, mostly by the GPs and hospital staff in Chichester to increase their training. Each of the consultants who had a speciality would lecture us all on his speciality.

Nurses attended any para-nursing subject, but they also, of course, had their own meetings within the Medical Centre. Thanks to our generosity [laughs] because the Health Service didn't provide any of this. There's a library there, too; anyone, not just the nurses, may visit our Library, which is a very fine one indeed, to look up any subject. We were very fortunate in having an on-going legacy from Mr. Dinwoodie who had been a patient of Dr. Mickerson, and when he offered to help the Hospital, Dr. Mickerson wisely chose medical education. Mr. Dinwoodie owned, and his family still owns, big quarry areas which still produce a large quantity of money, which has facilitated the on-going development of this Centre. Before Mr. Dinwoodie came on the scene, all the money was raised by the people of Chichester, and more than 50 per cent of that was from doctors in the area who produced this Centre. In many ways, the Centre has been pioneering. It has always been kept up-to-date. It has a lot of contacts with the London teaching hospitals, and of course more recently this has been furthered by setting up of a Medical Student Centre, to which the London teaching hospitals send down students for experience. They would stay in the hospital, seeing all patients in casualty and in the wards, over a period of six to eight weeks.

Bill Gammie

When I arrived, the Post-Graduate Medical Centre was being discussed fairly actively at that time, led by Jack Mickerson who had taken on the task of furthering post-graduate education at Chichester. And in fact I've always been rather intrigued at the total cost of it, £15,000. The initial Medical Centre, of course, was a hutted building built on one level. It had its library and its reading room and one lecture theatre, which was also used as a dining room and secretarial offices. So it was a rather restricted building but it was built with the purpose, on a site which gave it the opportunity for expansion in the course of the subsequent years. And that is only too evident if you look at the site and see that the whole of the site is now occupied by the building.

Nurses' sitting room at the Nurses' Home, c.1950.
[Courtesy: Paddy Whiteside]

At the time the building was being established and in the mid–1960s raising the sum of £15,000 seemed quite daunting but Walter Dinwoodie happened to be a patient of Jack Mickerson's in the ordinary medical outpatients. Jack mentioned to him that he was looking for funds for this centre and Walter Dinwoodie said that he would be very happy to make a contribution. At that stage the extent of his contribution was unknown. But he certainly made a contribution to the initial building.

Suddenly, he died in 1968. At that stage he and Jack had been discussing further developments of the Medical Centre. Fortunately, Mrs. Dinwoodie and the Trustees established a continued working relationship with the Trustees of the Medical Centre. We were able, therefore, to continue with stage 2 and the final stage development of the Centre.

In the early 1960s the British Postgraduate Federation decided that there should be established centres for postgraduate medical education at district general hospitals. In the region, Chichester was one of the first four of these centres to be developed. And we saw many advantages accruing to Chichester, if we could pursue this particular course. Because if you have a good postgraduate centre then you would attract better quality junior medical staff. And I think the spin-off from that has been only too evident over the years. It was quite up-hill work. I still recall on the surgical side that Roger Miles had been appointed clinical tutor. And in the early days we decided that we would set up regular Wednesday afternoon meetings with the junior staff. There was a slight sales resistance to this in some way because the junior staff were not all that enthusiastic initially. Partly because there were relatively few junior staff and their assistance was required by other colleagues. The junior surgical staff, for instance, had to service the orthopaedic surgeons as well as the general surgeons. And if the general surgeons weren't using the theatres on a Wednesday afternoon then the orthopaedic surgeons might be using them and they required the junior staff. And there were many of the early meetings that we set up when Roger Miles, myself and Nobby Clark and Colin Knowles—our enthusiastic pathologist—used to sit and wait patiently for the rest of the team, or some of the team to appear for the weekly surgical meetings.

It was a little easier I think when one got round to the 1970s when everything was focused on the St Richard's site. Then you had certainly more junior staff on site and you had a greater opportunity of organising regular meetings on a wider scale. And these became audit meetings—surgical audit came into the field. And one was increasingly discussing the audit of surgical activity which included morbidity as well. And it became a very much more formal event. In fact, during the 1970s the surgical meetings took off and they have increasingly established themselves and I think they have remained on a Wednesday afternoon since Roger Miles first established it.

It was a great fillip to Chichester, I think, when Roger Miles who had pioneered as first surgical tutor at Chichester—and was one of the leaders in the field in the South West Thames region—was appointed as Penrose May tutor by the Royal College of Surgeons. He was the first Penrose May tutor appointed outside the college itself in a district general hospital. And this was a mark of the esteem by the surgical establishment that postgraduate training in a place like Chichester had been effective.

In 1970, I was elected by my colleagues to chair the Joint Medical Staff Committee, which consisted of elected consultants from the Royal West, St Richard's and Graylingwell. We met on a monthly basis. Our part was to advise the then Hospital Management Committee [HMC] on matters medical. This related both to the developments of services and the provision of special services and any other factors that the HMC would put to the medical staff committee.

It was an interesting time because the government was then proposing a reorganisation of the Health Service, which eventually took place in 1974. Prior to this there was a scheme for developing more cohesive advisory committees within the Hospital. This scheme was called the Cogwheel Scheme, [*Ministry of Health,* First Report of the Joint Working Party on the Organisation of Medical Work in Hospitals (Cogwheel 1), *HMSO, 1967; Department of Health and Social Security,* Report of the Working Party on the Organisation of Medical Work in Hospitals (Cogwheel 11), *HMSO, 1972.*] and the idea was that the various divisions such as medicine and of surgery should set up small committees of all members of the surgical and medical teams. Added to them, of course, there were sub-divisions like anaesthesia and the pathology services and the radiology services. We opted in fact at Chichester to have only two divisions of medicine and surgery and the anaesthetists joined the surgeons as a small sub-committee and the pathologists and radiologists similarly joined the medical division.

This did seem to allow development of a more cohesive advisory structure within the district, in preparation for the setting up in 1974 of the District Medical Committee. In 1974 the administration of the hospitals within our district came under the care of the West Sussex Health Authority and there were district committees who looked after the interests of the specific hospitals within the Chichester district, as also within the Worthing district and the Mid-Downs district.

The District Medical Committee, of which I was chairman for its first three years, was made up of a group of nominated consultants and general practitioners because the concept of the reforms in 1974 was that there should be increasing inter-relationship formed between the general practitioner services and the hospital services. It turned out to be quite a useful working forum, certainly for a group of consultants and general practitioners to get together and discuss and air views as to how the services should be developed to the benefit of the public of the Chichester district. At that time, of course, the development of the district hospital on the St Richard's site was still anticipated to go ahead to completion on its eight separate phases, to provide a complete district hospital on the Spitalfield Road site.

Unfortunately, with the reforms of 1974, it was increasingly apparent that resources were not going to be available for this and there had been a change of government at that time and Mrs. Barbara Castle became the Minister of Health. Many promises had been made with regard to improving the lot for the staff in the Health Service, particularly with regards to their long-standing quest for higher remuneration. Unfortunately, as so often happens, these political wishes are not so easily granted when it comes down to looking at the overall resource of the service. And the only resource that the new Minister of Health could find was in the capital budget as opposed to the revenue budget. As a result of this, the developments at Chichester were suddenly halted in 1975 and we did not, at that time, achieve the completion of the buildings on the St Richard's site. This was to have a considerable impact on the Hospital over the next 20 years because in these plans it had been agreed that there should be eight operating theatres and new facilities for central sterile supply and also supplying sterile goods for the general practitioner services without the hospital. There was also going to be a considerable increase in the beds on the hospital site and other increases in facilities for the hospital service and, to some extent, for the general practitioners. We were cut and therefore we had to re-allocate our resources to various smaller areas in the development. I think part of the difficulty, and one found this as chairman, was to try and see a fair distribution of resource amongst the various specialities within the hospital. Chichester also had the added burden of a large psychiatric institution adjacent to the St Richard's site, all of which had to be resourced from the same finite source.

We came into a lot of criticism for the actual physical structure of the buildings. The lack of maintenance over many, many years. The lack of simple painting and decorating was only too evident to so many of us and this was going to consume quite a lot of our financial resource in the years ahead. At the same time the demand for medical services was increasing. The expectation of our public was increasing and with new developments in technology there was a further demand for special facilities to be provided.

'The surgeon was the boss of the ward'

THE WORK

> ❛ The surgeon was the boss of the ward, and you ran it, carrying out his order. And you were responsible for carrying out his orders. You were in charge of the patients' welfare and treatments and you were in charge of the domestics and you were in charge of seeing that the patients were fed properly. You were responsible to the Matron and if you didn't do your job properly the Matron would have you in the office and tell you so. It was still very hierarchical. We didn't quite salute but it was nearly up to that. ❜ *(Jean Monks, Ward Sister)*

The introduction of the National Health Service brought with it a standardisation of jobs and training. As new working procedures changed, so, too, did medical knowledge and peoples' expectations and demands from a health service which promised to take care of the welfare of all. Paddy Whiteside and Marjorie Semmens recall how the new grading and training affected those working at St Richard's at the time. They further recall how St Richard's was still, in many ways, a total institution in that the doctors and nurses used to be resident, and were presided over by the Deputy Superintendent and the Matron, who were undoubtedly paternal and maternal figures for them. Over this time period, however, this structure of benign paternalism was gradually to change and fundamentally to alter the way the staff viewed their work. The conditions the staff worked under were also slowly changing. Dennis Barratt talks of the Pathology Laboratory, for example, and mentions what health and safety standards were in retrospect and how by today's standards they were quite lax. May Burrows recalls working conditions in the theatre during the 1950s, and how they had to labour under what would now be considered arduous and primitive circumstances. There was, however, a gradual movement under the NHS to a centralism and, with this and the developments that were taking place in the expansion of medical knowledge generally, there came a transition towards more specialism, more compartmentalisation. This seemed to be an advance to many, especially as it was accompanied by an enlargement of services and a development of the buildings and infrastructures in which the services were offered. However, some saw this increasing specialism as a movement away from the family-like unity they felt they once had. Crom Polson and Eric Skilton discuss some of the management improvements they developed in administrative procedures; while Dennis and Judy Barratt talk of this move towards specialisation. Bill Gammie and May Burrows recount the gradual developments and advancements they saw in technology, which radically altered the way they worked and the attitudes they had towards their work. They saw that procedures were being made possible in a way that they never had been before and that these pushed forward the frontiers of their own and their patients' expectations in a radical and exciting way. The support personnel discuss the changes they saw in their work during this period. Heather Jeremy, a WRVS worker in the Tea Bar, recalls the spirit of volunteerism which pervaded and which, in many ways, still echoed the spirit of camaraderie fostered during the war. Trevor Hayes, from the Catering Department, recounts how his division, as other divisions in the Hospital, was centralised, and how the supplying and serving of food was increasingly mechanised. Bill Gammie, Paddy Whiteside, Judy Barratt, Crom Polson and Pat Saunders all comment on the expansion of facilities and services during the 1970s and how this changed the fundamental nature of their work. These changes, also, of course, influenced their own career development as they moved more and more into administrative roles and were responsible for ensuring the smooth running of newly introduced procedures.

Bill Gammie

In 1948, when the state took over the hospitals, it was decided that many of the hospital jobs should be regraded and this applied to all the senior Medical staff. Each of the doctors had to apply for their own jobs and would be graded as a consultant or a Senior Hospital Medical Officer (SHMO). The more junior doctors would become Junior Hospital Medical Officers (JHMO), or housemen. This was possibly understandable in that some of the hospitals in the country were not of a very high standard but this could not apply to either St Richard's or the Royal West Sussex Hospitals where all the staff affected had higher degrees in their own specialities.

Senior members of the London Teaching Hospitals, who had already become consultants, undertook the grading. They, of course, had little knowledge of the local hospitals and their staff. To take Chichester as an example, only two of the standing staff, Dr. H. Seward Morley and Mr. Douglas Martin, were graded as consultants. The remaining nine became SHMOs, with a large drop in salary and prestige. The anger throughout the profession, throughout the country, was such that grading committees were reformed and five of our staff, Dr. Guy Emerson and Dr. Paddy Whiteside, physicians; Mr. E.P. 'Nobby' Clarke and Mr. D.A. Langhorne, surgeons; and Dr. Edgar Wallace, chest physician were upgraded formally to consultants. The remaining staff, all of the Royal West Sussex Hospital, remained in general practice. Subsequent appointments, from 1948 onward were graded at their appointments.

Marjorie Semmens

The National Health Service was inaugurated on 5 July 1948, and one of the things that followed that was standardisation of training. It has changed since then, but not the initial training. You still have to do your year pre-registration and then you make a choice as to what you can do. Now, today, career training is a little more narrowed. You almost have to make your mind up at the end of your first year. I didn't have to do that because you were much freer to do things, so I actually had a run of doing a number of things.

As a student you worked and learned about surgery. Once you'd qualified you went and assisted. But it might mean just, if you were assisting at an operation, you were probably holding an instrument called a retractor, which meant you were holding the wound open so that the surgeon could see what was going on. As they got to know you, and knew that you were capable of doing things you would stitch up. But, of course, if you were doing casualty, you had somebody coming in who'd had a fall and split their head you just got the needle out and sewed them up that night: put a pad on and sent them home. Or you made your decision about admitting them because they had an awful headache, and they might have meningitis. Mind you, you had other people, you had your registrar behind you. There was always somebody to refer to, and if you were really in difficulty you got the consultant in.

Jean Monks

The nurse training compared with now it was as different as chalk and cheese. We had a PTS, Preliminary Training Core [School], and in my PTS there were about six of us. We used to have lectures on Mondays, Wednesdays and Fridays, and then on Tuesdays, Thursdays and Saturday or Sunday we were on duty on the ward. We had one day off a week. So it was either Saturday or Sunday. And my first ward was the ward I eventually became a Ward Sister on, the Male Surgical Ward. We had to do everything. We had to do the dusting. We had to do the meals. First of all in the morning we used to go in and make the beds on one side, because we used to work on both sides. There were two wards with a central office and a corridor leading out, and on one side were a lot of old men who'd got bladder trouble. On the other side, were the younger end with hernias, and we even did eye surgery in those days, and fractures, things like that, orthopaedics. Mr. Martin and Mr. Clark did everything. They did fractures, orthopaedics, gynaecology, general surgery, you name it. They could turn their hand to anything.

The Matron in 1948, she controlled the nurses. She organised the nurses and was responsible for them over-all. You could call her the mother. And we had a Home Sister who looked after the nurses. We all had to live in. And we had to be in by half past ten at night and actually the Night Sister would come round and see that we were all in bed. And the Nurses' Home was locked and it was known as 'The Virgins' Retreat'. Well, they were responsible for us, you see. They were in *loco parentis*. I mean, I was nearly twenty-one by this time but a lot of them were only eighteen. And in those days you didn't have the vote at eighteen remember. That didn't come in until a lot later. But if you were 21 you were adult, or supposed to be.

They were terribly strict. You had to have your hair a certain length. You were supposed to be clean and smart. I mean, they didn't actually do a sort of uniform thing, but if you weren't looking up to snuff you would get told about it. And if you broke a thermometer, inadvertently dropped it or whatever, you used to have to go and confess to the Matron to get a new one. You didn't have to pay for it because we really didn't have any money. I mean you can imagine, what we got, I don't know what it was, but it was an extremely small amount of money, because we were clothed and fed and our board and lodging was included in it and we got a small amount of money. But it was extremely small.

We had our food in the main dining room. That was in the main hospital on the first floor. We had shifts. To begin with we worked split duties which would be from seven-thirty in the morning until one-thirty, and then you would have, what was known as a two to five-fifteen off and then you were back on duty and you worked until eight-thirty. And then later they brought in what was known as a shift system, where you did two late duties, which would be from two to ten, and then the next week you'd do one week of early duties, which would be seven-thirty until four-fifteen or four-thirty. Then you would go on night duty on the Saturday night. You would work from seven-thirty in the morning till twelve-thirty; then you'd have your lunch; then you were off duty until ten o'clock that night when you went on duty until eight o'clock the next morning. The next month, you see, you'd be on one late, two earlies, and then night duty. It was quite exhausting really, because you never quite got used to one shift before you were on to another one.

We had a Miss Carol, who was the Sister Tutor; she was extremely good, and we did our anatomy and physiology and we used to have lectures by the doctors on medicine and surgery. Mr. Martin, Mr. Clark, Paddy Whiteside; we did have a series of physicians. We also had physicians from the Royal West Sussex Hospital, who were separate in those days, to give us lectures, as well, in the Nurses' Home actually, or in a bigger room on the hutted wards.

We did have a main kitchen, which cooked all the meals. And they came down in trolleys and you used to serve them out. In the beginning, when I was there, they used to be served from the kitchen and then they got these special trolleys which then you would put into the ward and then you'd dish them out from your actual trolley. But you didn't have them plated. You actually had a whole thing of potato and carrots and meat and whatever. And you would dish it out. You know, 'Mr Smith, would you like mince today or would you like chop?' Or whatever it was, fish and chips.

We used to make tea. We used to have to cut the sandwiches, cut the bread, butter the bread in the kitchen after lunch when the patients were having an hour's nap, and then we used to go round with the tea trolley, which had a great big teapot on it, and go round the ward dishing out cups of tea. And they used to send down cakes from the kitchen, but we used to butter the bread, and they used to have bread and jam, or whatever—Marmite. We didn't stop. We never sat down. If you sat down it was a disgrace. The Matron used to do a daily round and she used to do it after you were supposed to have dusted, and she used to do that on the lockers, and that on the lights. She used to wipe her finger along, to see if there was any dust. Oh, yes. There was no messing.

The doctor used to give the orders to the ward sister and she would then delegate the jobs to the nurses, depending to whether they were third, second or first, according to your amount of training. After one year you did a preliminary exam. And we went to Portsmouth actually, to do it. And then after three years you took your State

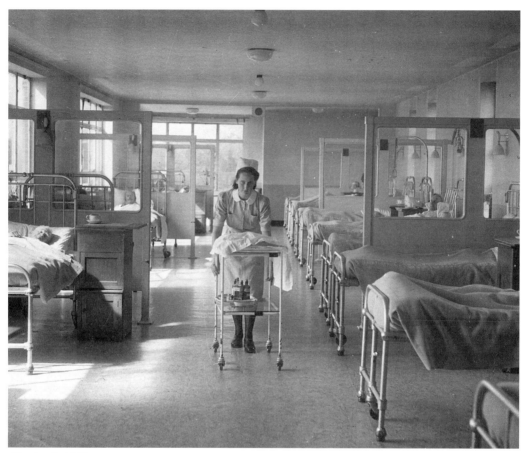

'On duty', 1950.

Registration, which again we had to go to Portsmouth to do. We did just mainly dressing of wounds and seeing that everything was as it should be and looking after the patients generally. You used to wash them if they couldn't wash themselves. They used to have blanket baths everyday, and you used to check that their pressure areas were okay, and walk them. Sometimes, because the doctors were so busy, I mean we used occasionally put up drips and things, which wasn't really legal in those days, and we used to take blood, which again wasn't really legal in those days. But they do all that now anyway. I mean they're taught to do it now. We weren't taught; we were just told to get on with it.

To begin with, you wouldn't have known the difference, it was a very, very gradual difference. So gradual that really you hardly noticed it, because things couldn't change quickly because there wasn't anything to change in a way. Treatments in those days were extremely primitive. I mean, for instance if you had a hernia repair, you had to have, what was known as a hip spica put on, which was a bandage which was round your thigh and round your groin and you stayed in bed for two weeks, I think it was. The difference between then and now, I can't tell you, it's so extraordinary. They couldn't get out of bed, they weren't allowed to get out of bed. We used to have to use bed-pans and things like that; I mean you weren't allowed to get out of bed.

By 1955, on the Male Surgical Ward, what they were able to do surgically had increased enormously, and the actual treatments themselves were changing quite rapidly. More and more things were done and people didn't stay in hospital quite so long. The average stay in those days was a fortnight to ten days and then it would be a week.

The surgeon was the boss of the ward, and you ran it, carrying out his orders. And you were responsible for carrying out his orders. You were in charge of the patients' welfare and treatments and you were in charge of the domestics and you were in charge of seeing that the patients were fed properly. You were responsible to the Matron and if you didn't do your job properly the Matron would have you in the office and tell you so. It was still very hierarchical. We didn't quite salute but it was nearly up to that.

We didn't really have an awful Matron. As I say she was very strict and very upright but we respected her. She knew her onions. She'd been a nurse; she knew what was what. Then we got in Domestic Supervisors who then took over the control of the domestics on the ward—that was the cleaning and the high dusting. The domestics didn't do the feeding. That was the Catering Officer who did the feeding. The nurses then saw that the patients had what they were supposed to have. If they didn't eat, we would know. I mean, after the war there wasn't a lot of variety of food. There was still rationing when I started my training. I could remember having my pot of jam, which had to last a fortnight. And the Home Sister, when we went to the dining room, she would be dishing out the food. She would notice if you weren't eating, or whatever. So she again was a sort of a mother figure.

Patients were very grateful to be treated because with the National Health Service it meant that they didn't have to pay. Whereas beforehand they used to have to pay in a certain fund and all sorts of things. I mean, they were extremely co-operative and they were grateful. Nursing was regarded as a vocation. So you did your best and that's the way it was. They didn't argue with you. The whole atmosphere was totally different. They were just extremely glad to be treated and said, 'Thank you very much'. Their expectations were not as great, of course. That's the difference between then and now, isn't it?

May Burrows

[In the theatre, we didn't have a lot of domestics or support personnel.] Not until we moved to the twin theatre and we had one domestic, one little domestic we had. The porters would help us with the mopping. You see, prior to going to the twin theatres we had no porters at all. We used to go up and get the patients for theatre from the wards and take them back, whoever was available amongst us nurses, or the technician. The doctor would produce an operating list you see, and we would get a copy to know what operations we were expected to be doing and we would just get ready for them. I mean, once you'd laid up one trolley, if you were working in that sterilising room—talk about working in a steam bath—you would take your first trolley up and then you would have your second trolley, while they were doing the first case your job was to get the second lot of instruments ready and so on, throughout the day. We weren't doing the instruments, we didn't touch them at all. You see the supply unit were packing all our instruments for us. The instruments came over on trays with big sheets on them, everything would be on the tray—your swabs, your abdominal packs, your knives, your scissors, all your instruments would be all on that big tray.

Eric Skilton

The National Health, well it suddenly came overnight. I know there were arrangements obviously building up to it, because the laboratory—we turned one of the huts into a laboratory—they were no longer County Hall's responsibility or the County Council's responsibility. And one didn't notice an awful lot after that except that we did get more staff. More nursing staff, more administrative staff, medical records. Because none of these other departments had been built. These extensions. There was no maternity block built at that time, so all these things came about during that period.

Dennis Barratt

I worked in the roof space of County Hall. The angle of the roof pitched down either side of the long narrow room and we had about three roof lights in it to give you some illumination and the benching at that stage was just scaffold planks with white paper spread over them. It was quite a long room, or appeared to be at that stage and there was one, a Mr. Edwards who was the Chief Technician, Mr. Dixon who was in Bacteriology. I can't recall the other chap, mainly because I was involved with the other two. When you are young like that you've really got tunnel vision; you're too frightened to look either side. You concentrate on the job you're doing, I think, just in case you make a mistake.

Well, up there [County Hall pathology laboratory], all we were really was skivvies. We did the washing up, and we did the washing up and we did the washing up. Test tubes, flat medicine bottles. All glass. We used to test waters, milks and waters for infections from various boreholes in peoples' wells. A lot of people had wells then and the water was checked on a regular basis for bacterial contamination. Milks were brought in, they were cultured as well. Ice cream, which sometimes was a good bonus, as long as there wasn't any bacteria in it! We used to get pieces of ham from Shippam's factory from time to time to culture out. That was really public health work in that sense. Then there was a lot of washing up, as test tubes were used for checking out the milks and they had to be cleaned.

We had a thing called a methylene blue test. I remember those tubes because they were marked at 10 ml circumference around a tube. There used to be dozens and dozens of those—you got sick of those things, washing them up that is. You had various lengths of twisted wire with bristles on the end as test tube brushes. We had some huge battery, glass battery tanks and what you had to do was to boil the glassware, you rinse it out, boil it up in soda water and after it had boiled for 10 minutes you poured it out from these buckets and you transferred the glassware there from the buckets into these tanks, which held potassium dichromate which was pretty lethal. It was potassium dichromate made up in sulphuric acid and these tanks used to hold about five gallons I suppose and they were all up at eye level. It's horrifying now when you think about it and we used to have to drop all this glassware in and make sure they sank, so you didn't get air bubbles in them. So you had to put your hand in there and turn the tubes over to get the air out. You could only do it for so long because your hands started to sting like blazes from the acid. You had to go and wash your hands and start again!

The other odious job of cleaning we had was to boil up microscope slides because the financial situation was different, you had to recycle slides and the majority of the slides that we had were from TB examinations, because TB at that time was quite rampant and with Aldingbourne Hospital so close we dealt with all the samples from there. These slides were stained with some stuff called carbolfuchsin which stained the tubercule bacilli red and counter-stained it with methylene blue. Then the whole thing was covered in cedarwood oil to be perused by highpower microscope. There were hundreds and hundreds of these things. Then we suddenly got presented with a baby bath; I can see it now, a baby bath, enamelled one with two handles; it was piled high; they couldn't get any more on it, which was why they had given it us, because every time they put a slide on it it slid off because the heap was so high. We had to boil these up; scrape off the cover slips, some still had the cover slips on that's right, which softened in the boiling water, scrape these cover slips off, which are very thin glass slips and you scrape off all the sputum, which had been stained with another slide and then transfer them to another bucket and boil them up again. Then you put them into the dichromate, which I spoke of just now, and then, after an hour in there, you used to take them out of the dichromate and then wash them in tap water then put them into distilled water. It took an age, an absolute age. There were thousands of microscope slides. We really didn't know what we were doing. We didn't know what was on them; it was only subsequent to this event that we found out what was on the slides, because nobody told us at that time. We were very much the lower level of employees at that stage, so we weren't told anything. Then we shifted all that stuff, all equipment, the majority of which I had no idea what it was for at that stage, boxed it all up, put it into the lift and run it down to the basement and put it onto lorries and transport it round to St Richard's.

One lad picked up TB and we're certain sure he got that from the TB bench because, horror of horrors, looking back at it, I mean we didn't think anything of it at the time. We used to get all the spit pots down from Aldingbourne, which were samples of sputum and in little glass phials and in plastic pots and used to write a number on each one to give them a sequence. We used to line them up along the bench, about forty of them and … it's dreadful thinking about it now, we used to go

The Lab Technicians, c.1951. (Dennis Barratt is fourth from left)

along and take all the tops off, the whole row of forty, put them on the back and leave this row of open specimen containers … mostly from Aldingbourne. He knew full well out of those forty or fifty pots, there was about twenty there that were positive TB. You used to get this piece of wire, platinum wire, with a loop on the end, flame it until it was red hot, to sterilise it and you take some of the sample out of the first one, spread it on this slide, and you warm the slide over the Bunsen flame, theoretically to fix the material and kill off the bacteria. Again, though, if you were in a hurry you didn't necessarily heat it very long to kill everything off and you did this all the way along the forty to fifty specimens and then you stained them and then you started putting the tops back on the pots again by which time you didn't know where this stuff had gone and, as I say, one of the lads picked up TB of the throat, in the gland in the throat and he spent a long time at Aldingbourne. That was the days when the treatment in Aldingbourne was to take a very large butter intake and the patients used to sleep out in open-fronted sheds in the grounds. They used to have a cot in there. They were wooden sheds with no front on. We used to turn them round to face the sun while we were out there. You used to see them dotted all over the grounds at one time.

When I was a junior still at St Richard's, in my first couple of years there, they had a blood test called a Paul Bunnell, which was a glandular fever test really, which required sheep blood to do it. It used to be sent to Graylingwell. They were self-sufficient at that time, had their own farm for vegetables and meat and they had their own abattoir, which in reality was a shed, with no windows, which I suspect was to stop the sheep from panicking when they were slaughtering the others. I used to go up there armed with a pint blood bottle, with no top on it and I used to have to hold this bottle under the neck of the sheep and cut its throat—it used to wind me up something terrible—I didn't like that at all, but it was one of those jobs you had to do. I used to stand there with this bottle under this sheep's throat until it filled right up. I was always getting it down my sleeve and everywhere else and put the cap back on and rush back with it while it was still fresh, before it clotted, so it could be dealt with in the lab. They were patients that were doing it, killing the sheep, as well, which was another worrying factor, for a youngster going up there … standing there with these great knives in their hands [laughter]. For killing their sheep. They used to butcher them, yes—because they were self-sufficient; they used to butcher their own meat up there. But at the time, of course, it seemed reasonable, or sort of until I had the job of doing it.

Crom Polson

I was Chief Administrative Officer, running the lay side of the Hospital. Trying to get a quart into a pint pot; finance-wise we were quite restricted. Nothing seemed to be easy. We were still under wartime conditions see in 1948, and supplies were restricted. There was really no freedom that we have today. I was also Supplies Officer. We had to start organising contracts for the supplies. In the mornings your list came down from the wards, how many number of patients. That was transcribed in a book register, a copy of which eventually [went into the] kitchen. The kitchen knew exactly how many meals to supply. When they wanted stores, they sent us another list down and they wrote this out and that was checked over and sent to the stores and the stores combined all the lot. On one day they issued china; next day they issued hardware, polishes and all that; the next day they did linen, and all this was done by transfer of information from the wards to the central office, to the stores and then issued. And signed for, don't forget, and signed for.

I maintained that the effort made by a ward sister telling the staff nurse we want some polish or we are short of this, put it on paper and order it, or get somebody to go down to the store with a chit, to the office first, then to the store and then get this issued, the amount of time spent in getting all your orders in, the time spent in the office booking them out to that ward, the storekeeper booking it out on his summary was extremely expensive. I worked it out that I could certainly save thousands of pounds by getting stores into the store and issue people with everything what they wanted from the wards without any forms filling. If a person wanted to steal anything, they'll steal it whether it's on the ward or whether it's in transit to the ward. One day I had a big discussion with one of the auditors and he said, 'Do you know, you've got something there'.

I was also the Clerk, the officer in charge of the Building Committee. I took that on when I arrived there and it remained with me until I left there. Our first building was the new theatre, the next one was the Nurses' Home, new Nurses' Home. Then there was the outpatients, new outpatients and then the maternity. So there was quite a bit of development. There was also the Graylingwell's, St Richard's, and the Royal West's combined boiler system with heating, steam heating for all those places and, I think, of course, the Chichester Festival Theatre also was tapped off from there. That was a great project.

I was also involved with paying the wages. My people went down to the bank, collected the money total, having already broken down what they wanted, whether it was notes and cash and all this, copper. They come up, they put it into a wage packet and that was the morning's work. If the staff were going off, afternoon off, they made an effort to pay those before the morning session finished, and they went in and they signed for their pay. Consultants were paid into the bank.

Jack Frost, my office manager, was a great forerunner of office technology, and I'm talking now about 40 years ago. We went to an exhibition of computers, it was IBM I think, it was in London. We went to the exhibition. He was clued up and he would have been a great computer expert today, there's no doubt about that. He was much before his time and he had it in his mind that this pay system could all be done by machines which was very much a thought in the distance then, but we got onto computers in about, it must have been about 1960 something because all our wages then were paid from a computer centre in Winchester then. It had to go to Winchester.

Eric Skilton

I took over Admissions and Discharges, which was obviously the record of keeping track of patients. We used to have a big Admissions Book, single sheets, which you clipped in daily, which was held in the telephone receptionist's office. She could immediately open that book if someone phoned or someone came with an enquiry. Because she did the lot. She did telephone, enquiry desk, the lot as regards reception. She could flick open the book—they were in alphabetical order the pages—she flicked this open, loose-leaf sheets in there, and she would see the admissions and what ward they were on. That's how she could tell where a patient was. What ward they were on. And I would receive from the ward notification of discharges for that day or any deaths.

The other system they operated then, going back to the visiting side, they had what they called S.I. Notices, 'Serious Illness Notices'. You issued these to relatives and there were three copies, one you kept in the book, one went to the ward and one was given to the relative and that allowed them to visit at any time. Any time during the day. There was a D.I. Notice, a 'Dangerous Illness Notice'; the same situation, three pages, tear off, one to the relative one to the ward and that meant that the relative could stay there all the time.

When it had been confirmed by the Sister of the ward, then we would issue these 'Serious Illness Notices', because, as I said before, there was only one visiting day a week, a half day, in those days. I also took on the responsibility for deaths and dealing with relatives. We didn't have any room where we could do them. We had to do it in the sort of hallway of the hospital. It was very difficult. You can imagine some of the distressed cases we had to deal with. Yes, I used to arrange the burials. If they said cremation, then I would arrange to get the form signed by the hospital doctor; there used to be two doctors who had to sign in those days. I had to collect a fee, of course, for the doctors signing them. Well, Mr. Martin always signed the first one in those days and then the other doctors around would sign the second part. I would contact the undertakers.

We had a set undertaker for, what we called, the 'people of no means'. We had a contract undertaker for that purpose. In other words what we called a state funeral. But it was no different to any other funeral, the same arrangement. I used to contact and get the release of the certificate for them and direct them to the Registrar of Deaths in Chichester. If they needed my help, I'd give it. Some would have their own undertaker and make their own arrangements. If they hadn't, though, then I would advise them on the local set-up, because Chichester didn't have a crematorium then. The nearest crematorium was Brighton so it was an expensive thing in those days to arrange a cremation.

Pat Saunders

It was very hard work in those days, portering. You worked 48 hours a week and you done a five and a half-day week. And I can remember our half-day started at two o'clock so it wasn't much of a half day. But that's how the rotas were worked out and that's what we done. About 1948, the government took over and things started happening. Prior to that we weren't really permanent staff. We were sort of a war-time measure, I suppose, or temporary staff. It wasn't until 1948 when the government took over in July we actually got a contract. With the contract, came superannuation which obviously brings in a nice pension. Of course looking at the beginning of that, I mean, that started off very small. And you wondered, well, will I ever get much out of this sort of thing, you know. But it's surprising over the years how this changes and so forth, that's how it goes. And prior to that, too, I mean unions were a dirty word and it wasn't until about this time, 1948, really that the unions were recognised. And I suppose, people coming out of the services demanded this as well. So where the management didn't allow it in the old days, they had to then.

Clive Bratt

The theatre at St Richard's in 1954 was a sort of day room. When I came there Douglas Martin said, 'We're hoping to get new theatres soon'. But it was many years after I left before the theatre block was built. So it was … pretty rudimentary. The brick wall, blast walls, hadn't been knocked down from the war, and it really was very rudimentary. We scrubbed up obviously for operations. And everything was sterilised. There was a steriliser unit in the hospital which sterilised dressings and gloves and instruments and so on. There were no throw away instruments. I mean, we hadn't seen plastic syringes. All syringes were boiled and needles too. And you just got rid of needles once they felt they'd got a hook on the end. [laughs] Mostly my job would be to hold retractors. We used to diathermy blood vessels. Diathermy is an electrical heated needle which just fries the tissue. I mean big bleeding points had to be ligatured off. But smaller points would be just touched with the diathermy to keep the operating area clear. I didn't do very well as a house surgeon in the fact that a surgical registrar came in at three months. She was a woman and she was anxious to get her teeth into things. And so whereas one normally did an appendix and a hernia and so on, I never got that far because the surgical registrar wanted to be getting all the experience she could. So I think the farthest I got really, to doing anything on my own, was just stitching people up after the operation. An awful lot then rested on the skill and the artistry of the surgeon.

I was in the first year of doctors who, when they qualified, had to do a pre-registration year. Prior to that, once you were qualified, you could go and do anything anywhere. So you had to get two house jobs of six months each, at a hospital that was recognised by the GMC [General Medical Council] as appropriate for junior doctors. And I came down to St Richard's and did a house surgeon's job, and fortunately, without going into details, a house-physician job came vacant immediately I finished my house surgeon's job. I did the junior house physician's job, then senior house physician. And then finally finished up as the casualty admission officer which was a post which you wouldn't have found in many hospitals in those days. It was quite unique to St Richard's as far as I know. Because on admissions I did all medical and surgical admissions from nine to five. So I had virtual control of the bed state. The only thing I didn't deal with was obstetrics and gynae; that was done by the obstetric registrar.

The house surgeon is the most junior of the surgical team. In those days, when I went to St Richard's, in actual fact we had no registrar. I was the house surgeon to one of the two surgeons at the hospital. And one's training was one's experience. I would say that if you were sensible, you listened to the ward sisters who were largely single women who had been in the job for years and knew a darn sight more about medicine than you did. And if you listened to them you learnt a hell of a lot. And then individual training from one's surgeon was purely working alongside him. Both the surgeons at St Richard's at that time lived on campus. They never left you swimming. You were encouraged to call them in the middle of the night if you had any worries at all.

There was a female surgical ward and a male surgical ward. Douglas Martin ward was split into two wards. One was Douglas Martin's and the other ward was E.P. Clark's, who was my boss. So each surgeon had a ward. You had two wards basically you were in charge of. A male ward downstairs on the ground level and a female ward on the first floor. We had alternate day intake, so one day the intake went into one surgeon and next the other. And the weekends were split.

First thing in the morning the consultant did a full round of the ward at nine o'clock. And then you attended out-patients with him. You obviously assisted him at operations on your operating days. And the rest of the time if there were any problems. I mean you might have a post-operative patient in pain or needing a drip or whatever, that was your job.

We had a laboratory technician who took the blood and the only time we took blood, and you know venepuncture is something you either quickly get into or don't. You only took an emergency at the weekends if the technician wasn't there. So it was a general looking after your two wards and out-patients and assisting at surgery. You didn't have any formal training, no lectures or anything like that.

The other job that you had to do, whether you were house physician or a house surgeon, there were the [other wards], the hutted wards, Willowmead as it is now, and they were large geriatric wards. They had about thirty-six patients in each and you were responsible for—whether you were a house physician or a house surgeon—you were responsible for one of those wards. I took quite an interest in geriatrics and I did a full round once a week and possibly got called over there during the week for emergencies.

The other thing, of course, was the new intake of patients and the discharge of patients. One spent, I think, quite a lot of time talking to the patients, or I did any rate. And I think so did my colleagues. We had the time to, when one did a ward round, go back and explain to somebody what the next investigations were going to mean for them. Or that we were going to send them home, and what to do when they got home. And, then of course, there was the new intake of patients who'd already been clerked by the admission officer but you made your own full notes on admission.

One interesting thing about St Richard's was that Douglas Martin was Surgeon Superintendent and he took his job very seriously. Nothing went on in that Hospital that he didn't know about. Regardless of whether it was another consultant's ward. I mean he went down in the morning to his office, read the Night Sister's report and was up like a shot if somebody had fallen out of bed, to find out why they had fallen out of bed. Or if something had happened in the night that was unusual, to see what was going on. All surgical and medical admissions during the morning—they obviously came in during the morning except for emergencies after lunch—went to his secretary's office first and he went through them, medical or surgical. It wouldn't be tolerated now but it made for a good hospital.

Dennis Barratt

We transferred [the Pathology laboratory] lock, stock and barrel to St Richard's, the hut, which was really exactly the same as the ward huts, except the middle coke boiler had been taken out, because the huts were heated by little straight-sided stoves and that was a sort of central heating, literally, and that had been taken out of the lab, but you could still see the raised circles, under the lino where it had been standing and school radiators had been put in and all the benches that were up in the County Hall had been transferred down and refitted into the St Richard's hut. They had teak benches. One Saturday morning job was, for the junior staff, to get up on these benches with bumpers—they are the long rods with a heavy cast iron weight on the end, with a cloth wrapped round them—and swing these bumpers backwards and forward and polish up the benches.

It was like moving from a cottage to a football field when you moved up to that new laboratory. It was massive, everything was shiny, everything was sealed, the floors were sealed off against dirt and all this kind of thing. It was very, very sterile and the, I don't know, the ambience was rather sterile as well in a way. It was fine; the conditions were brilliant for working in, but it was just different, that was all. I think it was just because we'd been brought up through the building blocks of it all. I think that the contrast was so vast and then eventually the staff got absolutely enormous and no it got to the stage when no department would cross over and help any other because it was nothing to do with them. So you lost this camaraderie between the departments, which was a great pity. The youngsters used to meet outside for tennis and things like that, you know the junior staff, which was fine, but the majority of it all was all separated out, everybody went their own way really. The amount of money spent on the new lab was quite something and the equipment was first class. At that stage we had one, two, three pathologists in histology alone, so that was how we'd increased quite dramatically. We began to centralise all the work at St Richard's, because it was a bigger laboratory, better laboratory; it had more facilities and so on. The emphasis was on the patient's work, but also we were still testing milks and waters. That gradually got phased out.

We had an animal house there, out back of the laboratory, a brick-built, purpose-built building. That was a saga. We kept guinea pigs out there and they were used for checking milk for TB. We used to spin the milks down in the centrifuge and then emulsify the deposits in saline, inject the poor guinea pigs and then kill them off after six weeks, post mortem them and see if there was any liver changes, kidney changes, lymph node changes and things like that, which gave you the answer to whether there was any TB. I don't know what happened to the milk in between time, I mean, I can't imagine them stop selling the stuff for six weeks while they waited for the result to come through. It's just occurred to me. It's silly, isn't it. Anyway that was what the animal house was primarily used for that.

We had a couple of rabbits out there for serological use, but I never saw them used. They were pets more than anything else. We had lots of cages and there must have been probably room for about a hundred and fifty animals, in cages. Then we had two runs with guinea pigs in, stock guinea pigs and they were all put in together and consequently you got inter-breeding, so you got lots of youngsters in there as well turning up; sad really, because they were a bit cannibalistic when the youngsters were born. Didn't like that very much. That was another one of the juniors' jobs looking after the animal house, cleaning them out as you'd expect and also included going in on holidays and weekends and stuff like that, and for which we were allowed to come in at 10 o'clock instead of 9 o'clock in the morning.

During the week one of my jobs was to look after these things, feed them in the mornings; we had a rota system. I used to get round the feeding problem by taking the runs outside on the grass and putting the guinea pigs into them and covering them over and letting them feed on the grass out there, which was fine. I did this on one occasion and I suppose there was about one hundred and odd guinea pigs in this run, white ones and I went out there at coffee break, to get something from the animal house. I happened to look across at the run and it was empty [laughter]. I had put it over a rabbit hole and these damn things had got out … [laughter] and they scattered everywhere. God, dear, we didn't get them all back, don't know where they all went. I think they got about fifty back, that was all. All the rest scarpered over the fields, the Graylingwell ground somewhere. There was no way we could have found them because the grass was very long. That caused a stir, to say the least. I nearly lost my holidays over that. [laughter]

The changes started later when people started to specialise. You started to take on university students, who'd already decided what they wanted to do and they went straight into bacteriology or straight into biochemistry and that's when the changes started. They then became unaware of what was happening outside, with the other three departments, so they couldn't understand, so at that stage because everybody else had gone through all four departments and knew what was going on, the newcomers — probably brilliant in what they were doing—in other words, there was some friction between the two types of intake, which lasted for quite a long time, well until the oldies moved on out in retirement, I suppose [laughter], really. It's all degree stuff now and I think you will only get taken on now if you have a degree.

We had great times, we really enjoyed the work, did an awful lot of clowning about, which was bad news from the Health and Safety Inspector's point of view, if he was about then, because we didn't have one then. Health and Safety didn't happen. But we used to go out in our lunch and coffee breaks. We used to have shooting matches out the back, so we would bring in .22 rifles, shoot coins off a stick and things like that. Because at the back of the lab, its totally different now, difficult to describe what it was like, but you went through the hut, out the other end, because there was French windows and things like that onto the animal house, which was linked by a concrete path. At the back of the animal house there was a small boiler, an incinerator, I beg your pardon, not boiler, where all the rubbish from the hospital went and then behind that again there was an open field, sort of dropping down to a stream that used to run through from Graylingwell, past the end of the lab, through to the back of the hospital and bordered round the cricket pitch that used to be there. And there were a lot of rabbits and pigeon down there and a huge, huge willow tree, which was leaning over, precariously over the water, it was very, very old, massive, not a lot of life left in it and the rabbits were actually, had actually burrowed into the trunk of this thing and they used to live in there some of them and Arthur [Edwards] he used to bring his shotgun in [laughter] and in between doing the odd blood test he'd go out and shoot rabbits. One evening, he suggested we went back there one evening and have a go at these rabbits down at the other end of the huts. The first huts, the first one was, if I remember rightly, the right-hand one was Physiotherapy and the left-hand one was Maternity, and then you got all the other huts beyond those two, ending up with the lab at the top. This stream used to run and there was a branch ran across in front of the Maternity hut and we got down in this bank with this shotgun. I mean, we were only about from here to that fence away from Maternity, what's that about fifty feet, I suppose and these rabbits appeared and old Arthur he leapt up and let go with two barrels [laughter] and the sister in Maternity went berserk. She came howling out there; we'd put some woman into labour with this explosion. All hell let loose, 'cor we didn't half get into trouble over that.

Another change I remember was formalin that was the biggest thing about. Yes, I suppose, the major change was formaldehyde, the preserving fluid. In the huts we had this little side room, which had butler sinks in it, with all the specimens in it, with normal saline and when Dr. Colin Knowles and I were in there cutting up the specimens for processing later, the formalin level became so high that after about ten minutes we just had to vacate the room, go out in the fresh air and breathe for about quarter of an hour before you could go back in there, because your eyes used to stream, your nose blocked up and you had a sore throat; it was dreadful stuff. When we went over to the new place they suddenly brought out rules and regulations and you weren't allowed to have more than one millionth of a part of formaldehyde in the air at all.

You had to have filtration systems and stuff like that, so you very rarely smelt formalin after that, compared to the other one, which was one of the reasons why I think I have lost the sense of smell, but I suppose they made a lot of changes, the Health and Safety Regulations made a lot of changes—fume cupboards suddenly sprouted up everywhere—all for the good obviously. There were so many built-in safety factors, that you lost sight of what you were actually doing, which was a shame, so you didn't actually get hands on things. I mean histology was slightly different. You could still damage yourself with the knives because they were incredibly sharp, so physically you could do yourself a lot of damage, but from the point of view of toxicity you are pretty safe now, which is obviously a good thing, but it did take the excitement out of it.

Judy Barratt

Science was my subject at school and I had had one visit to the Path Lab at the Royal West [Sussex Hospital] and seen the job and I was intrigued by it and wanted to do it. Of course, in those days you didn't have to qualify and then take the job, you qualified while doing the job. It was like an apprenticeship; you learnt as you went along. For the first couple of weeks I was in what they called 'The Washing-Up Room'. We didn't have throw-away plastic things in those days, everything was washed up, re-sterilised and used again and so a great deal of the work was thoroughly cleansing all the glassware, washing it, getting it ready to be sterilised again and sterilising it. Even the bottles we collected urine samples from were washed up and used again. We didn't have many of them so you always had to be doing that. They had rubber bungs, you sterilised the bottles eventually, after a lot of soaking in acid and rinsing with distilled water and drying in the drying oven and you plugged them with cotton wool, then you autoclaved them. Then you had this tray of rubber bungs, which you had to boil to sterilise and then you had to take a pair of forceps and put the rubber bung in as you take the cotton wool plug out to keep it sterile. Very labour intensive it all was and you didn't produce very many. The same ones kept having to be circulated again and again. You'd forget you were boiling rubber bungs and you'd boil them dry and you'd suddenly see a cloud of smoke coming out of the sterilising room and rush in and find they were all black and you had to do the explaining. I did washing up and sterilising, really; that was learning very much from the bottom and learning why everything had to be clean and sterilised. This was very important for the job, but very rough on the hands, that was how you learnt, though, and then you gradually were allowed to do more scientific jobs on the bench.

I think I went on to Bacteriology first and you were always supervised obviously, but you were gradually allowed to do a few urine tests and look at your own deposits under the microscope. Then you were allowed to put the odd plate up, the odd swab onto a blood agar plate and then you learnt how to make the culture plates themselves and then you were with somebody when you looked at the results of the cultures every morning. Gradually, you learnt by experience.

We'd have regular rounds then. Every morning that was your first job, to go round and collect the blood samples, having cleaned and sterilised the syringes yourself and sharpened the needles yourself. Then you would go and take the blood samples and you would also prepare the tubes into which the samples went with whatever was put in to stop the blood clotting, depending on which test you were doing, whether it was sodium citrate, or fluoride. Then you would go back with the samples and then you'd do the tests. So although people would laugh to think you only did two or three of a certain kind of test, instead of hundreds as they do now, you actually did the whole process from preparing the tubes to doing the tests, to writing up the results, the lot.

You had direct contact with the patients, and you could—it was interesting because you could—monitor their progress, their recovery and you got quite involved in the patient's history. I did see the beginnings of mechanisation coming in, not in a very grand way, but a certain amount of things were replaced. The first thing was the old metal and glass syringes being replaced by all glass ones which were easier to sterilise. I can't remember whether, I don't think we'd quite got to throw away plastic ones when I left, but in between me leaving in 1959 and then when I returned later in the '60s as a Phlebotomist things had changed to a lot more throw away, plastic stuff.

May Burrows

Between 1951 and 1954 I did my training. We trained three months rotation on the wards, out-patients, and three months on the geriatric wards which were over in the huts, as we used to call them, and three months in theatre. We'd rotate. We were working a shift system then. Lates, earlies and nights, and it was going on all the time, you see. We had a matron, a deputy matron and a home sister. There was Miss Chapman the Matron, Miss Barr was the Deputy Matron, and Miss Fleet was the Home Sister. That was for the nurses only. Because, you see, quite a large number of the students were resident. They weren't too keen on non-resident staff in those days for the students. I was a resident. I got paid, as a student nurse, four pounds a month. We were given our uniforms, but we had to buy our own shoes and stockings. There was many the time I was broke at the end of the month, and on my day off I used to walk from Chichester to Havant and my mum used to give me the fare to go back again.

My uniform was mauve and white stripe, and we had the bib aprons. And you had a different colour belt for each year of your training and the belts were … the first one I think was to match your uniform, then you had a white one and a black one. So that's how everybody knew which level you were at. We just used to wear the little square hats as student nurses. I think we were very proud of our uniforms and I always thought St Richard's was quite nice; it was an unusual colour to have the mauve and white stripe. Of course, that was all stopped when we joined up with the Royal West.

The School of Nursing was in one of the huts. All our lectures we had to take in our own time. You were never allowed to go to lectures on your duty time. So the first thing the ward sisters would always want to know was what lectures you had and when, so that she could always make sure you were off-duty for those lectures, and even if you were on nights and you had a lecture at two o'clock in the afternoon, you still had to get up and go to that lecture. So you had no lectures in your duty time at all.

The first year we were very much the drudges of the nursing profession. I mean the first job in the morning was to dust the wards. We used to have to pull all the beds out to the centre of the ward, and we used to do all the dusting. All the wheels had to be dead straight all down the ward, and nothing was out of place, the beds had to be looking perfect. We had a special way to make the beds. You had to mitre all your corners for a start [laughs]. You know fold all your corners so they were all nice and neat and, you know, turn the blanket down, the corners in, and the flap back, so the patient could always pull it up if they were cold. Of course, we didn't have any of these Airtex blankets they have now. We had ordinary blankets, and most beds would have at least three blankets on them and a counterpane. So it was quite heavy work making a lot of beds. Of course, patients weren't made mobile so much after surgery, so of course anybody that was in bed over 24 hours would have their pressure areas treated twice a day, which was our job. And bed pan rounds we were responsible for; also for washing patients that needed washing, feeding patients that needed feeding. It was a hard grind. Training lasted three years. Everybody changed over every three months.

We used to do Wards 1, 2, 3 and 4. And, of course, you see, Ward 3 was half children and half adults, half medicine and half children you see. Ward 4 was all medicine. The little four-bedded ward on 4 was where they treated the post-operative chest surgery. There were four beds up there, because we used to do thoracotomies, pneumonectomies, lobectomies and later on we were actually doing mitral valveotomies. That was the only four-bedded ward they had for them. It was up on Baxendale—what we knew as Ward 4.

As you progressed, like if you were on the surgical ward you would be responsible for doing the dressings and the special treatments like enemas and fractional test meals and the injections. At night, we used to have 48 patients on a ward to look after, because both sides of the ward, where they're double names now, was one sister and that was all of her ward. She had the two 21-bedded wards, she would have the four in the south ward and the two side wards, that was all one ward. Quite often of a night there was only two of us on duty, and we were taking responsibility for those wards, probably in our third year. A night sister or two night sisters would be down in the office, and if you had a problem you had to send for the night sister.

At the end of the three years you took exams. You took your SRN exam, which was a whole day written exam, you had a medical paper, a surgical paper and a general nursing paper, and you also had an hour's practical. Assessment was always based on your work during the three years. At the end of the first year you did what they call the first-year exams; you had papers on anatomy and physiology, hygiene and general nursing, and that was your first-year exam. Then you had no more exams, only tests within the hospital, but they didn't really mean anything; it was just a way of marking your progress. And then at the end of the third year you took your State Registration Exam. Then you became an SRN, if you passed.

The morning you got your result, you went to the Matron's office and she would ask you what you wanted to do. Some girls naturally decided to go on to do midwifery, or she would ask you what department you would like to work in, and they would accommodate you, if they possibly could. But I said surgical nursing, and I was asked if I would mind going into theatre to give them a helping hand, and I said, 'Okay', and there I went.

We were pretty much like slaves. I mean, if people realised the conditions in which we worked, they would be pretty horrified now. The theatre … we only had one small theatre which was in the four-bedded ward of Ward 1, Martin Ward. The sterilising room was as you come in to Ward 1. It was a little door on the right. And there is a very small room in there and in that room there was a large water boiler and a small one. The large one we boiled all the kidney dishes and bowls and hand bowls; the other one was solely for instruments. In that room, we laid up all the instruments that we used in the theatre. We used to lay them up with cheatles. They're the forceps to lift sterile instruments out of the … you couldn't take them out of boiling water, you see. They would be boiled for 10 minutes. You had these things and they were actually kept in long … well, you'd call them vase-like things … cheatal containers, and they would be kept in a sterilising solution. They would be boiled first thing in the morning and then kept in this sterilising solution for the rest of the day. That's all we had. They would all be just carefully laid on sterile mackintoshes with sterile towels on. We used to have to cover them up with about three towels and we used to have to wheel them from there all up the corridor amongst all the people walking around, visitors, ward staff, and into the theatres. The water boilers for the sterile water were upstairs, on the level of Ward 2. As you came at the top of the stairs there was a room up there, and there were two water boilers; one was hot and one was cold, which we had to fill. The hot one was left hot and the other one had a cooling device inside, which, once it was boiled, you could cool it down. We used to have to wash all the gloves we used, all the mackintoshes. We had to wash all our abdominal packs. Pack all the, sort of, lumber puncture drums and we had a little autoclave up there. We used to have to wash and be given sets for the wards.

We used to have to make all our own swabs. Every swab that was used in that theatre we made by hand. To make a swab you take a roll of gauze, wind it round and round and round, cut it both sides with a blade, then just fold it—there's a special way of folding a piece of gauze. So it wasn't very easy. We patched all the gloves; we tested them for holes and patched them. We sewed on all the tapes on the gowns. We used to pack all the drums that we used, the metal drums we used to pack the gowns, the towels, the swabs in, and we had to do all that before we went off duty at night. Besides that, the laundry would arrive in baskets and we would have to check it and fold it as well. There's a special way to fold gowns, towels and everything, and we would spend hours at the weekend making swabs, tying them in bundles of ten. The office of that ward was the surgeons' changing room, so during the daytime the ward sisters never had an office on that ward because the surgeons would use it as a changing room. The only area we had there was in three cupboards. They would put up a barricade to make an anaesthetic room; there would be a barricade up to divide the anaesthetic room, then there was a little corridor. There were three cupboards in that corridor, which were our storage cupboards, and our little changing room was in there. All we had to sit on was empty drums.

The big window in that ward—there used to be a brick wall outside so that nobody could look into the theatres—and there were three sinks along there for the surgeons to scrub up in. So the surgeons were scrubbing up with the patient, sort of, just behind them and while you were scrubbing up you could see little mice running along the windowsill outside—a lovely little place for them. We had to mop all the floors before we left, and we used to have to be responsible every weekend. We used to have to change all the needle trays, the scissor trays, and put them in this special solution; change all the catgut jars, put new blades out, because they all used to come un-sterile in wax paper. We used to have to get all the wax off the blades and lay them neatly in the trays. I think the solution was called Instrument Dettol 5%, we used to use. The catgut came in glass ampoules then, you used to have to snap them, and they were stored in a solution, I think it was carbolic 1 in 20 or something. When we used to do this chest surgery, they introduced this business of hypothermia for lowering the patient's temperature to do the operation, and if we had a patient that needed this sort of anaesthetic we used to have to get up early, order it the day before, go up to the kitchens, bring down all this load of ice. We'd have to put cold water in Ward 1's bath and put all this ice in it, and the patient used to be immersed in this bath of iced water. They weren't conscious. They'd give them something to just knock them out, and then they would lower their temperature by lying them in this bath of iced water, and our hands used to get absolutely frozen. On the table they were kept cold, you see. When they went back to the ward, they had to be sent back to the ward with wet sheets on them, cold wet sheets. I suppose they gradually raised the temperature up again.

It was supposed to be better for the patients when they were doing heart surgery. I mean, if you saw the conditions in which we worked and we were doing mitral valvotomies, lobectomies, pneumonectomies, all the general surgery, pinning hips, dental work. Once you're involved in the actual surgery, though, you're detached; afterwards, when you think back, you become attached; you worry what's happened to them; have they survived, you know. You get to know about them, and then they become more personal after the operation. Once they arrive in the theatre, you know nothing about them, but if it was something serious then we always used to make enquiries as to how they were doing; if it was just routine stuff, we didn't take as much notice.

We used to use the loo in Martin Ward; a sluice, that's all we had. When we moved to the twin theatre our infection rate was no higher—no lower or no higher. But you see, I think, we were so much more aware of the conditions we were working under that we were extra careful; we were very careful. If you honestly knew you were walking around in this confined space and you knew you touched something, you would immediately change it and get another one. You would tell the sister you'd touched that. I mean, we would lay the towel over the instruments; and then to wheel it up the corridor, we'd lay another towel that way so it hung right down, and another one that way so it hung right down; and when we got into the theatre we just took the dust covers off, as they were called, and took them straight away. As we had finished a theatre, okay, so all our dirty linen was kept in the theatre … we took it off, our gowns. We'd have a bucket to throw the dirty gloves in, and just one of those linen bins to put our dirty gowns in, and they were only taken out at the end of each session. So we were doing general surgery; we were doing 'gynae'; we were doing chest, orthopaedics, dental; we were doing quite a lot.

We were wheeling the dirty laundry up corridors where the patients [and] visitors were walking in and out all the time. Actually, one day, I put the trolley just outside the door in the corridor. I went back in to make sure my water boiler was low enough not to be boiling over—because many's the floods we had down there, it's nobody's business; and with the water boilers upstairs we used to forget to turn them off, and it would go down in the pharmacy—but when I came back I thought, this trolley's not wheeling very well is it, and you'd always wheel it like this, push it like this so that you didn't actually touch those towels. You bent your back and wheeled it up the corridor like that. Then I discovered what was holding me up, somebody had tied a Pekinese to the end of my trolley! She'd gone to visit whoever she had in the side ward and she'd tied her Pekinese dog to my trolley, and I was quite a long way up the corridor before I realised I had a Pekinese in tow. So then you can get an idea of how we were working.

You see St Richard's was never meant to be a hospital. So there was never a theatre made for it. It was meant to be an old people's home. Of course, being built with that in mind, they didn't build a theatre, you see. It was never meant to have a theatre in it. It opened early as an emergency because of the war, and then they had this makeshift theatre which carried on after the war until they built the first twin one in 1961.

Bill Gammie

In 1963, Mr. Douglas Martin at St Richard's died, and one of the features that struck me at that time was, although there was a slight waiting list built up by the fact that there had been a six- to eight-week hiatus between Douglas Martin's death and my appearing on the scene, there had only built up a slight waiting list. It was never more than three to four months. By the end of January, it had come down to about two months. I was doing gastro-intestinal surgery; gastric work; colo-proctology and a large feature, of course, was urology. There was no urologist in the district and so a lot of one's work tended to be urological. In fact this continued throughout my 27 years as a surgeon at Chichester.

My main interest had been gastroenterology. At that time, of course, colo-proctology had not separated off as a separate speciality so gastroenterologists had been trained to deal with upper gastrointestinal work, gastrectomies, gall bladder work, pancreatic work and they had also trained to do colo-proctology. So it was the total gastroenterological field. In fact, one was even doing oesophagectomies because this was regarded as part of the scenario for which one had been trained.

At St Richard's we had one Surgical Registrar. The Registrar when I was doing the locum was a chap called Brian Morgan. The next Registrar, the first one appointed after I arrived—and I still recall this because this was a gentleman called Mr. Robert or Bob Oakshot an Australian—and he was interviewed by Nobby Clark and myself. And our colleagues at Broyle Road were rather aghast that we had appointed an Australian. We had one Registrar at St Richard's helping us and we had two House Surgeons in the Hospital at the time. There was one Registrar at Broyle Road and two House Surgeons at Broyle Road and that was the total surgical staff at that particular time. There was also a Casualty Officer who was a—what we would these days call a Senior Hospital Officer—but in fact he was slightly more senior than that. During the locum period I just slotted into Douglas Martin's habits, so one in fact had an afternoon list on a Monday and an afternoon list on a Friday. And there were two out-patients sessions a week, one on Wednesday morning and I think the other one was on Friday morning, as I recall it.

After February 1964, we re-allocated some of the surgical services because, in fact, at that time, acute cases were being admitted on alternate days to St Richard's and Broyle Road. And after discussion with Mr. Miles and Mr. Clark it was felt appropriate that I should be allowed to do some operating at Broyle Road, mainly because emergencies were being admitted under my care and it would have been inappropriate to transfer the patients from Broyle Road to St Richard's just because they had been admitted under my name. At that particular time, of course, the surgical duty roster was one week in three, so all acute emergencies were admitted under—for one week Mr. Clark, next week Mr. Miles and the third week myself. And this continued for the greater part of my time at Chichester.

The new Accident and Emergency unit was built at St Richard's in 1970-1971. It was completed, and we had to take a careful look at the provision of surgical services in Chichester and orientate all the surgical beds on the St Richard's site. But during those first six years we continued to exercise most surgical activity—or carry out most of our surgical activity at St Richard's. In fact, at that time, we were also operating at Bognor War Memorial and all three surgeons had an operating session there once a fortnight and an out-patients session there once a fortnight.

It was a fairly busy programme. But when one looks back on it I think the demand put on us by the public was perhaps less, when we look at the waiting list situation. For that first six or seven years there was rarely a waiting list of more than three months for any surgical procedure. So all the acute work came in fairly quickly and even, what we call cold work—the mundane surgical procedures such as hernias and varicose veins and haemorrhoids and so on—they were all dealt with within three months of being seen in out-patients. I don't know what has produced this rapid increase. I think an increasing awareness of the public that many of these things benefited from treatment. I think a lot of it is due to changing expectations of patients. And, of course, part of the demand has been the increase in the number of elderly people and the readiness of surgeons to carry out surgical procedures in the elderly. I think the overall elderly population—over sixty-five population—is about twenty-four per cent, something of that nature. But in the 1960s many of these people were not regarded as suitable candidates for surgery over the age of sixty-five. I don't think age is a barrier to any surgical procedure really these days. Partly because of the increased facilities for post-operative care. I was always quite fascinated because we had no intensive care facilities in 1963-4. We didn't achieve any until after 1971. And the patients … You arranged an operating list so that the more major cases were dealt with at the start of a list and you assumed that the Ward Sister was going to stay on duty until the last case had left the theatre in the evening. There was no restriction on the length of time we were able to operate. You were able to set up an operating list and continue until seven, eight or nine in the evening. Without any hesitation, the nursing staff in the theatres, and the theatre staff and the ward staff accepted this. If patients needed an operation and you were prepared to go ahead with it, they were prepared to support you until the patient had returned to the ward.

As the years went by and with various little industrial hiccups through the years—I would label it as that—then the changing hours, nursing hours I mean, they went down. In the early days they were doing extremely long hours, many of the staff. The hours came down, though, to 37½ hours a week. That really restricted everybody. In fact, cold surgery was not undertaken after five o'clock in the evening. You had to adjust your operating list to fit in with this, if at all possible. There was an increasing amount of emergency work which they tried to fit in in the evening, but only in theory. Only one theatre was going to be staffed after five o'clock. There was a certain little leeway in this and, I think, you know, come six o'clock it was definitely down to one theatre. People were allowed to finish what they had started, but if you could accommodate your list within the allotted hours, then it was appreciated.

Marjorie Semmens

I was at the Royal West Sussex until December 1963, and then in January 1964 for three months took on a locum consultant paediatric post, with a Dr. Ivor Balfour. Now paediatrics was becoming a speciality in its own right during the '50s and '60s. Before that one of the physicians always looked after the children, and it was Dr. Emerson, when I was the house officer at St Richard's, who was conducting the ward rounds, and he also, I think, had to do some of the geriatric patient ward rounds as well. I drove over to Worthing to do a number of sessions in that district, and one of the things I recall was the limitations on the mileage allowance. It was suggested by the Administration that you should reside within ten miles of your main hospital. As there was no reason for me to leave I stayed at Apuldram Lane and I drove to Worthing. As this was further than ten miles, and I calculated that it was 25 miles to drive there, I got paid only for ten, and I was paying for 15 miles there and back every time that I had to travel.

Heather Jeremy

I started as a WRVS [Women's Royal Voluntary Service] volunteer at St Richard's in 1969. There were then, I think, 40 people in the late '60s, which sounds a lot but compared to the 80 volunteers we eventually got up to; there were 40 people in those days and possibly even less. There used to be three, there's always been three shifts a day, and most people came in once a week, and so that's why we needed so many because of the three shifts a day. It worked out surprising well, though. Some people did a regular turn every week and some would be on the reserve list, which was organised from the office in St Pancras.

What did I do? Well, at the Tea Bar, obviously, I unlocked everything and put on the boiler for the hot water which was an automatic boiler. We had gas to begin with which was a terrifying thing. We used to have to light that with long waxed tape. Tapers; that's the word and that was quite hair-raising at times because it was gas. It was a tall hot water boiler. I don't know how many gallons it held but it was quite big and it was automatically filled with water, thank goodness we didn't have to fill that up with ourselves but that was a gas boiler and then we went on to an electric boiler which was a considerable improvement.

What we had to do was literally getting ready as you would in your kitchen at home. You get the sugar and milks ready and the sandwiches. We used to make our own sandwiches in those days, which was quite a performance because we had very little space to do it. We used to have to get in at least half an hour earlier to make the sandwiches and you generally got ready, that was it really. The cost of a cup of tea, of course, was very low then. It compared to something like ten pence or something like that.

We always wore the green tabard which was a plain green with the WRVS written in red on the front and then the head office improved on those so we got those that had red edges all round the edges of the tabard. Eventually, very recently, we were asked to wear white blouses to make it look more uniform, which we did and it did look better, but that was the only uniform. In those days, I used to have to get the things we sold myself. I used to take my car, I mean it was so little, well it was fairer not that much nothing like today, but go to Book, oh it was not even called Bookers in those days. It was the local wholesalers on the industrial estate and we used to leave packets and boxes of things in the boot of my car which nearly ruined the springs and haul them all the way back and empty the car here and bring them all in on a trolley. It was quite hard work. They eventually got someone to help with that and then it got so much that we had to get wholesalers to deliver it to us once a week or once a fortnight sometimes. Now that's how it was done right up until the rebuilding when we started to get the things like chocolates and tea, coffee, and so on, through the hospital catering stores because it was cheaper for one thing. We just joined our order on to them which made a considerable improvement on how much we spent.

In the beginning, we had a little drawer with little compartments in it and that went on for many years. We eventually got up to a proper cash till. We have several of those and I think now; well it is now an automatic one which we've all had to learn how to do, so the money is counted at the end of the day and it's all listed in to what is called the 'Day Book' where we sign our names at whatever time of the day we come in, and at the end of the day you put in how much we've taken and that was all parcelled up and it was put in. It used to be taken down to the General Office to be banked and I think it's still the same, as far as I know. One year on we still do it the same way and, of course, it's all banked generally at the WRVS headquarters and that's how it all mounted up.

We don't actually give the Hospital cash. We didn't. We used to buy equipment. There used to be a meeting with various people in the hospital, and they used to bring in a list of what they would like and it was mostly … I used to be very keen that we bought medical equipment. We used to buy all sorts of things for the hospital. We eventually bought some climbing equipment and general equipment for disabled children and there was a sort of club, which was run from the Royal West Sussex Hospital in those days. We bought a lot of equipment for them. It at least made the local paper, which was nice.

Trevor Hayes

At one time, each hospital had a butcher's block and each hospital had a person who used to hack the meat up. They weren't called a butcher, they were called a Chef. And then, at one time, they said, 'Right, let's centralise this over at St Richard's' and they pulled me over from the other hospital, Royal West Sussex, to actually be the butcher. Being a butcher's nephew to three butchers and a butcher's grandson to a butcher, I knew nothing about butchering [laughs] so I had to learn very much. We supplied the meat to both places. It came on carcass and we stripped it down from there. Eventually that went up to Graylingwell Hospital so that we centralised at Graylingwell Hospital up the road, all the hospitals, Bognor, Midhurst, Arundel, Royal West Sussex and St Richard's, that all went up to Graylingwell so we didn't need a butcher down our way, so it changed.

Eventually, after leaving the butchery, I had to be the Assistant Head Chef in the kitchen to sort some things out over the Royal West Sussex. Then I was asked to come over here for a couple of months to St Richard's to sort them out, or help someone sort them out, and after about six months I went back again. If you stay in the same place, you actually tend to move around a little bit but it was for various reasons, whether it be political for other people or whether it be actually to move into the future a little bit.

For the patients' menus, they filled out forms. They used to write the first patient's name on the left-hand side, the ward's name at the top left, and they used to put down if they wanted porridge or cereal, like P or C. Then they put down 'Main'; so they used to order from a choice of four possibilities; well, there's one, two, three or four. So there's been slight changes. You used to get the name, roughly what they ordered, and if there were a diet on the end here. They used to send them back; we used to collate them, what portion size they wanted, and that used to be read by hand. If you want beef casserole you had to have the creamed potato. If you wanted the vegetable and aduki bean curry, you had to have the rice. If you wanted the minced lamb and savoury dumplings you had to have the cabbage. No individual choice.

Paddy Whiteside

During the 1970s, I was mainly concerned with the daily routine of being a doctor, and working on the educational side of things. When you specialise in a subject you don't get the ordinary run of patients of all abnormalities, you get referred to you by the GPs, a much higher proportion of patients in your own speciality, and this occurred for me in cardiology. I saw a much higher percentage of cardiac patients than any of the other physicians. Sometimes I lectured. I am not a very good lecturer, being partly dyslexic [laughs], but I did lecture, when I could, in my own speciality.

Bill Gammie

The clinical work, of course, was continuing to increase. On the other hand, one did find a means of keeping the balance amongst all these things over the years. And, I think, it was just a question that one didn't have any problems coping with the clinical activity, if one had been trained to do that. One of the problems, however, I think, was, and I always said to myself that one thing that may cause me occasional sleepless nights was waking up and thinking of how to cope with tomorrow's administrative problems. The clinical problems never gave me a sleepless night at any time.

Judy Barratt

By the 1970s, the lab was moved into the new block and there were a lot more members of staff. Gradually, after each department got bigger and bigger, so that people didn't then move between departments. They stayed in one and, in fact, were taken on specifically as a Biochemist, or as a Bacteriologist, for example, then they didn't have any experience of the other chap's job. You then got four different departments all involved in the same patient; instead of, of course, in the old days when it was the whole lab that was involved with that patient.

Crom Polson

During the 1970s, one of the biggest changes was that finance was rearing its ugly head: COST. You could show on a ledger that you had £10 or £2,000 overspent, but nobody was going to tell them that that £2,000 was spent on the life of a patient. I think that accounting was becoming a big part of the service when I left. Accounting is good. We know that it's to be; someone's got to account for the service, but I don't think that hospitals, surgeons, physicians should be restricted with the thought of someone looking over their shoulder and whispering that's going to be £1, £2, £3 too much. They thought, I am certain, that a hospital service could be run by issuing an edict, you know, black and white. Hospitals are not like that,

Meeting of Area Supplies Officers, 1972. (Crom Polson right.)

illnesses are not like that. To say that three people were treated for pneumonia and, you know, great, one person could have taken the cost of three people. It could have cost, oh it could have cost a lot less. So I think statistics can be misleading. It was almost a Government cry. We can do so many patients and there are so many on the waiting lists. We've got no idea what that waiting list means. That so many people could be toenails, or it could mean hip replacements.

Pat Saunders

I became Head Driver in 1972, and I went up and worked in the supplies department under Mr. Davey getting these schedules together and tearing them apart and re-writing them and all that sort of thing. We thought we'd got it right. Then we had the meeting and presented these to the committee and they seemed to be accepted all right and from then on we, sort of, went forward as from that day, on transport. The three drivers that we had in those days, we had another one from St Richard's, one from Broyle Road and the one from Graylingwell. We wanted one more actually to get the system on the go. So we had the four drivers plus myself and we started actually as a district transport in the November. We visited all the local hospitals, supplies, specimens, mail etc. Case papers. You know, medical records, X-rays, anything like that. Then gradually it got bigger and bigger. As we progressed … the path. lab. used to have their own vehicle and a little while after that, the chap down there he was retiring, so we took over his duties on the path. lab. side of things and built it in to our schedules and gradually as we went on, sort of thing, well they started building all the different types of places. You had Health Centres springing up and of course that included Midhurst, Bognor's, then you got Selsey and Wittering, they came into it.

Obviously, we did do things wrong occasionally, but it was nothing that we couldn't correct. With the Graylingwell side of things, we had to take that type of patient down to the out-patients department at St Richard's etc., for X-rays and all that sort of thing. And also … which was something else we'd never had before, was absconding patients, you know on the psychiatric side. If they went locally, we'd take the nurse round and try and look for a few, if they thought they knew where they were. Some of these used to abscond some distances, though. They used to have their own favourite places; some would go to Brighton, some went to London, some went to Worthing or Portsmouth. Yes, they went. We've been to Birmingham everywhere for them day. But of course, early, too, in 1970-72, we started up another system of picking up the nurses at the railway station and bus station first thing in the mornings. So you could get to the hospital in time. That went on for a few years. They lived in Portsmouth, some of them lived in Portsmouth. Some lived in Selsey. Not only nurses, we picked up domestics; we didn't differentiate between staff or anything like that. If they wanted the transport, we were there to do it. That went on for about four or five years and then gradually it fizzled out. The Hospital didn't think they were responsible for any transport of nurses. So that was stopped. A lot of people didn't like it but that's what it had to be.

In the 1970s, we started a daily trip up to Guildford collecting radioactive isotopes from St Luke's Hospital. Yes, that was injected into patients for the ultra-scan. It was a very low content actually. They were in isolated boxes and it was kept in the back of the car. You didn't carry them up the front with you. You carried the radioactive signs to go on the vehicles. They were very low content and of course all the time you were travelling down from Guildford it was losing its content anyway.

May Burrows

I was the Nursing Officer in charge of theatres in the 1970s. I was in charge of all of them, the porters, the auxiliaries, the domestic. I very seldom got help from outside the theatre, most of the problems I was able to deal with within our four walls. I always made it my policy that I could do everything that I ever asked my nurses to do and if, right up to the end if it was needful, I would go and help clean the theatres, if they were really pushed. I would still scrub up and help with lists, right up until the very end. If we had a new surgeon with a new technique I always did the first case with that surgeon and then I would write it out, what his likes and dislikes were, and how he worked. I'd make him a Cardex, you know, so in future anybody doing that person's list would know what he liked to sew up with and what needles he used. I'd have it all written out on a card.

Of course, in the latter years, I also had a secretary, which was a luxury. We used to do all the theatre lists and used to do a lot of typing, which was a real luxury. And all the theatre secretaries I had were all exceptionally good girls. They still had to come in and wear the same garb that we wore, you see, change into trousers and tops and wear caps all day; the same as we did. But she would bring all the messages into the surgeon, she would take all the messages. They were wonderful helps and we really needed them. There was no computer in the theatre even by 1982, nothing like that.

From 'very primitive' to 'avant-garde'

THE TREATMENTS AND TECHNOLOGY

❝ Lung function equipment was very primitive and consisted of a crude spirometer for measuring vital capacity and there was really no attempt to have a full pulmonary function laboratory, such as there is at present. ❞

(Robin Agnew, physician)

❝ I was trying to get this Assessment Unit built and there was no money…Then we were just right. Just at the right moment to capitalise on this. So we got the money. We got the thing and it's set up. And it's been running on its own for ages. We've got a consultant in charge. Super. So in that sense, I suppose, we were avant-garde. ❞

(Bud Robinson, paediatrician)

During this period of the NHS, treatments and technological advances expanded rapidly. At St Richard's this affected all areas of work, so that, while in 1948 one doctor could talk of treatment being primitive, by the end of it another could recognise that St Richard's was in the forefront of medical developments. Clive Bratt and May Burrows discuss some of the existing treatments at the start of the NHS. Paddy Whiteside and Robin Agnew elaborate on some of these treatments, particularly for tuberculosis, which caused a great deal of discomfort to patients. The patients, however, tolerated far more, in many ways, then, with a somewhat blind trust that has been, in large part, lost now. Gradually, there was a shift to a reliance on machines and electronics for diagnoses and treatment. The acceptance of the reliability of these pieces of equipment was initially slow, but obviously was eventually to be pervasive. Jean Monks comments on her reluctance to rely exclusively on machines, however. By the early 1950s, the hospital had evolved its structures and systems and become a more organised hospital. Similarly, the science of treatments had evolved so that it was no longer what doctors could do but what, as Clive Bratt comments, they should do. The 1960s saw the expansion of medical knowledge and the development of potential treatments. The widening of medical knowledge fostered the increase in specialisation, as Paddy Whiteside recounts, with new types of surgery, more buildings, more beds, more patients, more work. Bill Gammie and May Burrows recall how they gradually used fewer and fewer reusable commodities, such as sutures and needles. Disposables became prevalent and this altered procedures and routines. The increase in technological developments made it possible to achieve more for patients as more sophisticated surgery became routine. Despite all the technological improvements, however, as Bill Gammie comments, the doctors and surgeons still relied a great deal on their art and their instincts.

Clive Bratt

Even when the National Health started medicine was still very rudimentary. We'd got antibiotics, but as far as hi-tech medicine, there wasn't really any.

Paddy Whiteside

We had improvements in the theatre and they continued right through from the opening of the National Health Service in 1948 with better services, better units being opened, more staff and, of course, less rationing, so that equipment was all the time improved. We got a proper X-ray set for the first time, and we could do the extra examinations, like Barium meals, Barium enemas, kidney X-rays, which had not been possible previously, except by referring the patient to the Royal West Sussex Hospital or the Bognor Hospital. All the finest hospitals in the land had very good equipment and we were hoping that, as the rationing reduced, we would get the necessary equipment ourselves.

In those days there was no suing for mistakes, because I suppose mistakes were more frequent, but patients were very much more tolerant. To give an example: My outpatient room was a biggish room where I had four theatre trolleys, and I saw and examined all my out-patients in that room, taking histories that all other patients in the room could hear. This is very disturbing. I asked them to write to the governors of the hospital and ask that they improve this but the patients refused to write. They didn't want in any way to criticise the service they were getting.

Robin Agnew

The Sister on the Children's Ward taught me a lot. I particularly remember she called me once to a child who had an empyema, with a very swinging temperature and very ill and she insisted that I put a tube in the child's chest, a thing which I had never attempted before. I was well aware of these awful cracking noises as I put the cannula in between the child's ribs, but the satisfaction when the green pus came out and we got an under-water seal going and the child recovered. As Senior House Officer (SHO) of the Chest Unit, I was expected to know all about these things. I was very much helped by not only Paddy Whiteside, but also Vince Powell, the Consultant Thoracic Surgeon, who came down from Midhurst to do a weekly operating session in the theatre.

Most of the cases in those days were for pulmonary tuberculosis, which was still very common in 1953. We also had a polio epidemic, I remember, and the unfortunate patients who were placed in the iron lung to help their respiration and trying to communicate with them, the awful noise that the machines made when they were forcing the air in and out of the patient's chest. They were known as Aaron lungs. We usually had about two or three of these on the ward at that time. The dreaded complication was acute dialatation of the stomach from which the patient inevitably died. All young people. Horrible. Eventually they sent me up on a course to the Western Fever Hospital in London where they had a positive pressure machine, which was very much better as a means of assisted ventilation. There was a doctor there, a Phil Bromage, who did a very neat form of epidural block, which was quite a pioneering way of giving an anaesthetic without gas in those days. These unfortunate patients, though, would come back to the ward and, when the effects of the anaesthetic had worn off, we were left to cope with them at night-time. We used to fill them up with pethidine to relieve their pain, which made them sweat a lot, and they were really very miserable. We also had to aspirate their chest when fluid collected in odd places called Semb's space.

I welcomed the new technology. Lung function equipment was very primitive and consisted of a crude spirometer for measuring vital capacity and there was really no attempt to have a full pulmonary function laboratory, such as there is at present. The simple peak flow meter only came in in the 1960s. The advances in the management and diagnosis of asthma have been really outstanding, as it has for other respiratory diseases since then. The great advance in the treatment of poliomyelitis was a number one preventative by vaccination as was the treatment by the positive pressure breathing apparatus rather than the old fashioned iron lung.

The other outstanding change was in the treatment of pulmonary tuberculosis in which the role of surgery became less and less and the role of chemotherapy more and more. This reduced the need for long hospital in-patient treatment and the need for such places as Aldingbourne Sanatorium, with which we had a very good relationship. Similarly, King Edward VII Sanatorium at Midhurst changed its role from that of being a sanatorium to being a major Chest Hospital, although less surgery was performed there for tuberculosis and more for bronchial carcinoma.

Paddy Whiteside

Constantly drugs are improved. New principles may not be developed but improvement of the previous drugs has gone on all the time. I did some early research in ultrasonic diagnosis. I did a lot of work in testing the new drugs for blood pressure by a number of the pharmaceutical firms in Britain. What would happen would be, I would have a fairly large clinic of hypertension patients coming up, a new drug would come up that would seem very promising for them. I would describe this to them and ask them if they would like to try it. And I would give it to them and see if it gives them a better control of their blood pressure.

Jean Monks

Eventually, we got monitors, alarms to record breathing and heart beat, and we got all sorts of other things, which we never had before. I mean, in the beginning it was the nurse who observed and she would notice if somebody wasn't looking very

The Hospital Chapel in the 1980s.

well. You wouldn't have a monitor to tell you. You would know just by looking at him. When they first decided to put monitors on we had one in the ward, and it was on a very ill patient. It was a very basic one, of course, but it told you whether his heart was beating properly or his blood pressure was getting low. Being a bit sceptical, I also put a nurse there to special him and also do his pulse and his blood pressure and everything. Anyway, this man was extremely ill. A nurse came to me after a very short time really, and she said, 'Mr. So and So is looking terrible and although the monitor doesn't show it, his blood pressure has gone down; I'm sure it has'. And I went to look at him, and just look at him. So I got hold of the doctor and he came down and it was while he was actually examining that patient that the bleep went off to say, 'This patient isn't very well'. I must say, after that, I'm afraid, I never ever trusted a monitor. Because if you train the nurses properly—you'd only got to look at somebody, hadn't you? Now you get the reverse, don't you?

Dennis Barratt

Electronics started to come in, but really when we moved to the new lab, at the top of the new block, that's when money started to be spent in large sums and equipment started to come in then, all electronically orientated. The technical staff got further and further away from the actual tests themselves. I mean half the excitement when we were doing things like urine ureas, when you had a 24-hour urine sample, I mean you had to work out the urea content; it consisted of measuring out about half a litre of this stuff and scratching the end of a capsule of bromine, and you had to throw this capsule of bromine in this bottle of urine, so that it smashed, rapidly push a rubber bung in, which was attached to a device which measured the amount of gas given off. It was very fine, but the only trouble was [laughter] occasionally somebody would miss the bottle of urine when they threw their ampoule of bromine in and the stench from that was unbelievable. You couldn't stay in the room, because this huge volume of brown smoke used to appear. But that was exciting, you know; you enjoyed that and even the basic things like sterilisation.

We had to sterilise all the urine bottles for the wards, because we had the equipment. At that stage they were like the old-fashioned milk bottles with the narrow neck. When they were up on the wards they had a label on them with a rubber bung, but they all had to be sterilised before that. So they were put into the autoclave under steam pressure and sterilised. They all had cotton wool plugs in, though, and when the thing had cooled down, you had to transfer the rubber bungs from a boiling water bath into the neck of these urine jars, taking out the cotton wool plug. Sometimes you couldn't let it cool down because they were short on the wards for these urine bottles and it was getting near 5 o'clock. So you'd undo this thing and it was damn near red hot and you were tossing these bottles around because they were so hot you couldn't hold them. Then the instant you put the rubber bung in the theory was to

The Lab, 1950. (Dennis Barratt is standing, third from left.)

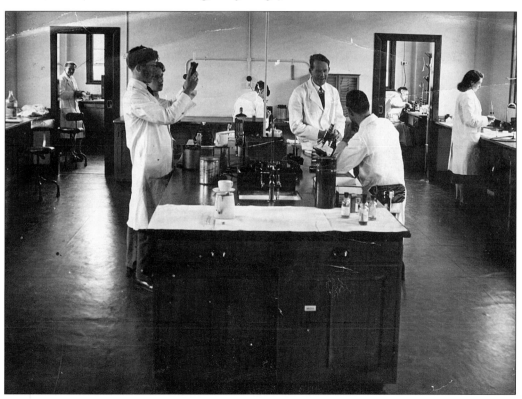

stop any contaminated air getting inside the bottle. You also had to flame the top of the bottle as well, as a sort of secondary measure. Like I say, when it was getting near 5 o'clock and you were in a hurry, these bottles were hot, the rubber bungs you couldn't touch them, boy did you get some blisters and all sorts of things and flaming the tops of these bottles with the Bunsen burner, on the end of a long lead. And more than once, more than once somebody would flame it and forget to take the cotton wool plug out first and this sheet of flame would go across hundreds of these bottles plugged with cotton wool. We'd get a towel and try and knock the flames out—so you could get the cotton wool plugs out and these bungs in quick so you could get home. Oh, dear what a caper! We had great fun.

Sylvia Dadswell

By 1953, the hospital got bigger, and it was an organised hospital. And, of course, we were getting sterilised bottles of blood. Oh, it altered vastly in those few years. Infusions of everything all in a bottle, exactly what they wanted, you know. We still had the South Ward, the theatre wasn't built then. And they used to do all sorts of very complicated surgery, with almost no equipment. It was in the days when the TB patients had lungs removed and lobes removed and all this sort of thing, and it was all done at St Richard's. And no Intensive Care wards or any of this. They had none of the gadgets that they have for the heart surgery now.

Clive Bratt

Diagnostically there really wasn't very much equipment. Obviously there were pathological investigations. ECGs [electrocardiograms], of course, were used on the medical wards. But I can't think of anything on the surgical side that we had really that was essentially diagnostic other than, you know, what one was familiar with in the surgery really. I mean there was the X-ray department. But X-rays were X-rays. There were no scanners or anything like that. We had a radiologist who interpreted the X-rays. Surgery was still very much in its infancy. I mean, transplants weren't thought of. As a dresser, that's a clinical student at St Mary's, I was on the professorial firm and the professor on almost every ward round preached the thing that he felt most about which was that we'd got to the stage that it was not what can we do but what should we do. Things were beginning to happen; bigger things being done.

Paddy Whiteside

In the '60s more specialising took place. In adult patients and with special diseases, for example. Also, there was one other factor; tuberculosis had previously been looked after in the sanatoria, but with the control of tuberculosis, the chest physician developed beds at St Richard's Hospital and he would look after a lot of the chest patients, which previously we had cared for. Tuberculosis got less, but cancer of the lung got much more common. With cancer of the lung, operation had to be considered often for removal of the cancer, or the whole lung, and that was done at

King Edward VII Hospital. During the '60s, there was an outbreak of poliomyelitis, quite a serious outbreak of poliomyelitis in England and Wales.

Changes in treatment are occurring all the time. There has been a great improvement in drugs and the management of hospital treatment. Patients with a coronary are mobilised very much earlier and should return to exercise as soon as they can, but it should not bring on breathlessness, chest pain or undue fatigue. Exercise is a coronary preventative and is known to help in prevention of a recurrence. St Richard's has been a pioneer in early mobilisation.

I was interested in cardiology and I rapidly trained by visiting the National Heart Hospital in London for resident and out-patient visiting. In 1963, I visited the Cleveland Clinic in the United States, and saw Bernard Lown resuscitate a patient, whose heart had stopped, with a defibrillator, and this was a miracle to me. A defibrillator is passing a direct, electric current shock through the heart, which will stop it and, if the heart is in suitable condition, it will re-start again in a normal rhythm. When the abnormal rhythm is present, there is, on many occasions, no output from the heart at all, and the patient will die very rapidly, probably within four minutes. I was very impressed by the defibrillator and very interested, and on my return to England I managed to persuade the committee to let me have a defibrillator that year. The next year my cardiology staff joined with our social club and ran a Mediaeval Fair in Bishop Otter [College] garden; this included jousting and all, and it made £3,000, which was quite a lot of money 33 years ago. With this I managed to buy some monitors and then by 1968 we managed to put aside a four-bedded ward for a Coronary Care Unit. This was probably the first Coronary Care Unit in a district hospital in the country. At the same time one of our enterprising Chichester citizens suggested that we should have a Coronary Care Club, which we started, and this has run ever since. It has made enough money for us to keep the Coronary Care Unit and the Cardiac Department absolutely up-to-date with the best equipment. It was a constant drain to raise money because most of the cardiology equipment costs anything up to £20,000, and it takes a lot of raising that amount of money fairly continuously. We put in, for instance, for fresh better monitors, further defibrillators, and a unit for ultrasound, which were just being introduced, and fortunately being produced by a firm in Bognor, which has helped us a great deal, not only for cardiology but also for obstetrics, and other abdominal disorders. We had an exercise machine, which would help to diagnose coronary artery disease.

All cardiac surgery is now specialised. We did do some of the more simple type of cardiac surgery at St Richard's, and here again it was probably a first in a district hospital. We did mitral valve disease, which

Preparing for 'A Medieval Banquet' outside Willowmead, Summer 1963. (May Burrows is far right.) [Courtesy: Jean Monks]

was done with a very able surgeon called Vincent Powell, who was consultant to the Royal Air Force in chest disease, and did do a lot of work during the war on cardiac injuries by bullets and that type of thing, which was the first war, of course, in which this technique was used. But with the improvement in cardiology with the use of artificial hearts during surgery, we gave this up. The defibrillator was purely treatment, when a heart either stopped or went into a fatal-type abnormal rhythm, but the ultrasound was diagnosis and when we got a simple condition such as a narrowed mitral valve we might do this ourselves, but the majority of abnormalities were referred to one of the London cardiology units.

The Coronary Care Unit was one of the first in Britain. We developed non-invasive investigations and did some minor cardiac surgery, but subsequently the cardiac patients requiring surgery were transferred to St George's Hospital, London for treatment. One of the benefits of starting a specific Cardiac Unit was that it included treatment of hypertension, which was then just coming in, and the reduction of the pressure, which the heart worked against, reduced the pressure on the heart very considerably. These patients would come up regularly to the Cardiac outpatients and be seen and their treatments guided. Once the treatment became standard, the GPs took it over. Cardiac surgery is very considerably used for coronary artery disease, and also for narrowed valves, and congenital abnormalities; all of these have to be diagnosed, and perhaps referred for surgery. Gradually, treatment for cardiac disease improved. Once it was mainly rest and drugs, the drugs being mainly digitalis and diuretics. But it was rest, particularly, and reduction in activity, reduction in weight and especially reduction in smoking. Eventually, there was to be an enormous expansion in the possibility of diagnosing heart disease.

There were changes in the treatment of cardiology all the time. One of the most important advances was drug treatment and control of hypertension. Drugs, of course, are constantly improved. In addition to that, there was the question of surgery, and later on coronary artery surgery, all of these were important. It was difficult to keep up with new treatment, extremely difficult. But this is why we had, and still have, a very active Society, the British Cardiac Society, where we met twice a year and for four days, and we went over all the advances that had been made since the last meeting.

Drug companies influence us all the time, of course, always. They have been pretty ethical, though, but they always, of course, assure you their own drug of a particular kind is the best. But there were clinical trials of all drugs done in various hospitals, and these were discussed in the Cardiac Society meetings, so you knew what was worth trying and what was not. As we do today. But the main method of diagnosis in medicine is very careful history of things like pains and breathlessness and coughs and things like that, and diarrhoea and so forth. Very careful history taken of these matters would give you the diagnosis, or lead you to the diagnosis of many diseases in some 70 per cent of cases, and you would only need to confirm that with investigation. Several of the more difficult cases may not ever be diagnosed until post-mortem.

Bill Gammie

I think, when one looks at it, the surgeons always look at the facilities that the anaesthetists were in a position to provide. Anaesthetics had come forward quite a long way in the '50s. And by the early '60s anaesthetic skills had increased significantly and their ability to allow you to undertake lengthy procedures had increased. The monitoring facilities were very limited. The monitoring skills rested really with the anaesthetists and their own perception of how things were going. Certainly there was not the extent of monitoring that one sees in an operating theatre these days. It mainly relied on the skills and the experience of your anaesthetist.

I was always brought up to feel, and I think this was evident in the earlier surgeons when you look back to surgery over the last 60-70 years, that so much that was achieved by the surgeons in the 1920s and '30s was achieved out of their own technical skill. They didn't have resources—particularly in the field of anaesthetics. The anaesthesia was in many ways somewhat primitive in those early days. It was mostly inhalation anaesthesia and it was only just before the war that injection anaesthesia first came in for the induction of anaesthesia but it was maintained by inhalation anaesthesia through that time. So it was really transformed considerably in the 1950s and '60s. That greatly increased the ability of surgeons to undertake more major procedures with greater safety. And, of course, blood transfusion was another feature that had come in before the war but advanced considerably during the war-time years. It became a feature, increasingly, in allowing major procedures to be undertaken with safety.

May Burrows

We did new types of surgery, you see. We started putting in hip joints, knee joints and did the occasional ankle and elbow joint; well, they didn't exist before, you see. Then we started doing all this facio-maxillary work, and, of course, we did no eye surgery until the Royal West closed and then eye surgery was brought over to St Richard's. Mr. Alan Scott came and we started doing vascular surgery. We never actually did neurosurgery because we would take them to a special unit. The only neurosurgery we would do is in the case of an emergency where the patient was too ill to be transferred to Southampton, and we used to do just the bore holes, and perhaps stop the bleeding and that sort of thing. But we didn't do any major neurological surgery at all; we would do just an emergency procedure just to save a life.

We had our own sort of sterile unit where they dealt with all our instruments and everything, and at the end of a session you just put the whole of your dirty instruments in a hatch in the corner of the theatre. They would come round and collect them from the outside all the time. So we had none of this extra work. By this time, you see, we weren't making any swabs and all the gloves were disposable, all the syringes were disposable, all your swabs came ready made and tied in bundles for you; so, I mean, there was nothing like that. They were just all over the theatre; they were just packed in boxes for us.

They were increasing the amount of work we were doing then. You see, by this time also, don't forget, we'd got more beds. There was more acute stuff in the hutted ward. We had the 'gynae' block. We had the orthopaedic block. The Caesarean sections were being done in their own unit but we were still having to go over there to do them. When I first went there the Caesarean sections were wheeled across from the huts to us to do, but they were done on the site after that new ward block opened. So the beds were increasing, you see, and consequently the number of surgeons were increasing and the work was increasing.

The core of our work was assisting in the operations, and assisting the anaesthetist. A lot of my nurses used to help the surgeon as well. He might want somebody scrubbed up to hold on to things, you see. We could do all that; keep all the equipment going. You rather felt the surgeons were always under a lot of pressure with the quantity of work, because we were always being pressurised to try and push more and more work through. I mean, a morning list was supposed to stop at one, but quite often the morning list would often run almost into the afternoon and it was quite an effort to get the theatre ready for the afternoon session. We'd be really running around trying to get it ready, and quite often we never got a lunch break. We'd grab a quick cup of coffee or tea and that was it.

When they first had a TSSU (Theatre Sterile Supply Unit), I typed them out their first Cardex. I used to type a card for every operation, and they used to work on those cards. We used to have to train the girls over there and they would work from this card and pack according to this card, and then there would be a label put on the top, who packed it and who checked it, and what set it was in. And these sets were wrapped up in paper and brought across and put in the sterile store that we had in the theatre.

We were still responsible for our own instruments. We still washed and autoclaved our own instruments. In each we had actually—we had a sterilising room, we had a theatre and we had a scrub-up theatre and an anaesthetic room in each theatre. So, I mean, the anaesthetists had their own little area to put their patients to sleep and do everything, then they were taken into the theatre; the scrub-up area was just around the corner.

We used to pack on trays. You'd look at your list, find out what cases you were doing. You had to get your own instruments out of the cupboards, pack them on a tray, put them in the autoclave and autoclave them. Then once you'd scrubbed up you went to the autoclave. We had these trolley bases. You just lifted the whole tray of instruments from the autoclave on to your trolley, and you worked from there and got out all your needles and your scissors as you required them—they were still in trays, you know. You never autoclaved your scissors. You had to pick out your blades and your needles and then you would ask what sutures you wanted. But by this time the sutures would come in packets. They were gradually doing away with the glass things, and, of course, by the time I left, all sutures were in packets. We virtually did away with needles, because most of the sutures had needles attached to them, and this was developing over the years.

When we first went to the new block, we had a—well they called it a CSSD [Central Surgical Supplies Department] really, and they kept us supplied with towels, gowns—that was their job. They would keep us supplied with all linen, but we did all the instruments still, until we got the four theatres—then we had a TSSU. They would pack all our instruments, wash them and do everything for us. The only things we never sent across to TSSU were our scopes because we felt they were too fragile to be dealt with in TSSU so we used to do them ourselves. The CSSD also supplied sterile equipment to the wards and later to the GPs through a hospital delivery service.

There's one operation that sticks out in my mind. It was quite a marvellous thing in the end. I think they did about a six-hour operation to cure it one day. A young woman, she was involved in a car accident, and the cars in those days, the passenger seat very often had a handle in the front on the dash board; you know, they used to hold on to their handle. It was in the '60s, and they had this crash locally and there were no seat belts, of course, and she was thrown forward and her neck caught across this handle in front of her on the dash board. She was rushed straight into theatre. They didn't even stop in out-patients, and we virtually had to hold this girl down while they did a tracheotomy, because she couldn't breathe you see, her tongue was all badly cut, we held her down and we put the tracheotomy tube in in the anaesthetic room, then once we got the tube in her neck, we were able to put her to sleep properly and explore her mouth and everywhere. It turned out that her trachea was crushed, that's what had happened, you see. So for quite a long time she had a tracheotomy tube permanently when she went home. She was a very pretty girl I remember; she always used to wear it on a velvet band. Then they decided they would try and rebuild her trachea. So I remember we had to send to America for this special mesh and we had to do it on a Saturday and we started at ten o'clock in the morning, and I think we finished about five o'clock at night. They actually made her a new trachea and inserted it, joined it top and bottom, but it didn't improve her voice volume very much. It was rather strange, the tracheotomy tube was left in. She could have done without it; but she wouldn't do without it; she always felt that was her safety valve. But she was able to perform … she had a much better life … well, she knew she wasn't depending on that tube. She could talk much better. We did make up a trachea, that was one thing that we did. When Mr. Williams came we started doing all these badly smashed faces you know. We had horse riders coming in with all these badly fractured jaws. We were wiring all the jaws together.

I didn't actually ever get frightened. I think the work always intrigued me and actually I enjoyed doing it. I know we had this case where one night this boy came in with a stab wound, and he died on the table. We had quite a time trying to save him, trying to find out why he was bleeding so badly, and then we discovered the hepatic artery had gone so there was nothing we could do. There was another rather spectacular case: a young boy came off of a motor bike one night and his leg was really shattered. I looked at his leg and I thought, well, they'll amputate that you know; there's no doubt about that, and when Mr. Wilson came—was one of our orthopaedics—he looked at it and he thought we'd have a go in trying to save it. How he managed to cobble that leg up I shall never know; and eventually we saved that leg. They did some pretty marvellous jobs there. They were specialised you see, in their own field. As years went on you were being able to do more and more for a patient; I mean perhaps things, when I first went to theatre, they wouldn't attempt; the technology and the knowledge had so increased they were able to do more for people. Some of it was quite dramatic, some of it was quite spectacular, really. I mean, I think they did some marvellous work in those theatres. We were only a small affair but there were some very marvellous operations done in there.

Marjorie Semmens

Paediatrics was becoming a speciality in its own right—the '50s and '60s. Before that one of the physicians looked after the children.

Bud Robinson

I was the paediatrician to St Richard's and Worthing. I also had responsibility for patients at the Royal West Sussex, but particularly the maternity unit at St Richard's. I had a place called Zachary Merton at Rustington. I had about a thousand, twelve hundred deliveries a year there, just babies I was responsible for. I had a ward at Worthing, and about four or six hundred deliveries a year, a little maternity unit at Worthing. And a ward at Shoreham, which is Southlands Hospital, and about two thousand plus babies being delivered at Shoreham.

Twice a week I would do a ward round in one place in the morning and Shoreham in the afternoon. I would do an outpatient at each end, at Worthing, Shoreham and Chichester. And I went to Zachary Merton once a week. So if I did two ward rounds in the big units, which was Shoreham and Chichester, a week, and then one at Worthing, because it was not so big. So I didn't have any time off.

The only person I had that was responsible to me was a peculiar arrangement. I had a registrar under my care at Shoreham, and supervision. A medical registrar. He was appointed medical registrar and at night he looked after the whole of the hospital, but in the day he just did paediatrics, and worked for me. Back up was just a pre-registration houseman, and so it was very, very thin. I was called out many, many nights. I used to sleep in occasionally. Come into the hospital and sleep. I was up, out of bed, I should think, two or three times a week.

In those days, what did a paediatrician do? He used to do exchange transfusions. I suppose that was the most dramatic; it was bloody boring but it is perceived as dramatic. There were a lot of exchange transfusions to do and I would be up all night doing those sometimes. You know, for Rhesus incompatibility. Of course, junior doctors can't do lumber punctures; they can't set up drips. I mean putting up drips in those days was a major surgical operation. We used to cut down on these babies with a knife on their ankle, anaesthetise it and cut down. We used to isolate a tiny sliver of a vein, which we used to half cut the vein open, half cut it, and that took a bit of a trembly hand, because if you cut it across it just disappeared. So you cut it half and then used to have to thread a metal tube in the opening and then tie it all in. That was a drip, so although you didn't operate, that sort of exercise could … I mean if you didn't get it done first time it could … you know you could be two hours putting up a drip.

We used to do what we called sagittal sinus aspirations. I personally never did one of those. I helped at them and I've been in a position where people have encouraged me to do it. But that was sticking a needle in the big vein that runs right across the brain in a baby. It's only about a millimetre wide, but in diagrams in books it looks enormous. And you get diagrams in books with a needle going into this it all looks very simple. Of course, you've only got to do it badly there, and there is bleeding inside the head. So in that sense … I used to have to cut down on the neck occasionally. I used to stick needles into the head to take out blood collections we call subdural haemorrhages from non-accidental injury particularly. They used to get these big collections of fluids. I used to put needles into the ventricles of the brain to put in drugs in children that had had, say, tuberculous meningitis. We used to believe that putting, tuberculin, purified protein … PPD, purified protein derivative tuberculin, to try to create … when they tended to get blocked, so they used to get internal hydrocephalus. So we used to do funny things like that, which today you wouldn't entertain.

The subdural haemorrhages we used to do … I mean, once you start doing them you may have to do a subdural stab into the brain, one side, one side, every day, and you might do that for a month, until it dries up—hopefully. Today you would send them off to neurosurgical unit. You know you either did it then or your patient perished. We used to give intravenous feeding 30 years ago, directly into a vein, not just clear fluids that sort of thing, but fat and protein and amino acid solutions. This is still done I might add, but it's now done only in Intensive Care Units and specialised units, but then we used to do that. I supposed we did it in a very hit-and-miss way and so on, but gradually it became recognised that it was a very sophisticated thing we were doing. And people began to specialise in that and take it on board. So we did exchange transfusions. I suspect because they were boring to do, they were still left in the District General Hospital province. But an unconscious child with meningitis, I've had them three, four days under my care and treating them. And then they've come to life again and woken up as it were. Today if you had that situation it would be away in an ambulance to Great Ormond Street like yesterday.

Jean Monks

They brought in newer and newer kinds of operations. And we finally got to doing arterial surgery at St Richard's, which I had actually done in London. In London we did arterial surgery where, you know, you removed the clots in arteries and put in a vein upside down to produce a good blood supply to the toes and things like that. And that was quite new then in the '50s. But eventually we got it down in Chichester and it was very interesting, you know, having done it 20 years previously, then to, sort of, start up again. And, of course, they could do a lot more by then.

It was changing all the time. One thing that was much better was prostatectomies. I can't tell you what we went through the night before on prostatectomies, because they used to bleed like stuck pigs. I mean you really did have nightmares about it because really it was awful. And when they started doing Millen's prostatectomies, because the other ones were called Freyers. And that was unbelievable. I can't go into it; it was so dreadful. Then they did Millen's operations which were much less blood-letting. And then they did these transurethral resections which are absolutely fabulous. In a Millen's operation you have to open up the bladder and what is known as enucleate the prostate and then you sew. It's rather like taking out a plum stone and then sewing up the plum skin afterwards.

When you get an enlarged prostate, it presses on this thin tube known as the urethra and stops them passing urine and they are extremely uncomfortable. And then they can get an enlarged bladder and be very poorly. And then you get back pressure on the kidneys and they go into uraemia (kidney failure) if it's not treated. And then you see when they brought in the transurethral resection you didn't have to have your bladder opened. They used to put in a thing like a telescope and just, sort of—like sharpening a pencil really, and get the passage or urethra bigger so it was fine, there was no problem. And you very rarely got any bleeding. I mean, patients were in and out much quicker. And then we started five day wards, you see. As opposed to having people who had minor surgery next to people with major surgery. So that you could do major surgery all in one place. But even that, you know, they got quicker and quicker in going out. Well, there was a great emphasis on getting them up early to stop thrombosis and clotting. We didn't get that many deep vein thromboses but it did happen, and they realised that it was happening. The more surgery they did, the more the percentages were getting a deep vein thrombosis. So they then thought the answer is to get the patient moving as quickly as possible, so then you used to get them out of the bed the next day.

Bill Gammie

In my particular time, on the general surgery side, there was really very little change that one saw. We used all the standard surgical instruments that had been used for many decades. I don't think there was anything very special. Apart from, let's say, the advantage of the new endoscopes in urology which were considerable, because the lighting systems were so much better. The fibre-optic lighting systems made a considerable improvement to that. Because initially, over the first decade or so we were using instruments with end lighting, which meant that the light was produced … the source was at the end of the instrument rather than through a fibre-optic cable. And it was frequently doomed to failure. There were a lot of difficulties and technical difficulties with that. No, the other instruments were those that had been designed— and I had used—ever since I started training in surgery, or took an interest in surgery in the 1950's. A lot of the skills one developed in one's hands, and one's perception and feel of things really, was more important than anything else.

The nurses knew rather routinely what you wanted. In fact, in so many occasions you just put out a hand and the exact instrument that you wanted appeared. You may have to indicate what particular steps you were taking. I mean, one of the interests that I had initially was in upper intestinal gastric work. And gastrectomy in the 1960s was still very frequently performed with a large number of patients with peptic ulcers. A routine gastrectomy was a procedure which one had had a lot of experience in, and one of the burdens on the nursing staff for these operations was, in fact, threading needles. I suppose the eyeless needle and the advent of the eyeless needle towards the latter part of the '70s did take a little bit of the pressure off the nursing staff. But threading needles … And if one was a fairly swift surgeon—as I always felt that I was able to undertake so many of these procedures successfully within about an hour— meant that there were lots of stitches and lots of needle threading. They were often very small needles. And I used to have my leg pulled quite a lot by some of the nursing sisters, some of whom were better at threading needles than others.

There was no Central Sterile Supply Department until the buildings were completed in 1971. Up until then all instruments were boiled. I mean, there were a lot of advantages in boiling instruments. I don't think many people will recall that. But the advantages of being able to boil instruments between cases is that you didn't have to have vast numbers of instruments in an operating theatre. You just had one set of instruments which you used for a whole afternoon. Or two sets of instruments, one being boiled ready for the next case and one that you had in use. If you dropped an instrument it was very easy to put it back in the boiler and re-use it, which was not an infrequent occurrence. It's very easy for things to slip off onto the floor from either the operating table or from the nurse's table. It was a feature of the structure of buildings that you had to have a sterilising room, which was just a set of boilers. When the new theatres were built and they had to be re-equipped, then we had to order vast numbers of instruments to allow for having several packs for different surgical procedures. It became quite a costly business. And I don't think the administrators really took that into account fully when they started assessing how much it was going to cost to set up a four-theatre unit as opposed to a two-theatre unit.

Any diagnosis hinges basically on taking a careful history from the patient and then following that up with a careful clinical examination, and one had been offered certain help from the pathology service and the radiology services. Now for much of my life these had all been somewhat basic, certainly in radiology. But during the 1970s with the development of the CAT scan and changes in radiology, hands-on radiology, as I would put it, became a very definite feature. Then obviously the facilities for diagnosis were steadily improving. I think all this contributed towards having a better understanding of what one was aiming to achieve surgically. Once you'd diagnosed a particular condition you could get a more specific identification of where a lesion might be; in which particular organ it might be. You could also, perhaps, get a better indication of the lesion, and perhaps save a number of people surgery. If, for instance, a malignant lesion had become extensively invasive the radiologists were able to give you more and more information to say whether any diagnostic laparotomy was justified or even going to achieve anything.

Marjorie Semmens

The treatment for polio? Well, in those days we had hot and cold packs. Anybody who had a weakness, or initially a discomfort and a tingling. The symptoms are progressive to actually paresis, but there are symptoms before-hand. Once the diagnosis was even provisional, treatment was started. I think the physios did most of this, rather than the nurses. They put the hot packs on, which eased the pain and then, of course, they manipulated the limbs so that they would keep the muscle tone as high as possible, as normal as possible. Then, hopefully, one waited for recovery. I certainly recall one lady who was down in the end, the sixth bed along at the end of the ward, and I'm pretty sure she was pregnant. This was certainly, I think, found in association— I mean there was a risk with pregnancy of getting polio.

I suppose, really, nobody realised how emotionally upset sick children were. They limited the time parents could be with them, and by limiting the parents being there they didn't have the crying sessions that the children usually had when the parents left. I think just nobody realised the importance of visiting. Even adults had limited visiting, too, you see; it's again quite changed. I mean that was quite a profound difference when I was a medical registrar. I really, at one occasion, and I said to the ward, I remember standing up and saying, 'I'd be most grateful if they could ask their visitors not to come when we were doing ward rounds'. It isn't so bad with the children, because on the whole, people who sit in with their children, perhaps, don't mind the case-histories being given and the discussions around the bedside being audible to the next patient. But for the adults … I always felt if you were discussing something with a lady and the next lady's husband or son was sitting there, it was a bit difficult for her, and a bit difficult for me sometimes. This was why I made that request. After a time, I just got used to everybody being there and if I wanted particularly to talk either to the relatives or the patient, we just went to another area where there was nobody.

With regard to the children, if they had a really bad chest they probably needed oxygen; well, we had cylinders. We still had cylinders in some wards when I finished working, although piped oxygen is really the in-thing, if you have a new ward and it's plumbed in, so to speak. Suckers and things we needed. Otherwise, you know, looking after children, in particular, there is a limit to what you need. It's with the babies, particularly, where extensive treatments developed. Babies just didn't survive in those earlier days.

They had the delivery suite and again, probably, what I knew of as the little interview room, which may be something else now, since I have left. But that was our Nursery, and we could accommodate four little cots in there. And so if we had any ill children we used to put the children in there; otherwise, they went into an area roughly where the cubicles are which was the Nursery part of the ward. And that's where the well babies went. They didn't even, at that stage, room in with their mothers.

Now everybody has their baby alongside them, of course; they don't stay in the nurseries, though they may go there for sleeping at night time, to let the mothers sleep if they want them to. If they want a quiet night.

As a student, you had to deliver a certain number of babies. But then in an obstetric job, you learn how to do the problem deliveries, forceps and assisted Caesarean sections. The midwives usually do the normal deliveries or again, the student, if there's a student. As a student, you usually went two at a time. We had to deliver ten babies, I think. When I did the obstetric house-officer job, I delivered babies. If there was a patient and there was a problem, however, either the registrar or the consultant came in. I might be the other end doing the anaesthetic. You were Jack-of-all-trades in those days. I learned to take X-rays, give anaesthetics. Nobody has that range of experience now. They're all specialised jobs now.

Bud Robinson

When I first came, to have a child on the ward for two weeks was nothing. Today you'd be saying, 'What on earth is going on?' I mean I used to do domiciliary visits, perhaps two—three hundred a year, see children at home, which was marvellous really: a) because I got to see what the environment of the child was like, b) I met the GPs, and it's an educational thing: a) they were educating me, and b) I was educating them. But I used to see children at home. I mean, by chance, with the most grotesque … I mean I've been stopped in the car park by a GP, and told, 'Oh I'm glad I've seen you.' He said, 'I'm just popping in to see so and so. But while you're here, I wonder if I could tell you about a little girl I saw yesterday … ' etc. And then they tell you about it. And I say, 'Do you want me to go and see her?' He says, 'If you can find the time, could you pop in some time; I'd be grateful.' So you take the name and address, you go round, and you find the child has got meningoccal meningitis. You find the child with a septic arthritis, big swollen infected joint. Things like that, awful. So you know, I didn't think … I wasn't alarmed about that. [laughs] It was par for the course. But looking back on it! I found a boy at home who'd been off his feet for about two weeks, not able to walk, paralysed legs for two weeks. He had a spinal abscess. From a congenital abnormality that should have been picked up at birth, and he was about six.

It's the structure of medicine that has changed. There was only one paediatrician in the UK earning his living in 1939, before the war, doing paediatrics. Only one person in England. All the paediatricians at Great Ormond Street, places like that had adult medicine or a practice where they did insurance work or something like that, to earn a living. The paediatrics didn't bring them in anything. So paediatricians didn't exist. So the teaching of paediatrics almost didn't exist. Even in my day the teaching of paediatrics was bloody awful, it put you off. So GPs learnt on the hoof, and it took them about twenty years to feel confident with a child. They were frightened to death.

When I was casualty officer at Guy's Hospital in London, and I had a bit of support at Guy's, I'd be able to call the paediatric houseman, if I was worried. A child would come through the door and six casualty officers would disappear. 'Sorry sister

I've got something … ''I'm ever so busy, I'm just going to put a plaster … ' Nobody would see the child … and somebody would be … the sister in charge would get hold of somebody's ear and drag them along, 'Look at this child.' Well, they didn't know what was wrong. We were always told children become very ill very quickly. That their presentation of illness is different to adults. And as we didn't get well taught, or we weren't well taught, we always felt we were going to be bowled a googly, as it were. And people were bowled googlies. The reason was, the GPs had never been trained. And they just didn't know what was important. The standard of education, medical education since then has gone up … oh, it's unrecognisable. I had to teach what heart failure in a baby would be like. I mean I would bore the pants off a group of GPs today talking about it. In those days they were anxious to know.

Nurses that look after children, nine out of ten, are very kind, sensitive people; they wouldn't be doing it if they weren't. When I first started at St Richard's, though, in 1965, I said, ' I notice there isn't a television on the ward, Sister.' She said, 'No and there's not going to be one Dr. Robinson.' She said, 'When children are in my ward, they're here because they're sick; they're not to play.' [laughs] You're laughing. Do you know that was a perfectly reasonable answer. Most people accepted that as an answer. Yes. [laughs]

Parents were not allowed. Not much before that, if you were sick and went to hospital, you know, you'd got scarlet fever or some perceived terribly infectious illness, your parents were allowed to look at you through a window, half an hour a day, or half an hour a week. You were isolated. And, of course, we used to be taught about isolation. You know, that children became disturbed for the rest of their lives, if they went into hospital. And I inherited that sort of culture, that people were just about to see. But parents weren't on the ward when I did ward rounds to start with. 1965, no. They were allowed to visit most days. Only parents, not siblings. You know special care, only the mother and father. There were rigid rules and they gradually went. The reason was not so much that the doctors did it, it was the mothers, you know. They got fed up, and said, 'It's my child. You're looking after it, but you don't dictate to me everything.' You know. 'I know when my child wants me, etc., etc.,' Some paediatricians took this on board and it became general policy that we should loosen up a lot of this abnormal rigidity that we had.

The child's vision was not perceived as important. The ward sister's or the hospital decorator's vision was perceived. And, of course, putting things on glass, you couldn't get it off perhaps because of the glue, or something like that, so it wasn't put on. I always remember at Southlands we had a very austere superintendent midwife, and she used to walk around like that, and she allowed decorations on Christmas Day and they all had to be gone by Boxing Day. Literally, you know. 'Why is this here? There's a balloon over there.' You know. So the night nurse, come Christmas midnight everything was taken down. It's true. Now, they perceive that part of a child's recovery process is that emotional disturbance must be virtually nil from a hospital experience. But then kids were in for weeks, as I say. It wasn't a two-day affair, which most people can sustain. In those days it was literally weeks and weeks. And, of course, with some illnesses like tuberculosis, it would be months and months. So it's totally changed; totally changed.

Community paediatrics didn't exist when I started, and what we call the Developmental Assessment Unit didn't exist. But I started to get one off the ground where children would come for neuro-developmental assessment, backward children, handicapped children, in some way. You give them short shrift in the normal hurly-burly of paediatrics, so they really wanted somebody to look at their multiple problems. We were getting this set off the ground, but we couldn't finance it, I remember. You know, it was going to cost money and I was being attached to the old maternity unit where I used to see these premature babies through the port-hole, suddenly became vacant when the new maternity block was built, and I had patients over at the Royal West. And I said, 'Right, I want that Maternity Unit for paediatrics'. And it was two great big huts, and they agreed that I could have it. I mean, other people put in bids but mine was the pressure, and I left the Royal West Sussex. I got everything on one site. I'd got babies being born at least on the campus, not on the same building but on the campus where the children were. And the children were where they could get an X-ray. They could get blood tests on St Richard's campus. Before, they were over half a mile away.

They said they would do one ward up, alter it from being a maternity ward to a children's ward. But they wouldn't do anything else. There was no money. I was trying to get this Assessment Centre built and there was no money. Then I got a phone call from the region saying, 'Had we got an Assessment Unit?' I said, 'No, but we're planning one.' They said, 'How far are you along on the planning?' And I said, 'Oh, well, we've got it …' And they said, 'Have you costed it yet?' And because I knew how much the paediatric ward cost to alter, I said, 'Well, yes.' They said, 'Well, how much is it?' And so I just gave them this figure. In those days, I think it was something like £18,000 or £25,000 or something. You know, an astronomical figure. It's like saying £200,000 today. And they said, 'Right you can have it'. And what had happened was, there was

a national outcry by a pressure group which had lobbied the Minister, that children with special needs weren't being addressed, and hospitals ought to have these. So the Minister desperately wanted to be able to say, 'And we've set up, you know, twenty new Assessment Units in the UK.' And we were just right. Just at the right moment to capitalise on this. So we got the money. We got the thing and it's set up. And it's been running on it's own for ages. We've got a consultant in charge. Super. So in that sense, I suppose, we were avant-garde.

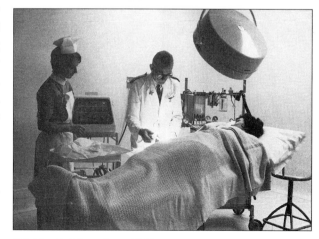

Working in Maternity, c.1952.

'A certain teamwork'

THE PEOPLE AND THEIR SOCIAL LIFE

6 There was a certain team-work in the '60s that was so evident. The Theatre Superintendent, at that time, was a great character and saw that everybody in the team was there to do a job. Surgery does involve team-work. That team-work goes right back to the porters that deliver the patients from the ward, take them to the theatre, transfer them in the theatre. And then it's the nursing team, the runners in the theatre—as the nurses are that are mobile. And the scrub nurse who is assisting you at the operation with instruments and equipment. There was a great, sort of, feeling of supportive help and if one ran into, as inevitably every now and then in surgery you run into some difficulties, you could feel that the whole team rallied round to make sure that you achieved success in whatever procedure you were carrying out. 9

(*Bill Gammie, Consultant Surgeon*)

The management of the Hospital changed over this period. It gradually moved from reliance on one dominating figure to government by a medical committee, and to systems that could be measurable and more accountable. At the same time, great efforts were made to integrate the staff: to make some attempt to break down old barriers of class and privilege and to bring some concerted social cohesion to an increasingly compartmentalised workforce. This was a time of many social activities: sporting events, social get-togethers, parties and the inevitable Christmas show. These events, however, became increasingly difficult to engineer as staff no longer lived on the site. As people lived away and commuted to work, so they were less likely to want to participate in events that were once the norm. Some, such as Crom Polson, regretted this; others such as Bud Robinson felt that it was a natural development of modern life and the increasing demands placed on its staff. All were to agree, however, that this change in the way people lived their lives altered quite radically the once tight-knit social cohesion of the hospital.

Clive Bratt

At St Richard's there was a very friendly atmosphere. I mean, I would go down in the morning at nine o'clock and get to the ward where Mr. Clark would almost certainly be already sitting reading the paper and he'd say, 'I see you were up in the night, bad luck. Have you had any breakfast?' 'No sir.' 'Well you go and have breakfast and I'll read the paper.' So we had a very close relationship, especially at the first three months when we hadn't got a surgical registrar intervening. I mean, one answered to her when she was appointed. She was almost a go-between, but it was very relaxed … I mean I did as many hours as the junior hospital doctors do today. But one has to remember we weren't in the field of medical hi-tech and probably the most serious decision we had to make was whether to send out the 'Dangerously Ill' notice to the relatives. You hadn't got to battle with complicated apparatus.

Jean Monks

We had what was known as a recreational room where we were allowed to have dances, and play table tennis and things like that. We used to have a club, a recreational club, and we used to hire a bathing hut down at Aldwick for our use only. So it was good. Everybody knew everybody, and you knew all about them as well. I mean, Mr. Martin would know where you came from, how long you'd been there and whether you were any good or not. He would, if you were in the kitchen setting up something or other, he would come in, and he was a very lordly man. I mean, he was the boss. He was known as the boss, and you were the children, really, in that sense, but he would be looking after you in a fatherly way. He was adored. I mean, he really was. He was strict; I mean there was no nonsense about him. But that was the ethos in those days, and you were glad of it. If a patient really wouldn't co-operate at anything, they'd be out, because he wasn't going to stand any nonsense. He was an extremely good man.

May Burrows

There was no question of us calling the doctors by any Christian names, you know, they were Mr. Clark, Mr. Martin, Mr. Cray, Miss Shippam. They were very nice to us, and I think they were very helpful. Because I think they realised that we were working very, very hard and we were always willing to push in all the extra cases for them, because at the time I left we'd gone up to 7,000 in a year, which was considered pretty marvellous in those days.

Robin Agnew

I suppose that we as doctors tended to take decisions which we felt were in the best interests of our patients, these decisions being based on our ethical teaching. Our first consideration was never to injure the patient and make his condition worse by our treatment. I think the chief difference being that the Ward Sister had a much more responsible role as regards both the nursing care of the patients on her ward and the management of diets, and certainly helped to teach the Junior Doctors. The Ward Sister was the person one always approached to find out about what was going on a ward and if she was off duty she made it her business to see that there was a competent Staff Nurse who could answer any questions about the patients. There also seemed to be more time as regards carrying out ward rounds and the Consultants were very much more looked up to I think in those days than they are now.

You were dealing with much more major surgery than you had in the beginning. And the turnover was much quicker. And also there was an enormous amount of writing and records to be kept which grew enormously, which you hadn't had before in the '50s. I mean, if you wanted an ambulance for the patients to be taken home all you did was ring up. I mean, for instance, after that you had to write it out in triplicate. If you wanted a light bulb changed you just used to ring up the electrician and say, you know, light bulb. Then you had to write it out in triplicate and you might have to wait two days—that sort of thing.

Clive Bratt

The staff seemed very, very close indeed. You had the senior nurse, the Sisters who'd been there many years, who you looked up to. And as I say, you learnt a lot from. And if you showed yourself to be willing to learn they would teach you the rudiments of ward work which you really had very little experience of. Then there were some of the younger Sisters who socialised with the young doctors. A lumbar puncture, for example, where you put the needle in to get the cerebrospinal fluid off to test it for infection as in meningitis or pressure. Well, I mean, I'd never done anything like that at medical school, of course, as a student. I learnt from a Sister I knew. She got two bedside tables, lockers, together with a towel on them. She stood on one side with the child lying down tucked its head under one arm, its legs under the other one, exposed the spine and I knew where to go in. I mean, she just taught me how to do a lumbar spine puncture. You know, I said, 'First time, lumbar puncture. I've never done one of these before in my life.' She said, 'Don't you worry, Clive.' We were on Christian name terms; and she showed me and I never had any trouble with children or adults after that.

Jean Monks

The rounds were all very formal and you had the houseman and the registrar and the consultant and you. Mostly, it was the consultant talking to the doctors. But you were allowed to say, 'I think so and so, because of so and so.' They would take that into account. More and more as time went on, if they trusted you, then they would ask you or you could say.

Clive Bratt

The Lady Almoner was there. Her main role was to see relatives of patients being discharged to see what benefits might be available to them. With the National Health Service coming in I think any charges had been dropped. Because that's what the Lady Almoner did, pre-National Health Service. She sort of gathered up the money for the patients who could afford to pay or were deemed to pay money for their hospital treatment. But, of course, the National Health Service dropped that side and so they became the embryo of Medical Social Workers.

Matron did a round of the Hospital every day. She was different. She was a slightly austere autocrat, I suppose, and the nurses were in fear of her. And one felt one's position was junior to her, even if you were a doctor. [laughs] But the sisters were superb.

Marjorie Semmens

There was a Matron, yes indeed. She came round fairly regularly. I imagine there was a deputy, otherwise it all was run by the Ward Sister. She organised everything, the cleaning, the serving of meals, the nursing, the care of the children. Now at that time parental visiting wasn't as relaxed as it is today. In fact, probably, there was limited visiting altogether. So she didn't really have to do very much with enquiries all the time, as you do now. But it was the Sister on the ward who was the person who ran the ward. As a junior doctor you were told about this when you were a student.

May Burrows

Miss Chapman, the Matron, came up to visit us on this Christmas day. [*Miss Victoria Rose Mary Chapman was the first matron of St Richard's in 1941, retiring in 1961, when she endowed the Chapman Prize to reward nursing achievement.*] She was pretty disgusted when she saw us all dressed up as bunny girls. She was a bit prim and proper, and she just walked in and walked straight out again. We all laughed about it, never gave it a thought. We did something different every Christmas; we did the Beatles one year and we did, you know, *The Carnival is Over*, that group. We dressed up as, you know, when they were on about the pills; you know, more pills. Then we did the Flower Power, where we all wore short skirts of flowers and all this rubbishy old garb on, and we did something different every year for the wards, went round the wards and amused the patients for a few hours.

I didn't have a Christmas day off-duty, only the once and that was when I was in hospital, never had a Christmas day off. We were more or less expected to work at Christmas. When I first started working in the theatre you never employed a married girl in the theatre, because I think they felt there was too much commitment. You were expected to do a lot of overtime and therefore with married people it was a bit difficult, especially if they had children. As things progressed, over the years, we employed a lot of married women; and, of course, you'd get them ringing up saying they weren't on duty because their children were sick, you see, and they always wanted Christmases off. That sort of thing. You can see why originally they didn't want married people in theatre, and they wouldn't employ you if you were married. If you got married, they asked you to leave; no question of you staying in theatre, if you were married.

It changed in the late '50s, I suppose; it was getting so hard to get staff, you were grateful to take anybody that was willing. And, of course, then they brought in the

'A Midwinter Night's Scream', Christmas 1955.

rule that if you became pregnant, you had to have your job back after you had the baby. But the condition was that you were coming back to do the same hours that you did prior to having the baby. So this is where a lot of my staff tripped up. They felt they couldn't do full-time staffing, or full-time, once they'd had the baby and I used to try and be very helpful to them so they were quite willing to go down on a lower grade, and perhaps do two nights a week or something, just because they needed the money.

Pat Saunders

Of course, that was another thing; that, like the laundry, a lot of the ancillary staff like domestics and so forth who were the cleaners in those days, called ward cleaners, they were very much family. You had mothers and daughters and sisters and all that sort of thing. In actual fact, it was those sort of people that kept the place going, you know. Also, with orderlies as well, you know, the nursing side of things. We did have a whole family there. As a matter of fact, there was a family lived just outside the hospital gates. There was the mother and father and the daughters. I don't know about sons, but mostly daughters that used to come along and work within the hospital. Mostly domestics. They were called ward maids in those days and kitchen maids and so on. Domestics was another thing that came later. We had a hairdresser there, who was another very good chap, learnt his trade locally and he was very well wanted in

Laundry staff, late 1940s.

the Hospital. You had the patients requiring hair cuts and shaves. Well, that was his job actually, just hair cutting and shaving the patients. I mean a lot of these older patients in the hutted wards, the geriatric type, I mean obviously they couldn't shave themselves, so it was quite a boon to them to have somebody to do this. You know these men they're very proud of themselves, like to be clean, clean shaven.

Crom Polson

I must pay tribute to the work staff there. Tom Porter was the engineer, we had George Drake, carpenter, Ron Mason was the fitter, Fred Wallace the electrician and he had a little runabout boy, Norman, at the time. They integrated, there was no question of, that's his job or that's my job, or we must do that or leave it to someone else. They got on and did the job and how a Hospital like that ran with four men basically in the works or the artisan department shows what wonderful men they were. We had two gardeners, George Horn and his assistant. George was a lame man but they kept the whole of the grounds, plus, of course, the cricket pitch [laughs] which we now established in perfect condition. Our portering staff was run by a chap called Alan Eyles. He was the Head Porter. He was also the Mortuary Technician. He was also a spare driver for the vans, again, the same spirit camaraderie and of help to anybody or any of their staff that was always evident. They fully integrated. At that time there was no such thing as sterilising, central sterilising. We had our own sterilising plant built. This was run by the porters. The portering staff took the sterilising as part of their duties and they kept that going month in month out. They were really great.

Bill Gammie

There was a certain team-work in the '60s that was so evident. The Theatre Superintendent, at that time, was a great character and saw that everybody in the team was there to do a job. Surgery does involve team-work. That team-work goes right back to the porters that deliver the patients from the ward, take them to the theatre, transfer them in the theatre. And then it's the nursing team, the runners in the theatre—as the nurses are that are mobile. And the scrub nurse who is assisting you at the operation with instruments and equipment. There was a great, sort of, feeling of supportive help and if one ran into, as inevitably every now and then in surgery you run into some difficulties, you could feel that the whole team rallied round to make sure that you achieved success in whatever procedure you were carrying out.

Jean Monks

At the end of the operation, of course, you did have to detain the patient a little while in the theatre until they'd actually woken up before transporting them back to the ward. There was not even a theatre recovery room where people now are currently monitored until they have actually woken up and are stable within the

Students in the sitting room of the Nurses' Home, 1950. (Jean Monks is seated first right.)

theatre confines. They were just taken straight back to the ward and you relied entirely on the ward staff for the immediate post-operative care. We worked as a team. We always had a team spirit. And when you gave the report to your nurses, I mean, you would get come-back. Then you worked as a team, because every person was as valuable as the next one. It was your job to assess things and tell the doctor. Women were becoming more independent; therefore, you did notice a change. It wasn't gross but women were having much more say in things. Because, I mean, really when I started my training you couldn't say they were in the least emancipated, you were a dog's body and that was that. You did as you were told, and you got on with it. Oh yes, the whole of society was changing at the same time and it was bound to be reflected.

Bud Robinson

A paediatrician cannot work alone. A surgeon admittedly needs nurses to hand him things, but really he can get on with it. He needs an anaesthetist and he can get on with it. A paediatrician needs input from Health Visitors, all sorts of people. What I really mean is a paediatrician tends to be very much a team worker. And I think people that don't actually do anything for the patient in a concrete way, like cutting or whatever, operating, has to be more a team worker because he's using other sort of skills. So paediatricians have not set themselves up as Gods; they've not had pin-striped suits. They've always tended to wear their ordinary gear and they've identified a lot with the child, which is identifying with a patient, and you can't be stuffy if you identify with children. When I first started, the first day, Matron was from the old school, she'd been at St Richard's about twenty-five years, and she came up and she put her cuffs on and walked up and she said, 'Morning Doctor Robinson.' Everything was in a line, the beds, the patients all in bed, and everything. She was a super nurse, very kind and nice, but she set a standard and the nurses were terrified of her, but loved her. You know, one of those old creatures. So she perceived me as a God, although I can't say that I did myself.

Paediatricians have never been very important people amongst the hierarchy of doctors. They're a new animal, created post-war, what is a paediatrician? It's rather like geriatricians. A proper doctor is seen as a surgeon, physician. Fortunately because we had a technical expertise of treating very sick people, we were given credit as a proper doctor. But we didn't have a big empire within a hospital. So we were never very important. So the people that have lost out in this reduction of the Gods have been the physicians and the surgeons. Particularly the latter. Gradually, they've been, not totally emasculated, but very much reduced in authority. Nurses used to jump; they don't jump like they used to. We used to be able to say, 'We want this ... ' And as I say, my colleagues used to dictate when I wanted anything. I went to my colleagues because if they said it was to be, it was to be. Today you've got a manager, an executive, a nurse manager.

Paddy Whiteside

On my team I would have share of a registrar and I would have a house physician entirely on my part. In the '60s, we had three physicians at the Hospital, as opposed to myself alone without aid in the early days. The nursing staff on the medical ward would look after all three physicians and the patients of all three physicians, though there was a tendency to group a single physician's patients together.

Dennis Barratt

You can't say one day it was like that, the next it was suddenly different. It was a very, very gradual thing. I'm not quite sure what happened. The management changed somewhat, the old type of management, which was really Dougie Martin, Nobby Clark and Crom Polson and one other, that was the Management Committee that controlled everything. Dougie Martin was an amazing character. He knew absolutely everybody in the Hospital, from the cleaners right through and he knew all the first names. He walked round; he often walked around the grounds and if he passed you, he passed the time of day with you. Amazing character. The whole place ran very, very smoothly and easily, trouble free. Then gradually the admin. staff began to increase. They got directives, I suppose, from somewhere. Well, that's because, as the National Health Service got well underway, but I was unaware of it at the time. I suppose that gathered momentum and things changed from that way. Great pity, because the patients, I mean, the same atmosphere was carried through to the patients on the wards, so they were all very much at ease and happy.

Pat Saunders

At St Richard's we had a Medical Superintendent, Mr. D.G. Martin, you know, who was a fantastic man, wonderful surgeon. And he was very much for the ordinary working man. Didn't care for snobbery etc.; but they were excellent, the whole family. Matron, Victoria Chapman, she was a very nice woman as well. But everybody respected them in those days, you know. Then you started getting your Nursing Officers. Some of them were very, very good too. But the ordinary staff could never see why we had such an increase in Nursing Officers where it was only run by one or two in the past. When I first went to St Richard's in 1945 the actual kitchen came under the Assistant Matron and the Home Sister. They would deal with the menus and food and so forth, on a daily basis. They had the ancillary staff there working for them and it was round

Support staff, c.1950s. (Pat Saunders is third from left, back row)

about 1948 as the government took over that you started getting a catering officer and a dietician. Other than that things ran all right with these people. They had very much a firm hand. People respected them for all this. Besides being a firm hand they were friendly people as well.

Crom Polson

When we appointed medical staff we usually got round to the question, and it was not the first question, as to whether they played rugby or not. We were very fortunate that we had a good name for juniors and teaching. A lot of that was due to Paddy Whiteside and Douglas Martin because they were on the top echelon. We found that lots of these people played rugby and they played for Chichester Rugby Club. So we integrated our medical and surgical staff with the local community, and that was a great step. So virtually we had very good rugby players as well as good surgeons and physicians.

Robin Agnew

I certainly remember playing rugby for Chichester. I occasionally appeared on the First Team, but more often on the Seconds and we used to go round all the local towns who had rugby teams in West Sussex and even up as far as Dorking in Surrey. One of the delightful things was on a Saturday morning one met in the bar of the *Dolphin and Anchor Hotel*, opposite the cathedral for a sort of preliminary beer and snack, that is if we were playing at home on the pitch which wasn't very far from St Richard's. It is now more or less the site of the Chichester Theatre. There was a remarkable character called Sid Teasdale who played at scrum-half on Chichester Seconds and was alleged to be at least forty-nine years of age. I was about twenty years younger at the time.

In the summer, we had a magnificent hospital cricket team, which was under the general managership and tutelage of one Cromwell Polson who worked in the Administration. He used to put me fielding sometimes right beside the batsman because he said I was agile enough to get out of the way of a wild hit.

The Hockey Team, 1950. (Jean Monks is second left)

Dennis Barratt

We had several contacts with Graylingwell actually. We used to play football against them and cricket against them. We always used to try and get them to play down our end, because to play football up their end the patients used to pinch the ball and run off with it. The game used to stop. Cricket was very strong; St Richard's had quite a good team. They had to play where the theatre is, I suppose. That is where the cricket pitch was. Lots of tennis courts, of course, and before the maternity block was built that was all tennis courts, belonging to Bishop Otter College. That was quite an active area.

Bud Robinson

Christmas shows, yes. Well when you think about it—what was the structure of the hospital in the '40s and '50s—well it was doctors, and us, and them. So the doctors were us, and everybody else was them. The nurses came in between and the Matron, perhaps, had a seat at the consultants table, but right at the bottom. Now all the doctors were male, so being young and energetic, what they enjoyed were the nurses. Their life structure was such that they lived in the hospital, in the mess. Because they didn't get any time off. They weren't worked intensively or, you know, day in day out. They went through life in a sort of fairly plateaued sort of way. There was a lot to do but you had time off. You could sit and watch the television. You could have an impromptu mess party. And if you had a mess party you knew that the other doctors, if the hospital was big enough to have a few juniors they'd be there, because they weren't allowed out either. Not only that, you could always ring up the Nurses' Home and get a few over to see you. So you would then have a party. An impromptu but very successful sort of party. So that sort of life was standard in most hospitals. And because you lived cheek-by-jowl, and because you poked fun at Gods you let off steam at the end of the year. It was a psychological thing, wasn't it? It's been a tradition in medicine. You can take the most pompous consultant to pieces at Christmas shows and he's got to sit there and laugh. [laughs]

Some of them didn't like it, of course. Some of them reacted very badly occasionally, they'd walk out and so on. But it was a tradition. And that tradition came back from their medical schools. Because these were still part of Medical School medicine. And of course the ones at Medical School had been embued with this, would come down to, say, St Richard's. The ones that had got a facility for writing lyrics, or composing little songs, or ditties, or stage management, or something like that, would be very active. And if you'd got two or three of those at a Christmas time within the hospital then a pantomime would emerge. If you hadn't got them there is no structure for you to create it. There aren't set people in the hospital that will do this. If you've got a porter or a lab technician or something that loves doing pantomimes you'd get one every year. Because you can always recruit you know, new people, doctors or nurses to take part. But very often it's generated by the medical staff and you've got, by chance, to have the right medical staff on board at the time.

Christmas Protest, 1968. (Paddy Whiteside right.) [Courtesy: May Burrows]

Crom Polson

With the new developments that had been taking place at the Hospital, it was thought that some moves should be made in integrating the staff from nursing, to lay and medical and we made great efforts by running various sports sections, pantomime sections and anything that would bring the staff together. For instance we had a pantomime which was always written by the staff; everybody seemed to have a hand at writing. They all considered themselves as playwrights; it was performed by the staff after their working hours. They were there for hours and hours being drilled, cajoled anyway. They would put on this panto once a year and it used to run for six days. The object of the exercise was to scandalise or criticise anything which they were not able to criticise during their normal run of business. But, if you were not included in the panto, if you were not criticised it was considered you hadn't made the grade. It was a great honour to be mentioned in the pantomime and I can well remember a song that was sung to the tune of *Sweet Violets*. This was about Dougie Martin. He couldn't charge the fees and he didn't but they thought they would get Dougie immortalised [*He sings*]:

> *Doug Martin's a Surgeon who did operate*
> *On a very rich patient*
> *With a large sum of money, who had a large sum of money*
> *Which he charged as his fee*
> *And very soon after the old man could pass from the Hospital*

Of health a fine picture
Until two weeks later he returned with a stretcher

That was the sort of thing you had and it went right throughout. But that was the good thing for the staff.

We formed a hockey team. The first match was the medical staff versus the nurses and the nurses said that the medical staff were the roughest people they had ever met in their life and in the modern terms 'they were as hard as Vinny Jones at Wimbledon', but only more so, with less scruples. We had a table tennis section and played with the local leagues. Our great achievement, though, was with cricket. We had the cricket side and played regular matches each Saturday and mid-week. Doctors, stokers, clerks, you name it they were all in the team. And we also had a female Registrar, Surgical Registrar called Pearl Walker, who had played a bit of cricket in her prep school. In our annual match against the Royal West Sussex Hospital we didn't disclose our team until they arrived in the evening and they were dumbfounded to see Pearl Walker among our chosen eleven. They were more dumbfounded when their captain went in to bat and Pearl Walker bowled him first ball so we were truly integrated with the sexes.

Marjorie Semmens

We were a very friendly group. We used to go out and have dinners. We used to go down to the seaside because it was a very hot year. I was there from July through to January so in the summer time we certainly all went out together, either down to Wittering for the evening or usually to the seaside. If we had spare time perhaps six of us going off together leaving the other two who were still in the hospital to look after everybody. But towards the end of every year we always did a Christmas show, and this is the programme for Christmas 1955 when I was the house physician there. Now I prefer being behind the scenes rather than in front. But there were occasions when you had to be because of the numbers.

Jean Monks

The hockey team faded out, I should think, in the middle '50s, late '50s. Because when people started living out you see, that was different too. Well, the whole of society was different. And there was so much more for people to do. You see, in those days there wasn't very much in Chichester. You can imagine can't you, there was not a lot to do in Chichester. Kimbell's, which was a tea place, used to have Saturday night dances. And there were dances up at the barracks.

Kimbell's was in North Street. It's now Marks and Spencers, the clothing store. The soldiers up at the barracks used to have dances and we used to go to Thorney and Tangmere for dances and we even went to the Navy once for dances, on Saturdays. But that's all there was really you could do. I mean, that was the thing people did in those days was dancing—ballroom dancing. And then you used to have parties in the Hospital.

May Burrows

Another thing in St Richard's, the Deputy Matron, Miss Barr, she was very, very clever in making artificial flowers, exceptionally clever. Every Christmas, this was in the '50s, you go in the front door and there's that long straight corridor, she used to do from one end right the way down to the double doors into the hallways. She would make it like a garden, and it was absolutely spectacular. She did this every year. She would have trees with all these blossoms all up, all over the ceiling, and they would supply her with turfs all up the side of the corridor, and all this corridor was filled with flowers either side, with these big arches of flowers all the way up. And she did that every year she was there. It was false flowers. She used to make all the flowers, and she used to make them so beautifully they looked real. They used to come from miles around just to see that corridor. It would take her several days to put that corridor up. [laughs] One funny thing, when I first went there, there'd be one little woman, I always remember, she was a funny little woman and she had one big tooth that used to stick out over her mouth, and her job for the day was to scrub that corridor on her hands and knees from top to bottom. She spent all day scrubbing that corridor by hand. She did that every day, from top to bottom.

Jean Monks

We had hospital dances every year and we used to play hockey. It was like a great big family. And we used to play against Graylingwell Hospital who were mostly male nurses and you can imagine the injuries we went on with if we were on night duty that night and we'd had a good rough game. We never had any leave at Christmas. I didn't have Christmas off for twenty-odd years. You worked all day Christmas Eve day and all day Christmas Day without a stop. Because you had to make the jelly—we used to give the patients' visitors teas. We used to make jellies and sandwiches and goodness knows what. It all had to be got ready the day before and you had to carry on with your normal duties on the ward as well, and decorate the ward, and the corridor, with the Christmas tree and we used to do the corridor as well. And also the main corridor to the hospital from the main entrance, that was decorated every year by the assistant matron, called Miss Barr, and she was terribly artistic. It used to be absolutely gorgeous. And the patients' relatives coming up used to admire all these lovely decorations. I mean, she really was fantastic, she really was. I mean, we used to have the nurses and sisters dinners after Christmas but they used to make an occasion of it. We used to have parties in the doctors' flats, too; we used to have lovely parties. Everybody lived on the premises. And the registrars, they did, too, you see. And Mr. Martin and Mr. Clark they lived in special houses actually in the grounds of the hospital, so they were always there.

May Burrows

Every year we used to have a ball, held at Graylingwell. All the medical staff came, all the nursing staff came. And at Christmas we always had lovely parties, we always had the old-fashioned way. The Sisters, the nurses party we used to have to wait on the nurses, for their party we would serve their Christmas meal and wait on them. Then the Sisters would have their Christmas party. The doctors always came round the wards at Christmas. And like that Mediaeval Fair, that was something, that was put, on everybody took part in. There were a lot of things that went on that everybody participated in. Okay, and for that day you could be on the same level, you know, doctors, nurses, domestics, porters. If anything like that came up we all sort of mucked in. It was a group thing. It was a hospital thing and we all sort of joined in. There was a lot more of that going on, I think, in those days. Then, of course, the surgeons used to go and carve the turkey on each ward, the old tradition, you know, and visit their patients every Christmas morning. The consultants would come round and visit all their patients that were still in. We were always expected … when we were on the ward at theatre we used to go and help the ward, sort of, get the patients comfortable to start the Christmas day off, or do what we could to help so that everybody could have a good day. But when we moved to the twin theatres and the other theatres we were expected to go round the wards in some garb to amuse the patients for a while, you know. We used to dress up in something different every year

Clive Bratt

There were many sorts of parties. The doctors' mess was a centre for all sorts of parties of various kinds. Peoples' birthdays and so on. There was a hospital ball. And there was a lot of Christmas dinners. Christmas of course there were lots of functions going on. The younger sisters and nursing staff mixed very happily with the doctors and we all were on Christian name terms. There is a photograph of me standing outside the hospital Out-Patients with one of the nurses dressed as a fairy on the top of the Christmas tree. And she knew somebody who had a Shetland pony and cart, and we dressed up down at the Hope Inn and trotted up to St Richard's. And all the patients were able to watch us. They'd come up and we actually took the Shetland pony up on to the children's ward.

Paddy Whiteside

There was a proper recreation club which ran various expeditions up to London for shows, pantomimes at Christmas, sports against other hospitals, including our sister hospital, the Royal West Sussex Hospital. Everyone would take part in all of those. Patients that were fit to go over to the area where the pantomime was shown, would be allowed to go. There was a very marked community spirit.

There has always been a recreation club, it was called the Social Club actually, and in the early days we used to do a lot more travelling up to London to see theatres. This gradually dropped off because people were no longer interested, and of course when the houseman got married there was even less call. However, things like games, hockey— mixed hockey between Graylingwell Hospital and ourselves, or cricket between the Royal West Sussex Hospital and ourselves were quite common and successful.

III

1974–1994
RETRENCHMENT AND RENEWED HOPE
St Richard's and the Restructured NHS

The concept of bringing the hospital and general practitioner services under the West Sussex Area Health Authority in 1974 presented the hospital services with new problems at a time when the Salmon Report[1] had changed the style of delivery of nursing care. All too soon, however, hospital finances were stretched and by 1975 the capital developments at St Richard's were halted. The restructuring heralded major changes. Aldingbourne and Bognor Chest Hospitals were closed, as was the main ward block at Broyle Road, with its operating theatre. This was followed shortly after by the closure of the operating theatre at Bognor War Memorial Hospital. This reduced the district operating theatre provision from six to four at a time when advances in surgery, anaesthesia and intensive care were becoming more complex, and increasingly lengthy and complex operations were being carried out. It was a consequent period of retrenchment as staff made every effort under difficult circumstances to maintain the highest standards of medical and nursing care. The development of a maxillo-facial department at St Richard's during this time, whilst adding to the lustre of the hospital, increased the pressure on the theatres at a time when other surgery, like that for hip replacements, for example, was taking off. New consultants were recruited only as finances allowed, but new treatments and the possibilities of treatments developed without regard to the resources available for their use. More emphasis, therefore, was put on preventative medicine. In 1980, for instance, Alan Scott, a vascular surgeon, was appointed. His appointment coincided with improvements in the X-ray department, and vascular surgery soon became a regular feature at the hospital. Later this treatment extended to the community as ultrasound sought to detect asymptomatic aneurysms, before they became an acute surgical problem requiring more drastic treatment and longer stays in hospital. The availability of a CT (Computer-assisted Tomography) scanner and mammography investigations opened up new horizons for diagnostic possibilities for the medical staff and patients alike.

The early period after a further restructuring of the NHS in 1982 gradually presented St Richard's with renewed hope for the further re-development of the hospital and its staff. A new government, recognising that the ever-growing demands upon the NHS, arising both from increasing patient expectations and rapid advances in medical science, were going to bankrupt the country, prioritised reforms to the NHS. The Government planned to expand the consultant grade and this was seen as a great opportunity for St Richard's. The hospital infrastructure itself, however, was still dependent on the original ward block and war-time huts, which were originally built to last 10 years but had already been in use for 50 years. The buildings and infrastructure had, therefore, to be updated if the hospital were to keep abreast of all that was expected of it, especially in the imminent new century. Nevertheless, despite its limitations, St Richard's had built up a good reputation; partly as a result of the success of the postgraduate medical education facilities, which readily attracted high quality candidates whenever a new post was advertised. Consultants in developing fields like gerontology and rehabilitation were therefore attracted to the hospital. The appointment of a fourth surgeon in 1988 saw the introduction of a colonoscopy service; later with the co-operation of the physicians the hospital introduced a five-day gastrointestinal endoscopy service. Other specialist consultants followed. In 1992, a urologist was appointed; the demand for his services was such that a second urologist was appointed shortly afterwards. By 1994, there were 26 specialities available at the hospital. Gradually, the government was to push for further changes to the NHS, this time advocating a move towards privatisation and further accountability in terms of 'cost-effectiveness' and 'value for money'. This brought its own dilemmas and difficulties for management and staff alike. Nevertheless, in the face of all the constraints, management and staff together worked eventually to achieve Trust status for St Richard's and by 1994 a new hospital was on its way to being finished. In 1996, St Richard's was awarded the Charter Mark for excellence, and its future, as a centre for such excellence, seemed assured.

The interviewees who lived through these changes recall it as a time of enormous stress. They express the complexity of all the conflicting demands placed upon them. Most remember the particularly difficult periods being when they had to compete with fellow workers for their own and each other's jobs. They had to learn to be more flexible and to try to do more with less, at a time when medical knowledge and the whole realm of what was possible in health care was expanding in an exciting and hitherto unimaginable way. They had to struggle to keep up with what was possible and what they could realistically achieve. At the same time, there were tremendous changes during this period in society as a whole, especially in relation to women, and what was expected of them. As always, different generations with different attitudes and values would coexist simultaneously and, depending on their viewpoint, which in turn would be influenced by their own social, political and cultural backgrounds, they would see this turbulent time as one of loss or tremendous challenge and opportunity.

[1] Ministry of Health and Scottish Home and Health Department, *Report of the Committee on Senior Nursing Staff Structure*, HMSO, 1966.

'An excellent resource'

THE ENVIRONMENT

❛We're very lucky that we've got a very well equipped Medical Education Centre. It's an excellent resource where we utilise the lecture rooms and the seminar meeting rooms. I suppose its prime purpose, apart from the range of meetings that take place within the Hospital everyday, is liaising with GPs. And that's of prime importance, because they are so fundamental to our future, and it's so key that we meet them and discuss what service we can offer them. ❜

(Robert Lapraik, Chief Executive)

The period from 1974 to 1982 was one of immense fluctuation and change for all involved in the Government's directives to centralise health services. For St Richard's this meant a shift to an Area Health Authority. Buildings were developed, as Shirley Roberts comments, to facilitate better a more effective management system. The centralising of services, with its concomitant assessment of those services, including administrative, medical, nursing, financial, transport, and estates, though, brought with it a more rigorous evaluation of cost-effectiveness. This evaluation nurtured mountains of paperwork and documentation, not to say bitterness, resentment and some cynicism, which, as Chris Bateman notes, spawned many headaches. This was especially so as colleagues were forced to compete with colleagues for the same job. Yet this revision of services coincided, as it had always before, with an expansion and development of medical knowledge and possibility, as Paddy Whiteside describes.

Just as people were beginning to adjust to the new way of doing things, and the changes initiated in 1974 were starting to work their way through initial teething problems, there was another political assessment of the nation's health care provision. Based on this, a further restructuring was ordered in 1982. This time the reorganisation aimed to decentralise the service. This was a progressive process, which moved incessantly towards increasing privatisation of the service, with the hospital and the area's local GPs and other healthcare providers, as those all over the country, were forced to change radically the way they conducted business—philosophically and practically. The hospital had to shift to an identity, which embraced the selling of services, and GPs, as possible fundholders, to one where they bought services. The whole thrust of the NHS was to be based on market-place principles—a long way from an ideology which demanded that healthcare be provided free to all. Those who had suffered through and survived one restructuring with all its resultant trauma were subjected to another. Some chose to leave the service rather than go through the stressful process again; others decided to see it through. Ironically, as before, this was to happen at an exciting time in medical history, considering what was being made possible in terms of medical knowledge and treatment. The greatest difficulty was in trying to manage this change. A further twist, as Robert Lapraik comments, is that, while these changes were being played out in the general and wider contexts of a nation's healthcare, St Richard's was shifting internally to a less centralised management system, where responsibility was being devolved to Directorates. This was most certainly a far cry from the benign paternalism of an all-powerful Hospital Superintendent. Paddy Whiteside, Shirley Roberts, Chris Bateman, Donald Russell and a volunteer, Heather Jeremy, all comment on the effects these shifts had on them.

Shirley Roberts

In 1974, we were restructured. Everybody was affected. The Senior Nursing Officers and Nursing Officers remained, but at my level it was restructured, and I was then called a Divisional Nursing Officer. There was still the same Divisions, but Graylingwell was the Psychiatric Division. There was the General Division, of which I became the Divisional Nursing Officer and the Community Division. It was at that point that Midhurst Cottage Hospital became part of the Community Division. There was a change in the boundaries a bit because we created what was called the West Sussex Area Health Authority which had headquarters at Courtlands in Worthing. We had to go through all the business of applying for our jobs and everybody within the Region applied for their own jobs. It was quite a stressful time really and some people did and some people didn't get their jobs. These were all central government directives. There seemed to be so many Chiefs and not enough Indians all the way along; but it worked quite well, really, in some ways; except that the Area level seemed to be a bit superfluous, because there was a Regional Health Authority and the Area Health Authority and then the local Health Authority. It seemed a bit top heavy.

Christopher Bateman

During my earlier years at St Richard's Hospital, when time was a bit more available, when we weren't tied down with so much paperwork, with so much analysis of where the money was going, with so much documentation, and latterly with computers, we had a lot more time to do things, if I can say, properly. The lab was in the top right hand EMS hut in the Willowmead Block, high in the north-east corner. Haematology and Microbiology were in one room about the size of an average size sitting room and Chemistry and Histopathology were tucked in rooms that people would not consider adequate as an office now. At the time of my arrival, the new lab at St Richard's was being built and by 1975 we moved into that.

Donald Russell

I started as Hospital Engineer and latterly I became Unit Works Officer, which covered all elements and trades. When I started, there were three electricians, three fitters and the plumber. We effectively looked after the hospital as we know it now, less all the developments that have taken place.

Preparing foundations for the Day Surgery, Donald Russell, 1993.

In 1974, the Engineering Department was a very small affair at St Richard's; in fact, it still is. The buildings it occupied were the old mortuary, because the old mortuary, in fact, transferred down to the far end of the corridor on the east of the site, so we occupied that. We occupied a couple of garages, which had previously been used for ambulances and we occupied the stores delivery yard. There was a small hut there.

Unfortunately, the Engineering Department in which I've got to include buildings, which involves painting, carpentry, etc., the whole Estates Department, is ostensibly in exactly the same place—in the delivery area where the stores come in, the dressings, the flour, all goods are delivered in the same yard.

We did everything, in fact, in the hospital with respect to maintenance; that is, apart from those items which were contractually maintained. So our maintenance activities included covering the roofs, repairing leaks, maybe putting some new roof coverings on; also taking care of the roads and the paths. That's on the building side, and then we would maintain the ventilation equipment, refrigeration equipment associated with the theatre suite, for example; and changing filters, replacing bearings on motors, changing fan belts.

Looking at a hospital you can always look at a hospital as a small village; it has everything coming on to the site, steam is one element, but steam, of course, is created from heat in the boiler house and water, which generates the steam, which is, in fact, heat being transported along the pipe. Other elements are taken into the hospital in the form of electricity, gas, water and in the other direction sewage flowing out of the hospital. A hospital is, in fact, as I said, like a village, or a small town, where everything is encapsulated on one site. We have almost every form of engineering on that site and we have people who actually have a knowledge of those services and can work on them.

Sewage, for example. People don't really want to know about sewage. In normal terms, all's well that isn't seen. But what we did tend to do once about every month or so, we went round and lifted the majority of the main manholes around the hospital and actually swilled them out, using fire hoses and standpipes from around the grounds. This had a dual effect. We actually tested and ran out the fire hoses and tested the fire point, i.e. the fire points where the fire brigade, the fire hydrant points where the fire brigade would hook into, to make sure that they were free and clean. Not only free, but free to turn on, because there is nothing worse than going to a place and you can't actually turn the thing on when you want it. It also gave the sewers a good swill out.

There were, of course, special precautions we had to take. Again this comes down to health and safety at work, with the Health and Safety at Work Act, and more legislation that's come along since. Its very difficult when men will be men, and they're, if you like, the macho age, 'nothing will hurt me. I don't need to wear protection.' But all the men, in fact, were issued with gloves, goggles and waterproof and weatherproof protection, so that, should they have to rod the drains to clear them, we've given them at least the minimal protection. They also can have health surveillance and if necessary injections against the worst they could possibly encounter, hepatitis B, from the drains. Normally speaking, they didn't give any trouble; if there were any problems, they were tree roots growing into the drains from some of the big trees that grow around the hospital, and congealed fat from the kitchens, which found its way past the fat traps and into the drains.

Paddy Whiteside

The Lesley Goldsmith Centre was started in 1979; this is again an Education Centre, and it was built from money provided by Mr. Garfield Weston. The building that was produced took 19 medical students and had mess rooms for all our junior staff and the students. It is very on-going and, of course, it does keep not just the students up to date, but also our own staff.

Shirley Roberts

When 1982 arrived, there was another re-organisation and the Area level went and they sort of decentralised everything; Supplies became a bigger unit. I think they were based at Redhill and all the Catering was taken over by Catering Managers for the Region. If I remember rightly, at that point, we had another slight restructuring and I became what was called a Director of Nursing Services. But the job itself was basically the same throughout really. It was to manage the Nursing Service.

Bud Robinson

I was involved with the Medical Education Centre. I became a Post-Medical Dean. There is a Dean for each region. The South West Thames had a Post-Graduate Dean and then about five, six years ago they took on two Associate Deans and I became one of the Associate Deans. I did it half-time. I used to go round and mix with the radiologists and surgeons and interview them and look at the hospitals. I also looked at the post-graduate doctoring in the whole of the South West Thames area and got involved very much in that.

Princess Alexandra visits Howard Ward, April 1983. (Marjorie Semmens and Bud Robinson are seen behind the Princess.)

A Clinical Tutor is a London University appointment. You run post-graduate education; everybody is responsible. You're responsible for all of it and they're responsible to you. So anything the general practitioners did filtered through you. All the hospital training was your responsibility. Well, it got more and more an administrative role over the years, but it was copeable with. You used to get an honorarium which was about, effectively, one session a week it would be. You gave it a lot more. I mean, I was often in Saturday and Sunday; all day Saturday and Sunday in an educational programme, where people came to St Richard's to stay for the weekend to learn about this, that and the other. I ran courses; all sorts of things.

Dinwoodie, he was a real man. He went to see Jack Mickerson in out-patients. And I've heard Jack tell this story. He told it to me. I was a very, very good friend of Jack Mickerson. And he said to Jack Mickerson—he was an ordinary National Health Service out-patient, and he went to see him and he saw him for whatever it was, his heart or whatever, and then he said, 'I wonder if I could have a word with you, Dr. Mickerson?' He said, 'Well, what is it?' sort of thing. And he said, 'Well I'd like to give the Hospital some money'. And Jack said, 'Oh, right, well, I'm ever so busy at the moment, would you mind waiting until the end of the outpatients?' 'No, no, not at all, no.' So he went and he waited. I don't know how long he waited. I don't think it was an inordinate time, but he eventually came back and he said, 'Yes, right. Well, why not give some money to the Coronary Care Unit?' 'Oh no I don't want to do that, that should be the National Health Service should do that.' 'Why not give some money to the Library?' 'Oh no, I think the Health Service should pay for books and things.' And he said, 'Oh, gosh.' After a while he asked, 'How much are you—you know—what sort of figure are …?' He thought a few hundred quid or something. He said, 'What sort of figure are you thinking of?' He said, 'About one or two-hundred thousand a year.' Of course, Jack Mickerson fell over. And this money was hopefully going to come for years, and years, and years. So immediately Jack Mickerson, who was the Clinical Tutor prior to me, he said, 'Why not give it to the Post-Graduate Medical Centre?' And that excited Dinwoodie. Exactly what he wanted. It was divorced from the Health Service. It was an educational activity. All the good ideas about the Medical Centre excited Dinwoodie. And so then they started to negotiate. And they got as far as transferring all this money to the Health Centre when he died. But after that they generously honoured his intent, as you say.

Of course, it's a charity. And anybody can apply. It's oriented medically. And the Basingstoke Medical Centre has virtually been built by Dinwoodie Trustees. But originally they had exciting ideas, and as I say the visiting professor, Jack Mickerson said, 'Well, we could invite …' This is how he used to talk, 'We could invite the most

Chichester Medical Education Centre, 1992.

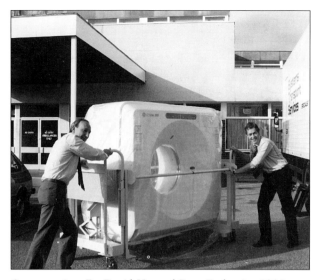
Scanner arrives, Dr. David Kay and Peter Ford assist, 1991.

eminent person in the world to come and stay with us for a week. I mean, people are coming from the States all the time, you know. D.E. Bakey could come over and give his lecture at the RSM [Royal Society of Medicine] or the College [Royal College of Surgeons], and then he could come down to Chichester and we could have him for a week on our own and pay him handsomely.' And we did used to get professors. I've had about five people down, over the years. I used to get them for half a week, three or four days. We used to put them up. We used to have a Medical Student Centre built and a flat for the visiting professor and his wife. So you could invite two. Or we would put them up in a hotel. And they were paid handsomely, not really handsomely, but reasonable well. They were wined and dined, and it was dinner parties and parties the whole time they were here. And they gave a couple of lectures, they'd perhaps show a surgeon how to do something, or they'd do ward rounds with me and my juniors would meet these people. One of them is now Sir Eric Stroud. One of them was just a girl called June Lloyd; she's now Baroness Lloyd. One of them was David Hull; he's Sir David Hull. They were only just paediatricians when I knew them, friends of mine. But these people met them, my juniors met these people, which was marvellous for them, you see; whole opportunity.

Robert Lapraik

We're very lucky that we've got a very well equipped Medical Education Centre. It's an excellent resource where we utilise the lecture rooms and the seminar meeting rooms. I suppose the prime purpose, apart from the range of meetings that take place within the Hospital everyday, is dealing with GPs. And that's of prime importance, because they are so key to our future. We meet them and discuss what service we can offer them. How we can change them. As I've mentioned previously, we're very lucky to be able to bring them into an excellent environment in which to do that. So really it should be seen as a hub of education within the local area for GPs, and in fact more widely. I mean, if we can bring people in from elsewhere and raise the profile of the Education Centre and the Trust, then that's excellent. I think we're starting to do that. We've had some excellent sessions now. Not just bringing people in from across the country but also multinational days and sessions which have been extremely good. So I see it as a key way of raising the profile of the Trust. And I think Chichester, going back probably the last ten years, has been seen as something of a back-water. It's been known to have this elderly population. It's been known to be below its capitation level of funding. It's been known to be complaining that it's had these problems and that really doesn't do you any good actually. What does you good is to get a reputation for being excellent. And, for example, if we can be seen to be providing good education, to have good standards, to have good clinical results, to have good medical audit and clinical audit, then these are all things that actually enhance the reputation of the Trust. And that's what brings good medical staff. And that's where I think St Richard's is very lucky that we do have a reputation that encourages medical staff to come, both consultants and also juniors. That's the key to providing a good quality service.

The Hospital was experiencing financial difficulties in 1992 which, as I say, weren't altogether of its making. They were, I think, a combination of factors but it was to do with the lack of resources that the local purchaser had, and therefore clearly the budget setting process was extremely tight. So it was operating on very slim financial margins. It was operating with very scant information and information which people didn't actually trust. And it was moving from crisis to crisis. And by crisis I mean that on a regular basis there would be patients queuing at A and E; there'd be patients on trolleys for long hours in the Accident and Emergency Department and staff being called in to handle the crisis. And this was having to be handled by those senior people. So the infrastructure in the Hospital wasn't there to enable people, at the appropriate level, to be able to resolve the issues. Now again, this wasn't necessarily the Hospital's problem because it was actually in a stage where the management of the Hospital was moving from centralised management to a devolved arrangement, under what are known as Directorates, which would be a Directorate of Surgery or Medicine. And the idea there is that this Directorate is led by a Clinical Director who would be a doctor, supported by a manager and they would be accountable for all the staff within that directorate and for meeting the budgetary requirements. And that could be, you know, two, three hundred staff, nurses, doctors, the complete range. This was just in the process of being implemented.

Well, I think like all these things, it's got advantages and disadvantages, but the key advantage is that you have the Directorate being led by a doctor who should be the person best able to bring the clinical body—his colleagues—on board with a future direction and strategy of that particular Directorate, and well supported by a manager. They should be well able to make sure that they operate as a team and that really is the concept, I think. That it's clinician-led and that it's focused on working as a multi-disciplinary team, where nurses are working with

Bill Gammie (left) and David Kay with Shirley Roberts at her leaving party, 1990.

doctors, with managers, with other staff to provide the end result. It's a recognition that the patient is central. Their treatment requires the team to operate well and it is a multi-disciplinary process. It's not, you know, on the one hand the doctor and on the next hand a nurse. It's actually nurses and doctors and other staff working together. So that's the theory. I think it's right—I think it's the right concept, and it's certainly right now; it may well evolve. It means there's a fairly flat structure. I've got, currently, 10 Clinical Directorates reporting to me, and other Executive Directors reporting, so it's quite a flat structure.

The first set of GP Fund holders must have been in 1991. Well, it'd be 1991 so we're now [in 1996] in the sixth wave of fund-holding, but in this local area, there was only one from the whole of the second wave and it's been a gradual take-off. But we're now—certainly over sixty per cent of the population are now—covered by fund-holders so they are actually in the majority.

The direction towards the Directorates had been established and so I think it was really a case of working on that and trying to get to a point where everybody owned and supported what was happening. I found that, I think, the biggest thing that you require is ownership. It sounds easy and coming from the Services, I was in the RAF, it might seem a natural style to be, sort of, more autocratic in approach where you tell people what you want to be done. But, actually, I think, that in a hospital and dealing with doctors, you really do have to work it through with them and they have to own and agree with—having had a debate—what is going to happen.

One of the biggest difficulties, I think, with Clinical Directors is to get away from the fact where they see themselves as a representative who is there to fight their corner but more to becoming a member of a corporate group that is actually working out the best future arrangements and the best decision in the interests of the Hospital and the staff and the patients. That, on some occasions, of course, will mean that a particular Directorate is disadvantaged. Then they have to get back to their Directorate and explain the rationale and explain why we as a group made that decision. Not them but we, us. And that's quite a big change. I think that's now actually just about in place but it did actually take a long time.

It's very difficult. I think we're expecting an awful lot of doctors who have been trained as doctors to be expected to play a key role in management and management decisions with probably little training, certainly previously. Although I actually think that it's quite a key to the future training of doctors that this ought to be brought in at a much earlier stage because it's fairly naive to take the view that you are a doctor and you make a judgement about the patient in front of you with no regard to how resources are going to be used. That's not the real world. And that's really the change that's taken place over the last ten years. That doctors are now much more aware of the consequences of making a decision for one patient. If that's going to cost a lot of money and take a lot of resources, clearly it does impact on what we can do for other patients.

There are a number of mechanisms for talking to the purchaser and having a dialogue with the purchaser. Because clearly they have a view and they have significant impact. Because they will, at the end of the day, say, 'We will buy this service and we won't buy that one.' So they are actually, clearly very important. The purchasers are the Health Authority which again is set up as a Board with executives, executives who have professional doctors in the form of the Director of Public Health and his staff. But it is interesting that the expertise and the real insight into medical advances is actually held by the providers, by the hospitals, which is where the doctors work. So there has to be this exchange of views between the people who are practising medicine and the epidemiologists who are really with the Health Authority. And they need, obviously, to be having a dialogue about what the health needs of the population are on the one hand, and the relative benefits of new developments and changes in the way patients are treated. And that information is really held by the provider in the form of all the doctors who are practising within hospital. So that's an interesting dialogue that needs to take place. Again, what we do within the hospital is to go away as a group with the Trust Board—that is the executives and non-executives, the chairman and the Clinical Directors; that's the core—to go away probably every eighteen months to two years and review whether our future direction is appropriate. For the first time we're about to go away again for a day and a half to work it through. We've actually invited two members of the Health Authority to join us because it's very important, obviously, we're not going out on a limb that they can't support. And it's important that they understand why we're proposing to develop a particular service.

Heather Jeremy

The Tea Bar was enlarged one more time. It was decided to rebuild it completely because it had got extremely shabby and we thought repainting it simply was not enough and the hygiene regulations were much more stringent than they used to be because of EC regulations. We had a huge amount of money in our savings account so to speak and we had to get all sorts of permissions [sigh] and the hospital said right we'll rebuild it, which they did. It was opened in July 1995, by Honor Blackman. There's a splendid picture of her down in the Tea Bar now.

Robert Lapraik

The new hospital wing has 16 new wards and those replace the war-time EMS huts—the Willowmead Huts—so that's really elderly medicine, some acute medical admissions wards, and also children's facilities. Now the children actually aren't moving directly into the new building, they're moving temporarily into West Block. So it's elderly, it's medical wards and it also replaces the surgical and medical wards in South Block. We're also going to move across the orthopaedic wards from West Block and that will enable us to turn West Block into a women's and children's centre, which I think is a good vision.

They will be demolishing the old EMS Huts and South Block, which was actually the original building. The idea there is either to refurbish it, which is looking more

St Richard's showing the new building under construction, 1995.

likely now, than to actually rebuild it and demolish that building. This has come about because it's likely that the capital that we are going to get, if we get it at all, will come through the Private Finance Initiatives (PFI) rather than directly from the government. And this has been a recent change. So that's now under review to get the plans together to go out to a Private Finance Initiative and try to bring in fresh capital. And that will enable us to develop those parts of the site, really, that are still in old accommodation. It will enable us to replace the kitchens, the restaurant. It will enable us to, I hope, move paediatrics and maternity across on to adjoining the new buildings as well. And, of course, part of the new buildings includes some equipment. There is an assumption when you build a new hospital now, that it's a replacement, that you can transfer your equipment, your existing equipment across, because of course you've been able to keep it up to scratch, which one should have done. But the financial pressure in Chichester over the last decade has meant that a lot of our equipment is old. So we're replacing some of it through the equipment that comes with the new building but we're also having to go out to public appeal, which I think is legitimate. Our target is to try and raise two million pounds from local people to allow us to have the best equipment in the new building. I didn't add that in addition to the 16 wards, the new building houses a six-bed ITU (Intensive Treatment Unit) and a six-bed Coronary Care Unit. And those are going to be separate entities.

The Intensive Treatment Unit deals mainly with severely injured patients or post-operative patients. Whereas, obviously coronary care is dealing entirely with people who have cardiac problems. The problem with combining it, that we've currently got, is that it's quite often the case that it's full of post-operative patients and therefore coronary care patients get squeezed out, which doesn't provide a top notch coronary care service. So our objective there is to separate the two so that when we have patients coming in with a coronary problem they can go straight into the coronary care unit. And there would be a 'step-down' unit as they become fitter and they move out of the, sort of, intense area into a normal ward and then obviously get discharged. It's a smooth transfer out, so it will be a much better service.

'The patients survived'

THE WORK

❝ The patients survived. They did; they did survive. I think the standard of nursing was very high myself. Because your ward sisters, their fingers were really on the button; they were good; they knew their patients. Many of the junior doctors used to get advice from the ward sisters. They were very knowledgeable in those days, and they really did used to have their patients welfare at heart. ❞

(May Burrows, Theatre Sister)

The political management changes during this period brought about much contention and personal trauma. There was a great deal of consultation, and some confrontation, with interested parties involved in the changes, not least the unions, as Shirley Roberts comments. The playing out of this scene of transformation provided the backdrop for some profound developments in the nature of work for those who worked in St Richard's. The work of nurses, for example, altered radically after the earlier introduction of the Salmon Report, which had changed nursing structures. The nurses' role shifted gradually towards one which demanded increased academic professionalism as they were expected to develop their technological skills and become more responsible for certain medical procedures, as May Burrows and later Lyn Robertshaw discuss. The whole thrust of this period was towards increasing speciality, a developed reliance on technology and drugs, a need to find the funds to meet the health needs of all those who required care, and a studied application of cost-effectiveness in all areas of work. The gap between what was possible and what could or even should be possible was an ever-present one. St Richard's, however, as in earlier days, was often at the forefront of district care. Its fine medical postgraduate centre continued to attract quality professionals and its community supported its funding appeals to help develop its new services, and its eventual new state-of-the-art hospital wing. David Allen, Chris Bateman, Robert Lapraik and 'Friend of the Hospital' Eric Lock all discuss how these changes affected them and their work.

Shirley Roberts

There was various union activity and we had to consult a lot with the union representatives and find satisfactory rotas. So there was a lot of consultation went on in those days. I think more probably than now, because the unions were quite strong and quite vocal and wanted to be involved, rightly so, really; but you couldn't introduce anything without consulting them. I used to attend the medical meetings as a nurse representative. I was the person that the doctors came to and we would involve them with the appointments of ward sisters and so on. So I would have to set up interviewing committees for appointing ward sisters and so on. But there was a medical division and a surgical division and the anaesthetic department, all these different medical meetings one has to go to.

When we knew all our jobs would be up for grabs, it caused quite a lot of stress. There was tension. I mean because you thought you were settled, and had got a challenge and a job to do and then suddenly for a political reason the whole thing was reorganised and you were going to have to start all over again. I can remember you were encouraged to apply for more than one job; you didn't just apply for your own job. I remember applying for a job at Worthing, at Cuckfield and Crawley, places I didn't want to go to work at, particularly, and go through all this trauma of a big interview. I mean, it wasn't just one to one, there must have been a whole panel with outside assessors. I can remember meeting my colleague from Cuckfield-Crawley who's now retired and he said to me, he came out as I went in, and it was my job that was being decided, he said, 'I don't want your job at all, you know, don't think I'm trying.' You couldn't help but sort of look at people as much to say, why is he applying for my job?

In 1974, I was managing the nursing service and being responsible, latterly, particularly for budgets. The costing became very important and making sure there were enough beds and staff to go round and that you got the right level of skills to look after particular patients. We did make a few changes. Medicine was changing and therefore nursing skills had to change. It was much more technical for the nurses. They had to learn a lot about looking after machines, anaesthetic machinery and ventilating machinery. They became much more of a technician, really. Doctors were becoming more specialised and nurses did the same; having got their qualification, in the old days, they would decide whether they wanted to do medicine or surgery. But then you got Coronary Care Units and people wanted to specialise, or they wanted to work in Accident and Emergency. Some people liked the quicker turnover of surgery. Medicine is a much slower nursing care because your patients are in for a longer period of time. Surgery is quicker—in, out and … at one point there was a philosophy of trying to introduce nursing care where the patient came in, had their surgery and then went in and progressed, progressive patient care they called it. Well they moved on until they became sort of convalescent and then were discharged. But the nurses didn't go with them, so the poor nurses didn't see their patients from beginning to end and it wasn't very satisfactory. It's much better that they admit their patient, they see them have their acute phase and then they see them get better and then see them go out—much more satisfactory, really. Now they talk about holistic methods. It's better for the patient too if they get to know their nurse, but this coming in and moving up progressing, was very difficult, except that you get that in your Coronary/ Intensive Care Units. I mean, your Intensive Care Nurses see their patients at the most acute stage and then they have to hand them over to their colleagues, into ordinary wards. But that is their choice, they choose that sort of nursing.

I look back on the role of the Matron with nostalgia really, because the patients knew who was in charge. They knew what a Matron was. I think the nurses too, whereas with all these changing titles, we never had them long enough. People didn't know who was who and who was in charge. I mean I'm not necessarily advocating you go back to the days of the old Matron, but at least people knew who she was and she had some sort of figurehead. Now I didn't wear a uniform, for instance, when I first came here, in my management role, so you didn't even look like a nurse particularly. A uniform gives you some sort of authority, I think. Now there is a person who is called the Director of Nursing Services, Lyn Robertshaw. Her brief was very different from mine, so her job description was very different.

May Burrows

In the '70s, our work conditions changed immensely because we had a lot more theatre sisters, because we had four theatres. We had a lot more trained staff. We'd incorporated a lot more SENs. State Enrolled Nurses. We'd also started this ODA training, these Operating Department Assistants, and I got involved in the first lot of trainees they had. They came to me for practical, and for lectures they had to go to Guildford once a week. At that time they, more or less, were assisting the anaesthetist, and as time went on they were beginning to encroach on the scrubbing-up side and all the other sides, working a little bit in recovery room. And, of course, that was the thing we never had when we were in Ward 1; there was never any recovery ward; once the patient was lifted off the theatre table, they were taken straight back to the ward, and it was the wards responsibility to recover those patients. But, of course, once we moved to the twin block, we had a recovery area and, of course, the patients were— not awake—but they'd come round from the anaesthetic, very drowsy when they went back into the ward. So once they were back in the ward it was just a matter of nursing them, which is another thing that we never had.

I didn't like the Salmon change very much. Where we did away with our Matrons and we had number 10s and number 9s and number 7s, you know. That was the grading. I mean, we had a Mrs. Bolton who was a number 10, and Mrs. Sparrow was number 9, and then there was number 8. And then myself, as nursing officer in the theatre, I was considered a number 7. And I thought it was very impersonal and to me that was the start of when nursing began to fall apart a bit. I felt personally that nursing—well, I felt it was a calling in our days, you either wanted to nurse or you didn't want to nurse. There was no monetary value to nursing. We were very, very poorly paid. We got no money for overtime, no money for weekends, night duty or anything. We were paid for a basic 40-hour week, and if you had to work overtime, you had to work overtime, that was it. There was never any question of walking away in the middle of an operating list. If you were doing that list, it didn't matter what time it finished, you stayed to finish it, maybe one hour, two hours, you just accepted it. My first experience of theatre work, our duty was 24 hours on and 24 off. We could go to bed if we'd finished. But as I say, by the time you actually did all your morning sessions, your afternoon sessions, and as I said before, washed your gloves, packed all your drums, fold all your laundry, you might get it all done, just ready to go off for a few hours and you'd get an emergency and you'd have to do the emergency, you see. I mean, we were lucky in those days if we had four hours sleep of a night.

The value of the Matron system was that Matron knew her nurses. She knew them all, each and every one. You respected your Matron, and I felt there was a very strong liaison between the Matron and the medical staff. You see, it all crept in. When I first went there the Surgeon Superintendent and Medical Superintendent were the king pins with the Matron. The administrative officers took second place. But now the whole thing has changed, hasn't it? The administrative is the top, the doctors and surgeons second place, compared to what they were. You couldn't really see where this change ever came; it gradually crept in; you realised it was creeping in. The administration were getting more power and the senior medical staff were getting less. Can you get my drift? And that's how it's all changed. I mean there were very few administrators in my day. The Matron knew everybody. She knew everything that was going on. The Surgeon Superintendents—I mean if we said anything to Mr. Martin— if we wanted anything, he would make sure we got it. If it was a thing that he felt we needed. They were always for us, if it was something that they felt would help us.

The Matron was powerful, but it wasn't powerful, it was knowledgeable power. I mean she must have gone out of her way to know her nurses, but she knew them all. Now I see these nurses with pins on and these fabulous titles, and I don't really know what they are. When Miss Chapman left, Miss Rice came from the Royal West because we had united, sort of, and she was the Matron over both hospitals. And then after Miss Rice went there were no more Matrons. We started with the Salmon structure where we had number 10s. The system was, I would have to report to the number 8, and if my prelim needed to go higher she would report to the number 9 and if it had to go to the top they would report it to the number 10.

Then she would make the decision the same as the Matron would in the old days. I mean, if you had a problem you would go to the Matron and she would solve it. She would say it was right or wrong and she would sort the matter out. But with our poor pay in those days, if we broke a syringe we had to go to the Matron with a shilling, and if we broke a thermometer we had to go to the Matron with sixpence. You see, we didn't have disposable syringes, every syringe was glass, it was washed and used over and over again. The needles were used over and over again, and you did a whole ward's temperature with about three thermometers, going from patient to patient. We just used to put them in a little jar of disinfectant, you know, go from patient to patient.

The patients survived. They did; they did survive. I think the standard of nursing was very high myself. Because your ward sisters, their fingers were really on the button; they were good; they knew their patients. Many of the junior doctors used to get advice from the ward sisters. They were very knowledgeable in those days, and they really did used to have their patients welfare at heart. They were really well looked after. I've been a patient since my nursing days and they don't look after you in the same way anymore, you know. The last time I was in this young male nurse came to me and said, 'I'm looking after you; I'm your nurse for the afternoon'. That was the late shift; that was all he said to me; I never spoke to him again 'til he went off. He never spoke to me and I never spoke to him. Before we weren't allocated specific patients. I mean, if you were told to do the bed and back round, you did the whole ward. You'd do the patient; you'd rub their backs and their elbows and their heels, and you'd make their bed, and you'd go the whole … so you would expect to know all the patients in the ward, all 48 of them. Now they're assigned so many patients for their stand of duty. We were never assigned any, and, of course, as I say there was only the one sister and there were 48 patients to a ward, and that was her domain.

Christopher Bateman

When I went to St Richard's in 1973, I was the first person whose role was solely haematology. When I started it was a purely laboratory-based speciality where the doctor's role was to ensure that there was proper quality of the work done, that the appropriate tests were available for the hospital in which one was working and that you provided an interpretative function for the clinicians as to what the results of various tests meant. The only practical work one did with patients really was doing bone marrow and making diagnoses that way. During the time I was at Barts, haematologists started looking after patient, up to then it had been purely physicians looking after patients, on the basis of the results provided by the haematologists. It became quite clear, though, that that was ridiculous, because the haematologists knew much more about the diseases than the physicians and so gradually clinical haematology started as a speciality.

Eric Lock

They brought me in on the Friends of Chichester Hospitals in 1973, which was a very small Committee in those days. I joined as a new boy and obviously merely tried to fit myself in to the activities, which the Committee had then been doing in the way of money raising. I think that we had as a primary object as I remember it providing curtains around all the jolly beds in the wards and that was always a major project. We helped finance the setting up of a Hospital Broadcasting system. In June 1973, we had a garden party at Parham which was much bigger than anything we had ever attempted in the past and raised over £6,000 which in those days was quite substantial money. I seemed to be caught up as a dogsbody to the Chairman and all the organisations that we approached had to have stalls there and the contact with the authorities at Parham as to what we wanted and when.

We visited Ford Prison and we were allocated to a forger who did some absolutely superb work in the way of signs [laughs]. We were allowed out with two prisoners and a warder to put these signs up and that was our first big outside venture. That level

Eric Lock and his wife, Hilda, with Chris Shepherd in the Friends' Shop, January 1985.

generally continued, as far as I was concerned, until 1975, when I was unwise enough to say at the Committee meeting, when they said what else can we do to raise money, to say in the Hospital, where I was Chairman of the Friends before, I came down here we ran a trolley service round the wards and a shop. Oh, heavens! Will you do that here [laughs]. And that was the start.

My wife and I started up on our own in the Royal West Sussex Hospital, which still had wards and did a trolley round in a small way there. We approached people from time to time to join us and within a matter of about six months I got enough volunteers to take care of the Royal West Sussex activity, transfer my attentions to St Richard's and start the trolley service there, which went on growing with more volunteers taking part, and with my

agitating, 'We want a shop; it will be much more successful if we had a shop.' And under considerable pressure at the end of 1980, they turned the Linen Room Manageress out of her office on the main corridor. We took over this room with about six feet frontage to the main entrance corridor and we started a shop and that grew and grew, until it was obvious that our activities could expand far beyond what we could run from that small room. The office next door was vacated and the shop was re-constructed with the intervening wall taken out where we functioned until 1983, when it was made into the much bigger shop. At the time we were recruiting new helpers, who started off originally by doing 2–5 on weekdays, and extending that on to Saturdays and Sundays and then the hours were gradually increased on Monday to Friday as they got more volunteers until we reached the present state we are open 9–6 on weekdays and on Saturdays and Sundays for limited hours. In our first year we made a net contribution of £11,056 to the Friends' funds and this has increased year by year. Last year, 1996, we paid over £27,500. Our biggest item of expenditure was in 1984 when Her Royal Highness Princess Alexandra opened the Friends' Dental Unit, which cost something in excess of £120,000. Expenditure has been on a variety of things since that date according to the requests which have been put forward by the Hospital and requests have been getting bigger and bigger as we have had more and more funds available and I think in the last ten years we've collected and spent over a million pounds and I, we, are well into our second million now as far as funds provided for the Hospital during the time we have been in existence. We've constantly helped the Hospital Broadcasting Association, for example; in 1991, we gave them

£3,000, and then put £5,000 that year into the Post-Graduate Medical Centre. In 1994, we bought medical equipment, contributing £73,000, refurbishing wards £14,000, computer equipment £14,000, just as an example. A baby tagging system £6,000, always at Christmas; we have always made a point of providing a sum for the wards for Christmas festivities and where there are patients who as far as it is known will have no presents we have always bought presents and distributed those to them; that's been a feature for years.

Christopher Bateman

In 1975 it was all manual, there was no electronic machines. It was all pipettes and calorimeters. It wasn't until a year after I got there that we had our first electronic particle counter, Coulter counter which became the standard haematology machine to the next decade and at that time, before we had our first Coulter counter, we used to send our specimens over to Worthing in a van. They would then send our results back down the telephone system and that caused absolute chaos and was absolutely unworkable, because whenever you wanted to do extra tests on a patient's specimen it was in Worthing and we were in Chichester; that was an experiment in integration, which very quickly proved itself impractical.

The practical implications of the 1974 NHS reorganisation for us were that the Worthing and Chichester Labs ran as an integrated laboratory service with a lot of interchange of work and run by a common administrative committee with representatives from both hospitals and that I stopped basically around 1980 because both labs got too big and there came a time when it was not sensible for them to go on working as one. I think it was the cogwheel system and there was a cogwheel committee which consisted of the consultants from both Path Labs, at Worthing and Chichester, plus the two Chief Technicians, the most senior technicians. We used to meet, I remember, at Arundel Cottage Hospital, as it was neutral ground, halfway between the two. The Director of Pathology was a Dr. Konrad Rodan, and he was the first Director but the whole system broke down in the early 1980s because it became unwieldy. I think that what happened was that there was the choice between having many more staff, or introducing technology and for obvious reasons the technology came in and the reason behind it all was the relentless increase in workload, which has gone on ever since I became a haematologist, the increase has been about between 5 and 7 per cent a year, which means that the workload doubles every seven years.

We had technicians, and when we moved into the new lab we got a dramatic increase in staff, which went with the modernisation of the pathology services, but there has actually been no significant increase ever since. So that staffing has and the introduction of machinery has, enabled the lab to cope with the ever increasing workload with more people for the last twenty years nearly, but perhaps one or two more people, but there are seventy or eighty people who work in the Path lab and that number hasn't changed significantly for twenty years.

As medical knowledge has advanced the importance of some tests has waned and others have come in and they've become more important. New diseases have been invented, like the accelerated coagulation diseases, where people are more liable to clotting, rather than less liable to clotting and diagnostic techniques have been refined, but the actual volume of work has gone up, both because hospital doctors and GPs are now so used to having haematology results available that they can't manage their patients without. I think logical thought has gone out of the window; its part of the background information that anybody needs to make up their minds about anything. Because it was so difficult, people used to go much more by the clinical signs, now they don't even look at the patient. Its like, you don't examine the chest anymore, you send them for a chest X-ray. It's cutting corners and its partly to do with business and partly, in some people's case, to do with laziness. But you don't have the same degree of clinical acumen that you used to have. They don't look at the mucous membranes, or assess whether the patient is clinically anaemic, they just ask for a blood test and that's gradually come in over the years.

To give you an idea, the number of routine haematology specimens that went through the lab when I first started was about 100 and now its 400 a day. The equipment is incredibly good. Most of the mistakes now are clerical or transcription errors, or muddling people up. The quality of the results produced by the equipment is outstanding. So there are fewer mistakes, technical mistakes and more transcription errors and that sort of thing. In the end there is always an interpretative function, which depends on your past experience and how much you've got your wits about you, which enables you to see whether what is apparently a simple problem or not, and you can't do that with a computer. But I think computers will get as far as pointing people in the right direction and keeping them away from going down the wrong diagnostic pathways, but it won't actually be the final arbitrator, because there is still an art and a skill to medicine.

I think the changes in my lifetime, or my working time were the reduction in the number of deficiency states and the total change in the way we investigated them. When I first went there folic acid deficiency, or B12 deficiency was, you investigated them fully before you started them on treatment, by ten years later we were just looking at a blood count, doing a B12 result and slugging B12 into people for ever. So the number of bone marrow one did for deficiency states to begin with a very high and then at the end very low, but then there was this dramatic increase in the age of the population and with the age of the population there's been a dramatic increase in other types of blood disease and over that period myeloma, myelodysplasia, which is a sort of an umbrella word for bone marrow failure, but without it being leukaemia yet lymphomas, particularly the chronic lymphomas, they have dramatically increased and if you went to the Haematology clinic now those would be the main disease entities that were being looked after. The number of acute leukaemias has always been pretty small, but again that has gone up with the elderly population and because the backup services have become so much better, the antibiotics and the blood products, older and older patients are being treated. So there is probably always one or two, three acute leukemics in the hospital at any one time being treated.

David Allen

In 1978-1979, I was a Houseman. A Houseman is a general dog's body, I suppose. It's a continuing part of one's training, but essentially you're the first person to see the patient. You're a bit of a clerk. You're also learning to organise your schedule and to organise the patient's schedule so that investigations and management happen in a, sort of, one hopes, a fairly logical and sequential fashion. I think Chichester had the reputation, even that far back, that they had a very go-ahead educational programme. So, as far as I can remember, it's the same as it is now, which is every Wednesday afternoon was set aside to teaching, both on the surgical and medical side. No, one didn't go away on courses. I think it is very much an apprenticeship really. And so you'd done your theoretical work at medical school and then the time was to put into practice and actually learn to talk to patients and see patients and so on down here. And, being the area it was, the patients were all delightful and it made life a lot easier than being up in London.

The Sisters on the various wards ran a pretty tight ship. If they said 'jump' most of the housemen jumped. I think the basic moral of being a good houseman then, and probably now, is to get on the side of the Sisters so that they tell you what the consultant wants. They tell you what a patient will actually need, and they are very much a fairly dominant mother figure, as it were. Steering one through, sort of, fairly difficult times, when one first becomes a houseman.

It was every other night on call. So one was going around a 120 hours a week as standard. I used to get here for seven-thirty. Go round the patients before going round with the registrar or whatever. Then, if I was off duty, I usually finished—I think it was usually about six o'clock, something like that, five-six o'clock. But every other night I was on call. When I was first on for medicine, there was a room in Intensive Care where you had to sleep, and they used to wake you up at seven to go round and see all the patients early on. I remember at weekends, for instance, we always used to have a 'second' on call. Their job on Sunday was to cook Sunday lunch for everybody. So the first one took the bleep and did all the calls. And usually Sunday lunch started at four o'clock when everything quietened down and everyone sat down and had Sunday lunch together. When it was a lovely sunny day in the summer Roger Miles would suddenly finish his ward round at sort of, three o'clock, and we'd all go off sailing. So it wasn't all—it all sounded very dramatic working 120 hours a week—but you weren't at the coal face all that time.

Jean Monks

In the early days, a lot of the patients had their physiotherapy in the department rather than on the ward. But obviously with somebody with a fractured femur that you had to keep up in a splint for three months, well obviously you did see that he did his exercises. By the 1980s, though, you got patients up earlier and you didn't need as much physiotherapy in getting them on their feet again. If you'd been in bed for three weeks, you know, with your hip spica on because you'd had a hernia repair, it was awfully difficult to walk afterwards. So that was different, you know; they didn't even come into hospital to stay in hospital for that you see, they just sent them home. It got so quick it was just unbelievable, really. I belong to the Royal College of Nursing, of course, but that was really from the legal stand-point in case you got sued. I can remember, as a student nurse, when they suddenly decided that we were not allowed to give patient hot water bottles in case they burnt themselves, and we'd get sued. That's the first time it, sort of, entered my mind that we could be sued.

Christopher Bateman

I think most of the reforms were just tinkering at the edges. They were altering things for the sake of altering them. They weren't trying to make any fundamental changes in attitudes, or to the way health care was provided. The last five years, which is why they have been exciting, have changed people's attitude completely. They have undoubtedly been more beneficial than harmful, the changes for the health of the nation, and for the provision of health care services … quite a lot of people haven't liked implementing them, but that's another matter,

During the '80s, we were just reinventing the wheel time and time again and getting the same problems. You'd have to ask successive governments why they kept on reorganising the Health Service, but there are various cynical ways of looking at it. I think that, at the time, though, they probably genuinely thought they were changing things for the better. The fact that it all ended up with no change except people changing jobs, or changing names of jobs, was another matter. I look back on those times as being a time of no progress and no change really. But in all the years I was involved, St Richard's only had one or two years without severe financial problems and that was 1982 and 1983 for some reason we got enough money then. The rest of the time we were always struggling and we were always way behind where we should have been by whatever formula they used to dish out the money and even now when we are getting nearer, it's causing such squeals elsewhere that they're trying to change the formula back so we won't appear to be short any more. They did that about four times while I was involved too. When you tinker at the edges to keep the people who are squealing most quiet and that puts more pressure where you have just tried to take it back from and so it goes on.

During the '80s, it seemed as though we were reorganising for the sake of reorganising and I think the answer was that if you put people in boring jobs they get impossibly bored unless there's some change and so you reorganise so that they get the appearance of change. I mean that's rather cynical, but that's the way it looks. I can't think of any major benefit to the Health Service that occurred between 1983 and 1990, from changing administration.

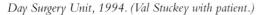

David Allen

In 1986, I was a more senior chap then and I was actually doing the operations, so I was doing the majority of the major surgery. I'd had my FRCS for four years at that stage, so yes, one's work had changed completely. One's responsibilities had changed. So instead of having someone standing the other side of the table it was a question of ringing Bill Gammie at home to tell him what I thought was wrong with a patient, what I thought needed to be done and him saying, 'Yes, go ahead'. By 1986, I think obviously various new drugs had come on the market and things like the anti-acid drug had come on the market at that stage. And so one was doing far less in the way of gastric surgery and duodenal ulcer surgery and that sort of thing. Otherwise, I think the basic techniques were the same.

By 1986, the Hospital was clearly undergoing quite significant changes. I mean, for one, there was another surgeon. Jay Simson had arrived, so there were four surgeons. The Hospital as a whole had got bigger. There were more people around. A lot of new faces. The reforms were beginning to be implemented, talked about, and so on, at that stage. One then became much more aware of the management of the Hospital coping with the financial problems and so on. The new Medical Centre had arrived and that was a dramatic change and was an enormous bonus for the Hospital and the proposals for the new Hospital were being talked about and we got the go ahead in 1993; the new Day Surgery Unit was about to be started. Things had changed significantly.

Day Surgery Unit, 1994. (Val Stuckey with patient.)

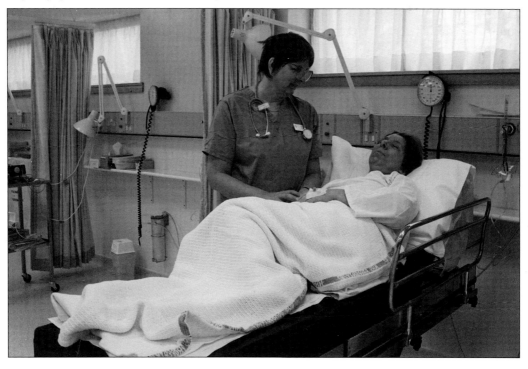

Christopher Bateman

I was going to leave completely in 1993 and then my colleagues asked me to stay on and be Medical Director of the Royal West Sussex Trust. I found that my job really involved strategy, looking at the strategic view of the future of the hospital, not getting involved in the day to day running of it, looking further ahead and making sure that people were informed when they took decisions on where we should go in the future. In order to do that you had to keep in touch with what was going on in the hospital. The next most important thing probably was clinical quality standards. Because of the change in the hospital, we had a very good system of finding out if there were unacceptable wrong practices developing because we had, apart from the clinical complaints procedure, we had a risk management strategy, which enabled potential hazards to be picked up early.

My job was, whether it involved the medical side or the surgical staff, was to make sure that they got dealt with. I'm talking about infections in theatre, ten hips getting infected within a few weeks, for example, that sort of thing. What's going on? Why is it in theatre, or is it on the wards, but all that is now picked up very quickly. Because that's all reported through people filling in forms and sending them in and clinical incidents, things that didn't cause chaos that might, anaesthetic bottles running out when they shouldn't have done, that sort of thing. It was a pretty good system and I think we did a lot to improve standards by picking up these things early and acting on them before they caused trouble. You know, a number of complaints about how a specialist was behaving from patients and once you got two or three of the same sort of complaint you know you've got to do something about it and it's much better to do something about it before it gets further rather than less. So there was that and the next thing that was new was the medical discipline, which was actually dealing with junior or senior doctors who weren't behaving. There were quite a lot of problems. I think all hospitals have one or two problem people. The problem will vary and the type of person will vary, but for the first time the latest reforms have allowed the hospitals to deal with these people themselves instead of them being fobbed off by somebody at Head Office who couldn't really care very much because it doesn't affect his day-to-day work. So there was that, there was representing the medical view on the Hospital Board.

I was made a Trustee in about 1987 of the Medical Centre, when the first part of the rebuilding had taken place and then two years later when the main rebuilding was faltering I was made Chairman and so I really oversaw the whole of the rebuilding of that centre and getting it running afterwards and deciding, raising

Medical Secretaries in CMEC, early 1990s.

the money for finishing off and how, who could use what and so on. So I enjoyed that, that was very rewarding. There is something nice about going and looking at bricks and mortar and saying I was at least partly responsible for that and its actually a building that's worked very well, too; so it's satisfying from that point of view.

Robert Lapraik

I think the staff do remarkably well because it really has been a roller-coaster ride of changes. The internal management of the Hospital has changed. Even the drivers of the Hospital have changed. This has really shifted the emphasis round now to what it should be doing which is that we're providing a service, or we should be providing a service, that our customers want. Our customers are the GPs and the patients. It's not usually the patients who say what they want. They may say that they didn't like a particular aspect of the service and we obviously pick that up. But it's primarily through the GPs that we hear of things. They will express what they want to see in terms of changes to the service.

Our clinicians meet GPs, and communicate with them regularly. We run forums where the GPs come in and we explain what we think and they tell us what they think. We try to crystallise out what is the best way forward for the individual services. There have been many pressures on the Hospital, and I think, internally, there has been a major move to improve the management of the directorates and devolve much more decision-making to the directorates and to the wards. I mean, ideally, a ward should be managed by a ward manager—a Sister who is actually managing the staff and the budget. It's taken some time to get to the point, which we are just arriving at now, where they do manage the staff and the budget. It has taken a number of years to do that.

The staff get training and I think it's a recognition that again, under financial pressure, it's easy to find that training is the first thing to be curtailed. It's actually very important that people do get training, I think. And that they are taken through it and they understand what is expected. But equally, that they are given appropriate training to enable them to do the job. I think that was a problem in the early days of directorates. It's easy to say, 'Right we've changed the system and here we are. You're the clinical director, and you're the service manager'. The professional manager supporting the director—and not actually to provide the necessary training. A large number of the proportion of the patients that we've got at any one time are elderly and very elderly. I mean, you know, people having hip operations at the age of a hundred or more is not unusual. Having pacemakers inserted at ninety-five or a hundred is not unusual. I'm sure it happens anywhere that the people we're talking about are so familiar with the type of patients that they deal with day in and day out, that it becomes a natural aspect. It's just that providing that service to an elderly population requires more resources than it would to a population in its forties and fifties, [as they] require more admissions to hospital than people at a lower age.

In labour relations, I think that we've been very lucky over the years that labour relations have been extremely good. Stepping back a second, I think St Richard's is fortunate in that it's seen to have a very friendly, happy atmosphere, which, you know, on the whole, survives the pressures that we have found forced on to the Hospital. So we've been extremely lucky. I think over the last few years there is a recognition that it's … from both sides, that it's helpful for staff to have their representatives. It's actually very helpful for management to have that. I think their capacity and their strength is growing, which is actually not a bad thing. I think as long as we are open with the trade unions about the constraints on the Hospital and they understand where we're trying to get to and how we're trying to do it. To have them reasonably well-found and well-structured and, you know, with some weight of ownership with the staff generally, is helpful. I hope it remains a constructive relationship.

Ordinary communications are surprisingly difficult. To try to get clear messages across to say—in the case of St Richard's—2,000 staff who are working quite complex shift systems. Many of the staff work part-time. To try and get messages across clearly is surprisingly difficult. We've worked very hard on a system, which is not unlike team briefing, but is designed to be two-way. That's the other thing, I think, about communications, that we ought to be seeking the views and providing a vehicle for the staff to say what they think. Because they are the experts in their area and they need to be able to get their views back. But to try and set in place an effective system, I think, is surprisingly difficult. You can't just blow a whistle, stop the factory and communicate. Life goes on. The nurses probably are working extremely hard when they come on the shift. There may only be four on one shift. There may perhaps be twenty or twenty-five nurses in total on a ward, so you're going to have to get them

'Spick and Span': Pauline Cardey at work, early 1990s.

in bites. And as I say they all work quite complicated shift patterns. And so it's not just the communications within teams and across the, sort of, multi-disciplinary boundaries, but in actually just even getting messages clearly out and feelings and views back from the 2,000 staff is surprisingly difficult. I think it's very important, and I think we need to be clear in the Hospital what our objectives are and where we're going. We need to be able to communicate that. But even that would be difficult.

I think in the directorate structure perhaps the staff group and the element that are the most difficult to embrace in this arrangement are, strangely enough, the doctors. Because the vast bulk of the doctors are trainees all the way up to the point where they become made a consultant. They're passing through, most of them, on six-month contracts with us and then they pass on to another hospital as part of the rotation. And so it really means that their interest in the future long-term success of this particular Hospital is very limited. Their stake in us in other words is slim. They're here to get their training and to pass on. But actually they're the people on whom our reputation rests. They're the people who make decisions about the patients and they're the people who commit resources. So it's actually vital that we communicate and we have them on board. But they're the people who are perhaps the most difficult to actually encompass within these arrangements. And I think where we've got to make most progress in communications is probably with that group. Across the board, I think we need to make more progress. We need to focus on it and we're trying to do that. But it's actually the doctors who are the key group and the most difficult group to communicate with.

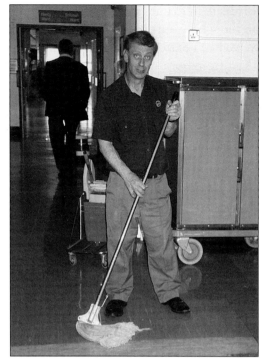

'Behind the scenes', 1994.

The NHS is fast moving. It's been changing an awful lot over the last few years. Over the last four years it's changed dramatically. And change is threatening. So people feel that even though the management style I hope is not a threatening one, people will feel that a lot of the decisions that are made are threatening to them, individually. Because the change inevitably will be seen that way. It's difficult, I think, to have. It's something that, as I say, we've been working on. To try and get a feeling that you can be open and express your views. I think that is difficult. And it's compounded by the fact that there is so much change taking place.

Christopher Bateman

The Salmon Report was a disaster, and it's only recently we've unwound and that's one of the benefits of the new system, that we have got rid of those: by not having a non-hierarchy that doesn't get its hands dirty. I mean at St Richard's there are probably only four people in the nursing hierarchy now who don't actually hands on patients, whereas I should think there were 40 during Salmon, so it's much better now. People felt, they've put responsibility back on the wards where it was taken away from. There's still a Director of Nursing Services, who doesn't like being called Matron, but that's in effect what she is. But no, the Ward Sisters have been given back their power and their authority, yes, which was taken away from them. It was a very degraded job at that time; that really was a disastrous change.

Lyn Robertshaw

A traditional perception is that the role of Matron was more significant than that of a Director of Nursing. However, a Director of Nursing still provides the same function as the old Matron, but there is a lot more involved these days. Nurses are now given an opportunity to contribute to a wider agenda. They have far more influence over issues relating to patient care and service delivery. Technology has changed, and education has changed. Nurses now have greater professional status. They have to have a college background, and their training is no longer conducted on site. We link with the university and our nurses are trained there. The core functions of my role, therefore, are to ensure that the nursing services are organised to provide effective delivery of care and professional leadership in nursing. I am involved with many aspects of nurse training practice. Importantly, I contribute, as Director of Operations and Nursing to the corporate leadership and management of the present Trust in areas not specifically relating to nursing. I also am involved in Human Resource Management and quality assurance. So my role is a much broader one than the old Matron's, although it incorporates it. I must ensure that the profession is nurtured throughout the organisation from its very roots to enable its survival in to the [next] millennium. I find my job, therefore, both exciting and challenging, but never dull! It is very much a balancing act with both corporate and professional roles requiring credibility in both.

David Allen

I'll run through my timetable because one has an all day list Monday. Tuesday is my private operating day. Wednesday is clinic in the morning, teaching in the afternoon and we're very keen, adamant, that half-day teaching stays in. Thursdays is mainly my Clinical Director day, I spend most of the day doing admin. type things. But I'm also on 'take' that day, so the idea is that, if an emergency comes in that I need to be involved in, I can go down and see it straight away. I can drop paper-work, I can drop a meeting, and just go straight in. Then Friday is operating in the morning and then out-patients in the afternoon.

In terms of treating the patient, I don't think the political reforms since 1974 have changed things a lot. I say that because emergencies still get dealt with, whatever happens. The urgent still get dealt with in exactly the same way. And whereas before the routines just got put on to a waiting list which may have been four years, three years, or whatever, now they still go on to a waiting list but it happens to be a little bit shorter, thank goodness. But in terms of actually dealing with the patients and managing them, I think very little has honestly changed. My practice hasn't changed enormously. But in terms of the paper work … in terms of what would you call it …? The hassle factor? That has gone up. I suspect, though, would have happened anyway, as a consultant. I'm not sure, however, that the amount of hassle and paperwork that's been created is off-set by enormous benefits to the patient.

Litigation does not come up in my head. I don't think that every time I see someone I might get sued. I think, basically, if you are competent and thorough and

Porters pause for a photo in the X-Ray Department, c.1994.

run a very tight ship with the whole firm, with the juniors, and talk to your patients and explain to them, and also are prepared to ask for a second opinion either from a colleague within the hospital or from outside if there's a case you're not certain about, then I think you're just practising good medicine, which also happens to be low risk medicine, or low risk surgery. Touch wood, I've not yet been sued in 20 years. I take out my medical insurance premiums in much the same way as I take out my car insurance. If you drive far enough, and often enough, an accident will happen, and if you have to pay for it then that's what you've got insurance for. I don't practise defensive medicine to cope with litigation. I think that's one of the advantages of working somewhere like Chichester. The patients are sensible and understanding and not out to get what they can get.

Marjorie Semmens
The catchment of geriatrics is getting bigger. The catchment of paediatrics is getting relatively smaller. That is the terrible problem about modern paediatrics. I had too much, massively too much work to do, properly. Today because they've got too little work to do, although they wouldn't actually spout this out. It is quite clear they've got too little work to do, but, of course, the big problem is their emergency on call. It's totally unacceptable to be like me, one in two for all my life. They say one in three or four is bad enough. So you've got to have four people to do that. Then they're on holiday and study leave and things like that. So you've got to have a big catchment. But the actual work load in the day is less. Plus they're all supposed to have an inter-mediate grade, [to help them] don't forget I started with one SHO there. There are

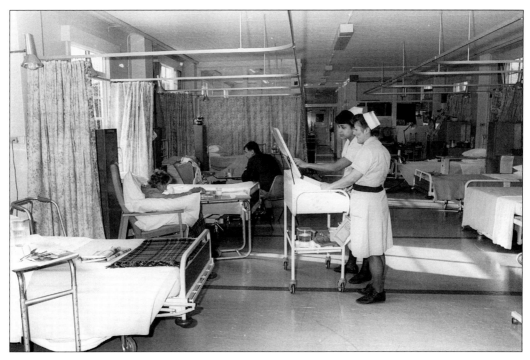

Care of the Elderly, Shippam Ward, 1989.

now five SHOs and two registrars, as well as four consultants. So the whole structure has, medically speaking, has gone like that, expanded but the patients haven't. So the patients admittedly in my day were under-serviced, I suspect. The GPs today are much better off. They are better trained, better educated, and so on. Education now exists. In my day it didn't exist. There was no post-graduate education at all.

I think that certainly the involvement of parents was one of the major changes in paediatrics. I mean, patients in paediatrics are not just straight ahead, they're out there, because they're the family. You've got mum, dad and maybe three other little ones or two bigger ones and they all have an input into the illness of the patient. I mean that exists for the adults but I don't think adult physicians recognise it sometimes. Another change was the recognition of chronic illness in childhood.

Most paediatricians deal with acute illness; that is, hospital in-patients. They see them on a domiciliary, perhaps. They send them into hospital, or the GPs send them into hospital, or they come in through Accident and Emergency. That's the route of all patients really, into hospitals. Then the doctor employed by the Hospital Service looks after them there. Now some children maybe have an illness, which is not going to get any better, like a cerebral palsy. They not only have health problems, but they've got educational problems; the family have probably got social problems. They don't come to hospital; there's no reason for them to come in. There's nothing acute about their illnesses; it's just a chronic situation. So you need somebody who is able to look after these children with their various problems, but outside the hospital. That's why the

Community Paediatrician Consultant has been developed and the team that's working in the community.

Before the Community Paediatricians actually came on board, the service was run largely by women doctors, and they were called Senior Clinical Medical Officers, SCMOs, or they may be just Clinical Medical Officers, CMOs, and they tended to be under the care of the Community Physician, not the Community Paediatrician. Okay he trained, he or she knew all about it but it wasn't quite the same as having the Community Paediatrician at the top in charge.

Now the children who are slow developers, again it's an educational problem, you'd have thought initially, but many of them have physical illnesses and so you need the Community Paediatrician is involved with schools to look after various problems. You've still got your speciality schools, perhaps, or not so much schools these days as classes. There's classes for the deaf, classes for the blind or partially sighted children, and so on. They weren't dealt with. Then the other thing that happened was the government recognising that you couldn't do anything about these children unless you assessed them properly. So there was the development of Child Assessment Units.

Psychologists were certainly involved there, and psychiatrists. And this is really where the one at St Richard's comes in. The first information I've got here is a meeting dated 1989, May 1989. But I think it was actually earlier that we had discussions about all this. The third thing was probably the recognition of mental handicap in childhood. So there was a whole change of emphasis on our work.

Heather Jeremy

We eventually got up to 80 volunteers but when I finished in '95 it had got right down to, I think, 60 volunteers. We were very pushed at times. People were not offering to volunteer. They prefer paid part-time jobs. That was a great consideration, I think, for some people. A lot of people, they needed the money. It's as simple as that. There was a problem with the age group eventually because we were also getting a bit old [laughs] elderly. Some of the people we had to draw the line at the age limit, or put a limit on their age. Eventually we got 75 and that was the cut-off point, but a lot of them were going on to work with us until eighty and they were perfectly happy and capable mentally, and physically. We had to have a cut-off point for age, though, because of the insurance. Nobody thought of it before [laughs].

Trevor Hayes

Mr. Richard Boyce is the Director of Estates and Central Services. Mr. Paul Hatcher is my boss's boss; he's the Central Services budget holder with domestics, catering and a load of other departments as well. He holds the budget and I muck it up for him, he says [laughs]. Central Services is like Hotel Services, catering, portering, telecommunications, general office and driving and security comes within it. Central Services links in with Estates Department so you could say facilities. Yes, the wider word for it.

In the kitchens, c.1993.

Food in hospitals, of course, has changed over the years. Half the dishes I have never cooked in my life. I never cook lasagne and moussaka because I can't stand white sauce with blooming mince, but some of my Chefs, and they've all been here, I think, bar one, longer than 10 years. (It's got to be something in the air, it can't be my charisma.) They have all been here boringly too long [laughs] like myself, and a lot of them have had to change. We've gone through the stodge and it's stuck on the stodge and lodge, you know. It's stodge in the mouth and it's lodged on the plate you can't get it off. There, we have been through the initial healthy eating bit and the cholesterol bit. We've been through the heavy duty, the aduki bean and whatever curry. We are still there with the healthy eating and they have had to do all this. They have had to learn all these dishes.

The quality of food, though, is that which we ask for against specifications. So if we say, right we want a digestive biscuit, we can say how many we want in a packet, what the quality is, what we want 'em for; we can flash it past the Dietician for calorific value or fat content or whatever, salt content and check it out. The Dieticians are a separate entity. At one time, they used to be allied to us, when we used to have one Dietician or one and a quarter Dieticians. Now we've got, oh we've got floods of them. They're brilliant and they all know their work. They are out there a long day sorting out the patients. We don't see as much of them now. They are actually sorting out the patient more than the diet.

We had numerous ways of getting the information to the kitchen and then back again. I won't bore you with the ones that lasted a week or two because it's called trial and error and there were a lot of these at one stage. Unless you get people that change things, things tend to last for a long time and then all of a sudden there's a hell of a lot of little changes to actually get it on stream to allegedly a better and usually a more streamlined and a better service for the customer and for the patients. So we had some ups and downs in various little things. Now people fill in a menu card and they have their own choice. They can order their own portion. You get a tray, a patient has a menu card, which they fill in the mealtime before and they have said yes, I want that and they tick this.

So much has changed in the little areas where our trolleys go. You could say in the old days people used to have more time to say hello. The pace was slower. The turnaround or the turnover of patients was less. This swifter pace now has affected everybody, not just the wards. Now twice as many people come through the Hospital. This actually means that people have got to come in and out and move along the corridor twice as fast. We see more people. We get more phone calls because we haven't got a meal for Mrs. So and So who came here five seconds ago. We sent the trolley up 10 minutes ago, so a lot of these problems are because of the actual pace of life here. The front interface is actually making patients better but the flack falls on our Central Services quite a bit. Domestics have to clean up more because there's twice as many people walking over the floors. It sounds weird, but Linen Department, which comes into Central Services again, has to change the sheets because there's an increase in patient turnover so that all affects.

George Cartlidge in the workshop, c.1994.

The first vending machines we had on site were actually to get rid of the night catering staff who were not cost-effective. We weren't serving enough people in the dining room to actually keep a dining room person on from 9 o'clock to 7 a.m.—9 p.m. to 7 a.m. the next morning plus also a chef because you might have had a female by themselves. We used to have a chef, though, and they used to try out the bacon and the breakfast. But for the takings they were not cost effective. The service they provided was brilliant, but it wasn't taking the bucks. So that's when the first vending machines went in. They were not liked. They were most hated. If you put pinky foam ears on them they might have taken to them but they are hard and fast they don't answer back; they don't ask you how you are. So we had some muck-ups when we have people rocking them and trying to get them off their legs and everything. I think more now, though, it's better. We lost a lot of customers. They started making their own provisions for the supper time. We didn't provide what they wanted; whereas the person on duty knew what their customer wanted. But these vending machines are very cost-effective.

'Medicine and Surgery is an art as well'

THE TREATMENTS AND TECHNOLOGY

6 The nurse now depends wholly on the electronics and it isn't good enough. You don't develop a sixth sense, do you? I mean medicine and surgery is an art as well. If you're dealing with human beings the whole time, you get to know what they're thinking and how they're feeling. You've only got to watch a patient walk in the ward and you know whether he's scared to death or not ... 9

(Jean Monks, Ward Sister)

Technological advances in both treatments and other areas of work characterise this period. The first computer was introduced into the West Sussex Area Health Authority in 1961. By 1994, many areas of work were operated by computers at St Richard's. Similarly, increasingly complex and sophisticated pieces of high-tech equipment became standard tools for diagnosis and treatment. This demanded greater technical skill on the part of the workers and above all dedicated and sustained training. The shift to 'high tech' was not, however, seen as a panacea. Jean Monks comments on the need to realise that electronics could not assess or solve all matters: much still depended on time-honoured experience and instincts. With this caveat in mind, however, what became possible in medical care because of new technology and new drug treatments brought with it new questions in terms of values and medical ethics. Medical professionals often had some very difficult choices to make in terms of who and how they treated patients. Paddy Whiteside, Clive Bratt, Bud Robinson, Robert Lapraik, Marjorie Semmens and David Allen each discuss how technology influenced their work and the daily choices they had to make.

Bud Robinson

There's been an increase in specialisation. Don't forget, say, at St Richard's, I'd have the children's ward with, perhaps, my one SHO, in the daytime, and at night I might have a pre-registered houseman, looking after the children on the ward. The maternity ward had a little side ward for prems. You could see into this side room through a port-hole, you know, and what we used to do is if a very premature baby was born and was breathing, we, well in those days you didn't do very much. You just said everybody cross your fingers and everything else, and let's hope it survives. But the little beasts used to stop breathing. Well, you can get them to breath very quickly by just tweaking them, you know, pulling their toes or stimulating them and they'll start breathing again. But, of course, you're supposed to do it straight away. So that meant you took a nurse away from the ward and put them specialing a premature baby or two premature babies. Now they put them on a machine. They'd ventilate that baby. But in those days … Well, we can't ventilate for very long even now at St Richard's. I mean, we stabilise for a few hours and then remove the baby to a special unit. I mean that's hopefully the next step. We'll be able to move into that. It's not because we haven't got the skills but you haven't got the all round expertise of nurses, junior doctors and everything. So the machinery's there, it's just the work-load. Is the work-load sufficient to justify a big increase in staff, or is it in fact … is it easier to transfer the baby away—cheaper, and all that sort of thing. So things gradually develop. And I've seen all these things gradually develop. There were a number of technological advances that I witnessed in my work. Ventilation, I suppose, is the main one, keeping very small babies going. I think aggressive management of the sick child. In the past you used to bring a child in and if it was very sick you used to put up an ordinary saline drip, give it antibiotics, hopefully wait and see. Today we monitor the oxygen saturation; we monitor continuously the blood pressure, all these sort of things. Automated monitoring. And we treat for blood pressure; we treat for falling this, that and the other straight away.

The management of electrolyte disturbance is an example. The Sodium, Potassium chloride—when that gets deranged, we used to in the past, we used to gently bring it … we're much more aggressive now, both in keeping it stable and by repeated tests. We could almost be twenty-four hours before I'd get a result back, in my day, when I first started. Now you can get it in half an hour; you know, a great battery of answers. I remember going to the leaving party—retirement party—of one of the ex-Mayors of Chichester who used to be the senior technician at St Richard's. He is sadly now dead, but he said you know, 'We do in a day six investigations, that was our job to get these six investigations through.' He said when he retired we'd be doing 666 investigations and thinking nothing of it, and, you know, we could up that even more. Because of all the automation and things like that. So a lot of things came in. Automated blood tests. Automated electrolyte tests. It has been a dramatic change. It enables you to have a view of a sick child straight away. Not get answers to say, well, yesterday, when it came in, this is what the state was, according to, you know, that time's gone. Today, you get a real time view of sickness, which you didn't get. That's dramatically changed.

Jean Monks

At the end of my time at St Richard's, we still had the Central Sterilising Department and everything went there. The other thing which came in, which was absolutely amazing to us, was the fact that so many things were disposable, like syringes and kidney dishes and things like that; and all our dressings were done up in little packets. So, in other words, instead of laying your trolley with sterile instruments and

'Packing them in',
Central Sterile Services Department, 1991.

things and putting out the swabs and things, it was all done and you did a totally different technique. Stitches didn't have to be taken out, they used slips and some stitches dissolved, and that sort of thing. Commodes came in, which was a good thing; but if a patient was on bed rest, he still had to have a bed-pan. They had those disposable insides—linings.

David Allen

Technology changed dramatically. I mean I think the whole business, of— where does one start—the whole business from the surgical point of view of laparoscopy, of key-hole surgery has transformed things. We've now got an extremely good Vascular Unit down here, no vascular surgery was being done here before. A CT [Computer-assisted Tomography] scanner had arrived on the scene, so we were able to do our own CT scanning. We were able to do our own angiograms, taking X-rays of arteries and so on, which could never be done before. We could stretch up arteries with balloons which were not being done here before. Ultrasound technology has come on enormously, so we can now use ultrasound to get pictures of what's going on inside peoples' tummies etc, and make life much less unpleasant, shall I say, for the patient.

If you're going to use it as a diagnostic tool or in treatment, you have to get to know how to use it. When one was training it was a question of—if there was a new bit of kit around—of going to the consultant who had most experience in that kit and being trained. But I think things change when you're a consultant and clearly over the 25 years that you are a consultant lots of new equipment is going to arrive. Some of it is just making life easier and so that's easy to adapt to and that's no problem. But when it's changing one's perception and approach to an operation totally, as for instance with keyhole surgery, I think, well you have no choice but to go off on courses to learn to do it, and become proficient in it. But it's not often that you have these dramatic changes that change everything so enormously. It's more commonly a gentle evolution, which is easy to cope with.

Shirley Roberts

We went into computers at that point, 1980s. I mean, they've probably got them on the wards now, but they certainly hadn't got them when I started. The

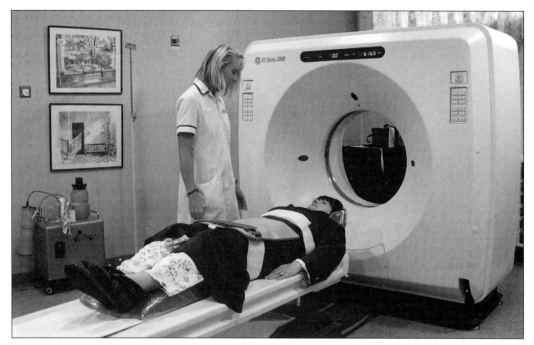
Scanner at work, early 1990s.

demand for information, though, wasn't as great as it is now. You didn't have to account for every single bit of plaster, or bandage in the same way that you do now because there's a cost put against it.

May Burrows

I think the drugs made surgery easier for the surgeons. Patients were more relaxed, and I think the anaesthetists were in far more control. They weren't relying so much on just gas and air. And, of course, people were anaesthetised for much longer periods for the bigger operations.

Heather Jeremy

There were some new pieces of equipment which were introduced. The electric till, and the electric boiler to begin with; yes, but that was some years ago. We managed, though, all those years with money in an ordinary drawer. We didn't have a microwave. Now as far as I know, we must remember I left nearly a year ago [1996], there was talk of a microwave, but I don't know if they've got one. They were talking about doing baked potatoes in there, things like that. We used to use a kettle. We've got tea bags which we were putting into separate cups and doing it that way with hot water straight from the boiler and coffee bags as well and sugar in bags. The only thing they kept was the fresh milk in the end. We did try little pots of milk but everyone objected. There was an unpleasant flavour to everything, so we went back to fresh milk, but everything else was in packets and jars and things like that. Yes, we used tea and coffee pots years ago, big four-pint ones, which were horrible. The great advantage to the new Tea Bar is the dishwasher, a commercial one which takes two to three minutes to go through the cycle so that's a great improvement.

Shirley Roberts

As we've seen when the NHS came in in 1948 I think the hospitals that were in existence then turned themselves into hospitals for their local patients. Subsequently things were like that for quite a long time, so it was St Richard's Hospital—the Royal West Sussex Hospital. They had, I think, different Administrators. I think there was a single Secretary, Mr. Williams, and we used to eat with him. And in the old days, of course, each hospital had superintendents. So when I first went to St Richard's Hospital the superintendent was Mr. Martin. The Deputy Superintendent was Mr. Clark. The little house at the entrance, on the left hand side as you go in, that's always called Mr. Clark's house.

After some time, above the hospitals were the Regions. And in this area we were the South West Thames Region. And then you had South East Thames, North East, North West Thames. And then round the country you had various different ones. I think there were probably 15 altogether, but I may not be correct on that. I don't know if it was for administrative reasons or what, but after some time Areas were formed. And Chichester and Worthing got together as the Area. And this of course was the easiest thing in the world for us, because we shared our work and so it was so easy when it was an Area, we could work things so very much better for the two sets of hospitals.

However, the next re-organisation led to splits again because they only wanted a certain number of patients per District Hospital, and we went back to Districts. And of course the latest one has been Trusts, which I can't really comment very much on because that was only just happening as I left. I can recall is that it was divided into two—the acute work, which is really the hospitals, and the community work which is called Priority Care in this District.

Marjorie Semmens

If you've got a seriously handicapped baby with, say, spina bifida, which is the abnormality of the back, which means there is a non-functioning nerve below that abnormality which gives splayed legs and no bladder control etc. you have to look at all the factors for keeping them alive. Because you may actually be keeping children alive with a miserable life in the end, and it kind of swung the other way. Quality of life became one of the top priorities for the individual then. And subsequent work has shown that you can probably pick out the ones who would have a reasonably good quality and those who can't. And I must have been involved with quite a lot of young adults who are now whizzing round Worthing in wheelchairs, with spina bifida. I mean they haven't got hydrocephalus, or we stopped the hydrocephalus, but they congregate in a place called the Guildhall in Worthing. And you see them sitting together because of course their limitations meant that they went to the same school, which meant that they got to know each other. So they've paired up and you just see couples of them driving around. And you know, these sort of things. Makes you think what have you done in your career. And so there are some bits that are less pleasant than others to look back on. Fortunately, with paediatrics, nearly all the children get better, with acute paediatrics, although you do lose them from time to time because of the severity of the illness, just like the meningococcal septicaemia that's going round at the moment.

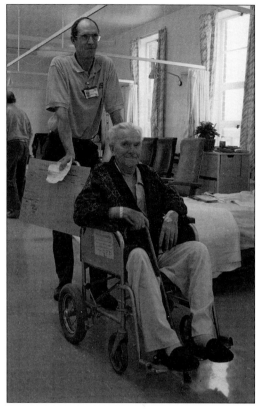

Returning from X-Ray, early 1990s.

Robert Lapraik

The money for the earlier CT scanners and MRI [magnetic resonance imaging] scanners traditionally came down in two sorts of ways. The first was money that was allocated through the Health Authority in the old days to a minor capital programme. So that would cover the, sort of, replacement equipment and the new equipment of a minor nature. So we're talking of certainly below a quarter of a million pounds. If you're talking about replacing equipment or buying new equipment of over a quarter of a million, then in those 1992 days that would have been a vote from the Regional Health Authority.

Now we're free to make appeals. We're free to enter into private finance initiatives. So clearly with technology like MRI there is the opportunity to enter into a joint venture with the private sector where we would get use of it for the NHS patients and they would perhaps sell the services on the private health side. So there are a lot of opportunities there; it's just choosing the right and most appropriate way of funding it. And like all these things of course—even under the new arrangements—if you're tight on revenue then it will impact on your ability to replace the capital stock. And that is an issue as a Trust. I'm afraid it hasn't gone away. If you run into pressure because there are more patients coming through the hospital than were anticipated, then inevitably that presents revenue problems and that will impact on your ability to spend capital money.

Which equipment we buy depends on the forward strategy of the Trust. This is clarified every eighteen months to two years, so there should be a background as to which services we're developing and which ones we're not developing. So that's the backdrop to it, and then when it comes to deciding on equipment we get all the clinical directors together, chaired by the medical director, and they're very good at

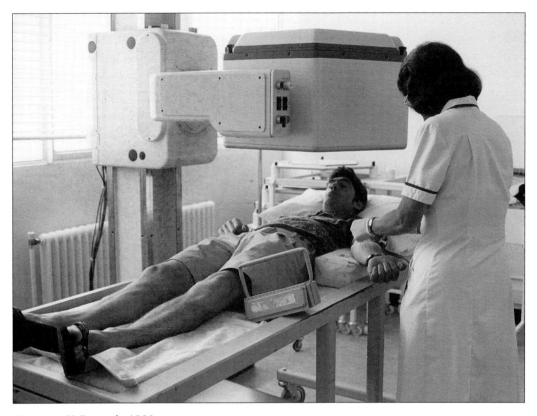

Having an X-Ray, early 1990s.

agreeing what the priorities are. And there are a lot of competing priorities. Inevitably the demands far exceed our ability to meet them. But they are very good at agreeing amongst themselves and producing a breakdown of what the priorities are. Secondly— or sitting alongside that—obviously we do go out to appeal. The CT scanner that we've got was raised by public appeal and that would tend to be the attractive item that the local population obviously would see as being a worthy cause and a key priority. So there is the opportunity to go out to appeal as well.

It would be wrong to say that we were a green field site in terms of information technology. Obviously we had a lot of computers. And we do have a very clear strategy for the future but it is an area where we have been lagging behind, insofar as the systems that we've got are not particularly good at what they do and they're not net-worked. So it means that it is difficult to link information. You can't put information in once about a patient and pull out a comprehensive, you know, across the board view of what's happened to that patient yet. That's clearly where we're trying to get to. We are now starting to put in a full hospital network. We're also now a pilot site for a new patient administration system. I think that we're really starting to take off in that respect. It may not be a bad thing because I think a lot of, sort of, false starts have been made. It's a highly complex organisation and to try to computerise it in a network way has been proven to be quite difficult.

I think the key issues really are being able to determine what level of information you require on the system. The approach we're taking now is to use a straightforward patient administration system. But also to use order communications, so that you order a test, you get the results. And the act of doing that registers, putting the results in the computer against that patient. So you actually will build up progressively, essentially an electronic record of what's happened to the patient. It's not quite as simple as that because doctors draw diagrams and they do things that you can't do on a terminal. But then again there is no reason, in the fullness of time, why that can't be scanned in. I think that's the direction we'll be taking. But it has meant that the operational aspects of registering patients results in things like pathology systems has been remote from anything else. It's only really brought together currently on a paper record, which is really pretty archaic when you think about it. It means that if one person has the paper record no one else can get hold of it. So there is a lot to be gained by going down the route of progressively putting it on to a decent computer system. It's very much making sure we get the right computer to provide what is required by individual departments, and then networking the results so that we can build up a comprehensive picture. A sort of management information system can be derived from that.

Paddy Whiteside

It was just gradual improvement. I mean, there has been an enormous expansion in the possibility of diagnosing heart diseases.[*] One of the early ones being, of course, catheterisation of the heart and the vessels. But also now special scanning, the use of ultrasound to look at the valves and now of course, magnetic resonance imaging. The MRI. I've never used that although I've referred patients for it but it has developed since my day. The bed numbers have not needed to increase to any great degree, because the medicine and surgery has improved and that means patients have to stay shorter times, and the same number of beds would cover a very much greater demand than had occurred in the past. This is particularly true now of the new surgical techniques, commonly known as key-hole surgery, where patients can be let out one or two days after quite a serious operation. The other thing is, many of the patients with diseases like tuberculosis, were hospitalised for six months, now of course two or three weeks is all that is usually necessary.

David Allen

Some of the instruments were pre-packed and some of them were sterilised in theatre. So there were still instruments in the big glass cases that you may have seen if you go into theatres. There are big glass cabinets. Then there were autoclaves out in the prep. room.

---

[*] Paddy Whiteside comments: 'We have been privileged to have Dr. Aubrey Leatham, Cardiologist to St George's Hospital, London and of international reputation here every 3-4 weeks as a visiting cardiologist, and the appointment of Dr. Colin Reid, a highly trained cardiologist, as our whole time cardiologist. Both consultants have encouraged the development of non-invasive cardiology.'

The early '80s, really, I think, was a transition period. I mean there was still plenty going on here. There was very little high-tech surgery being done, though. There was none of the complicated vascular surgery that is now being done. I remember when ruptured aneurysms came in, when I was a houseman here, having some very nausea-inducing journeys in the back of an ambulance over to the Royal South Hants. And delivering patients there to have their surgery done, and that didn't really change until Alan Scott arrived here, in 1981. So yes, I think it wasn't a cottage hospital, but it was in a sort of transition phase, really.

Bud Robinson

Today it's changing dramatically. I mean Community Paediatrics is a thriving industry. And then it's going to be Domiciliary Paediatrics, children are possibly going to be treated more at home, which would be kind of coming in a circle. I mean, you can't do very much, but children with fractured femurs, you used to see them like this, you know, in the ward. They'd be there for months, under the orthopods (orthopaedic surgeons). What the hell were they in a ward for? Being fed and watered, you know. They didn't need nursing care. But you know, it's very difficult to persuade … There was no paediatrician before me at either end. I was the first paediatrician. I could have created a lot of waves and resentment perhaps. It was a delicate path to tread. One wanted to change everything gradually, and I must admit I didn't have any revolutionary plans. But as change happens, you know, you take it on board and you want to do things. The only way I could get things was co-operation with my colleagues. And I had to, at the various committee meetings, say what I wanted and try and make a case for it. And I must admit, I didn't ask for a lot and so they were very, very generous. And I don't think I ever asked for anything that was turned down, in that sense, you know. Where they could influence anything, they supported me. So I always had tremendous support, at both ends, from the paediatric point of view, which allowed me gradually to change things. One of them, of course, is the pastoral role of the paediatrician. Although he looks after medical sickness, the surgical side, you've really got to try and get on with the surgeons too. And alter their way of doing things that is not strictly technically surgical. But the looking after of surgical patients. And that is an area still of a little bit of conflict. It's inevitable. It's a different mind-set really, isn't it? Oh, absolutely, yes.

Marjorie Semmens

From the administration point of view, it used to be staff meetings, consultant meetings. The decisions we were making were really to help the patients. I'm afraid they have now been split into your own speciality representative, or at least your own speciality vying for things. And paediatrics is a small speciality and so there's a bit of difficulty sometimes in vying for things.

The cost of paediatrics is quite heavy. You see the advance of neonatology, that's the newborn babies, and that has thrown paediatrics very far forward too. You are now expected to keep alive any baby that's 24 weeks plus gestation. You're involved with situations with ladies carrying deformed babies, so you're into genetics and ethics, resuscitation, all sorts of things. So this is why you have specialists in new-borns really. And that's a heavy—it needs a lot of equipment, neonatology—so that's a high-cost budget.

It isn't doing very well under NHS, with the result that you've usually got to fund things outside. I know at St Richard's they have had groups of mothers who've got together and got a name and fund-raised. And not only that, lots of other places. I mention 'The Lamb' who used to have, particularly, Christmas, fund raising efforts. And that was another thing that I found myself doing, going out to say thank you and collecting a cheque, and then inviting a representative to come and have a look at what we had bought with the money. Interestingly enough, people want only to get equipment. Now to run equipment you need people, and really it would be much better if they said 'Here's ten thousand pounds. This is the salary for a year for a nurse, to help look after the babies using this equipment.' Not £10,000 towards this equipment.

Now in the almost immediate past, even since I've retired, now we have recognition of children who have long-term care illness and terminal illness. And St Richard's certainly has a team now who support these sort of families with the children who have these problems. So it's still ever-changing. Yes, cancer, leukaemia and cystic fibrosis, muscular dystrophy, some of which you know, nowadays the children will grow into adulthood almost, well, I mean they will grow into adulthood. The response to child abuse has changed. It wasn't recognised initially. It was recognised during my career. I mean I'm quite sure we must have actually passed various bumps and bruises as bumps and bruises, well they really were not accidental. So this developed during the course of my career and I became accredited to the Police Surgeon's Department, an Associate Police Surgeon to deal with this, which meant I went on a course at Lewes, where the police have their headquarters. And before that I'd had a fair amount of experience anyway of analysing bumps and bruises, fractures with the X-ray Department and going to court with the lawyers, being able to tell whether they'd fallen off their bike or whether they were pushed, yes. They're sometimes very difficult to determine.

Unfortunately, the most difficult is sexual abuse, and that is still debatable. Sometimes it's clear cut with little girls, but very often it isn't. And you have to go on the emotional response a child is making to a situation or something like that. And I'm quite sure I must have caused some distress with the children in the past for not recognising what it was, and trying to undertake investigations which really shouldn't have been undertaken. I distinctly remember one little boy, and this must have been most unpleasant examining him and everything, when we discovered what had happened of course, but it was all retrospective at that stage. We were trying to get the evidence, so to speak, but in trying to do that I don't suppose we were really helping him very much with the actions we were taking. I was asked for an opinion, is this abuse or isn't it abuse? And if I said, 'I'm sorry I can't tell you.' It was recognised as 'no' until somebody else could tell you. Either the child could speak, or play or other methods of investigation enable you to arrive at a decision. I mean, what we tried to be was fair all-round, because if you made a 'yes' diagnosis that could lead to all sorts of litigation against you and the hospital. So you had to be as careful as possible in these situations.

Involving the family in the treatment, that's really become quite a big change. It's really a turn-about, isn't it? And there are, you know, all sorts of other things Management has changed anyway. Nowadays see, a lot of things are done for the children as a day case. There used to be times when children used to come in to have their squints operated on, their eyes straightened out. And they would probably be in bed with a pad on for three days. Well they go home the same afternoon now, virtually.

If you read about medicine now—everything has to be sort of substantiated before it's carried out. One word is audit. But I don't really think I mean audit. But now you're actually allowed to carry out a sort of surveillance for longer. So what you do, say you've got a child of five who 'glglgl' and you can't hear what they're saying because they've got big tonsils and they've always got problems with their nose, you would probably think, but my colleague down the road actually looked at 200 five-year-olds who were all rather like this, and out of them only three of them needed to have their tonsils out by the time they were eight. I think mum, we should just wait, don't you? And you would persuade the parents to wait. Now if they didn't believe you they took them somewhere else. And if somebody wanted to carry out the operation well there was nothing you could do about it. But you tried to explain to them that now we have had more experience with this situation and the options are … And you discuss it with them. So that's the way medicine is going now. It's quite different.

Jean Monks

The nurse depends wholly on the electronics and it isn't good enough. You don't develop a sixth sense do you? I mean medicine and surgery is an art as well. If you're dealing with human beings the whole time, you get to know what they're thinking and how they're feeling. You've only got to watch a patient walk in the ward and you know whether he's scared to death or not, or whether he'd say, 'Okay, that's fine, you just get on with it.' You've got to learn it, haven't you? You can't just read it in a book. This is where experience counts and merit shows up nowadays when they haven't the experience, I think.

Bill Gammie

The current field of laparoscopic or keyhole surgery evolved at the end of the 1980s. The first laparoscope at Chichester was purchased in 1990 so I didn't involve myself in that because our junior fourth colleague took up an interest in this and we encouraged him to do so. Because it was a completely new field and it was, I felt, quite inappropriate to start training oneself in something so—shall we say … It was a great advance and it needed new technical skills.

Dennis Barratt

As technology developed, it got very, very complicated and involved, testing was practically all electronic. Whereas you used to match up colours by eye against the

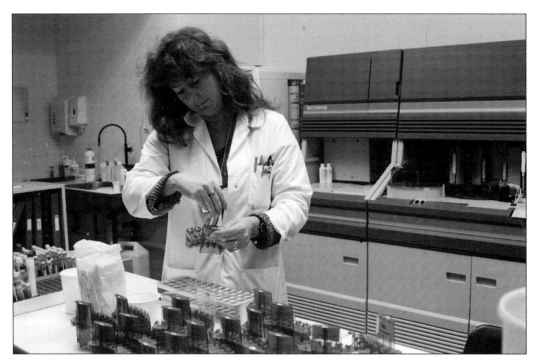

In the Path Lab, early 1990s.

window, you'd have the coloured solution you'd made up in one tube and you'd have a standard solution in another tube and you'd compare them against the light in the window and you'd make up your mind what colour it was—how deep the colour was and what the value was. Now machines came in where you poured the stuff in and the machines read the colours and it came out on a piece of paper and told you what the figure was, so you became divorced from the actual practical side of it. I personally, thought that was rather a shame, it lost a lot of its attraction, the job itself, which is probably the reason why I really opted for Histology, because that's very practical, very hands on; the whole thing is revolving around mechanical machines and so on; whereas Haematology now is totally electronic. You put a tube of blood up to a little spout; it sucks off a drop of blood and the machine does everything—the whole lot. Obviously, its got its advantages, because you can get repetitious results very accurately. But the job itself has lost something; I'm not saying it's worse for the patients; it's better for the patients, probably; although I think now the patient probably gets more tests done than is really necessary simply because the machine will do the whole lot in one go. I think it's not far off before were going to get a machine doing the diagnosis; we'll pull out the results and also written on there will be what this patient's suffering from. I don't know if that's far away. So in that respect it was a shame, its gone that far. Histology hasn't changed, that's basically the same as it's always been—hand cutting on machines, hand sharpening virtually, to do it properly.

'The Gods have gone'

THE PEOPLE AND THEIR SOCIAL LIFE

> ❝ Equally, of course, the Gods have gone, relatively speaking. Who now wants to go to see a pantomime that picks at someone you hardly recognise [laughs]. It's not quite the same thing, is it? ❞   *(Bud Robinson, paediatrician)*

A hospital is its own community and as in any other community its people are a key resource and influence. Each generation of members of that community remember specific characters: people who meant something to them personally or to the hospital generally. Obviously, there are people who have been part of the hospital a long time and therefore overlap generations; consequently, they are invested with disparate meanings at different times for varying people. Chris Bateman and David Allen, in particular, fondly recall some of the characters who have walked the corridors of the hospital. The kind of social life they have experienced together during this time period, however, has altered quite dramatically from earlier times. Although mess life still generates social activity and the Christmas show is still a feature, life in the wider social context has altered so radically that there is no longer the same set of shared assumptions to which they all can subscribe. The pressures of modern living pull people in diverse and often conflicting directions. Some see this as a loss of camaraderie; others recognise that social cohesion can no longer be generated by willing it to happen. Similarly, what was once considered an acceptable form of social activity by one generation is no longer considered so by another. Bud Robinson, Chris Bateman and Robert Lapraik reflect on the implications for the hospital of these fluctuating circumstances.

David Allen

Jack Mickerson was a delight. He was a very shrewd man. A very astute clinician and I thought a very good teacher of students. He always picked one up and pointed out one of the many mistakes one might have made in presenting a patient, giving him the diagnosis and plan of investigation. But he'd pick one up in the nicest possible way, and steered one back in the right direction. He was a great character. He was always very supportive of the juniors if there was a hospital party, or, as we often had, consultants' cocktail parties and that sort of thing. He was always very supportive of that and always came along to that. He was a true gentleman.

The expectations of patients have changed now. But I think that doesn't just apply to medicine. I think everyone expects a better standard of service whatever field that may be in. I think in earlier times it was much more accepted that doctor knows best. 'You do whatever you think is best, doc.' Maybe not wanting, but certainly not getting, explanations about what was done; not being offered any choice in the decision-making process. Whereas now, I think, quite rightly, and I feel much more comfortable about it myself, that one discusses things with patients much more. I hope we do anyway—involve them in the decision-making process. I don't think that's a bad thing.

Jack Mickerson

Christopher Bateman

No consultants at St Richard's have ever behaved like God. We've never had our share, of, fortunately, arrogant consultants There's always been a very good, co-operative attitude. To give you an example: when I started looking after the patients I didn't have any junior staff and so Dr. Mickerson just said well you use my registrar and my houseman. We arranged it so I didn't clash with his ward rounds and so on and that just happened. Whereas in many other hospitals that would never have happened.

I think also, like attracts like. I think you end up, a hospital's character depends on the people who sit on appointments committees. The people who sit on appointments committees appoint the people who they think they are going to get on with. So it's sort of self-perpetuating in a way and it's gone on. I mean, the number of difficult consultants at St Richard's now is tiny. We are jolly lucky, most of them are really nice, good people. So, well yes, I think the junior staff have always been treated well, which is why we have a very high reputation at the medical schools and we have no trouble getting junior staff. It's partly because the consultants are nice and partly because we have gone out of our way to always try and make sure they can get their training and so on. Relationships with management, between doctors and management, have varied over the years. They've never been bad. There's never been a big gulf like one hears about in other places.

Heather Jeremy

The Women's Royal Voluntary Service is not still all women. A lot of men have joined in the last 20 years. We never had any in the Tea Bar, oddly enough,

Outpatients Department, early 1990s.

though. Probably a bit daunted by having to work with two or three women [laugh], I don't know.

I think the most dramatic busy time in the Tea Bar was about two years ago (1994) when a coach load of elderly ladies suddenly arrived at the counter and we didn't know what on earth or where they'd all come from. We didn't find out until a little later that one of their members, poor dear, had had a heart attack and died in the street, as it were, in Chichester. They'd all been driven round to the Outpatients to be given tea and sustenance, generally. That was quite dramatic actually because they were terribly nice and they wrote us a letter afterwards to say how much they'd enjoyed being in there and our help towards them, which was very nice.

We used to get some strange people coming from Graylingwell Hospital. I think the most amusing one, that's a long, long time ago, was a man who came in dressed as a pirate [laugh] and he was waving a knife about, too, so it was pretty unpleasant but [laugh] the hospital porters, one of whom was a very large man or was, they had to overpower him, literally, and take him back [laugh]. That's the only excitement I can remember [laugh].

David Allen

When I look back over my life at St Richard's, there are particular characters that stick out in my mind. May Burrows certainly. I can't think how to describe her without offending her because I certainly wouldn't intend it to do that. But she ran a very, very tight ship in theatre and she's the sort of person that you were terrified of as a houseman, but then you look back on and realise that she was bloody good at her job. I think I learnt from her that if you didn't get your theatre list in you'd have your wrist slapped. Or if you were disorganised and that resulted in a patient being cancelled, then you'd get a clip round the ear. On the medical side, I vividly remember a chap called John Addison who was one of the orthopaedic surgeons here, [*mimics*] an 'Austraaalian'! He was always a good source of ammunition for the Christmas shows. He was an incredibly brusque and almost abrupt man who many people considered very rude. But he was none the less a great character and actually cared for his patients a lot.

There was another chap called Mr. Partridge. I think he was a clinical assistant. He designed a thing called the 'Partridge Strap' which is used to join—or help—get fractures sorted out, and very magnanimously called it the 'Chichester Partridge Strap'. But he was the first man to encourage me to write papers. And one amusing story— I think I mentioned earlier on—my great, great uncle was a very famous orthopaedic surgeon called Heygroves, and one of Brian Elliott's favourite questions to his housemen when holding an instrument, which is called the Heygroves burr-holder instrument, was to say, 'Who's Heygroves?' Of course, most housemen sort of said, 'Oh I've no idea'. So I stopped for a while and I said, 'Well, he was my great, great uncle, Mr. Elliott'. And he literally … It was the one time I've seen Brian Elliott speechless. And then when Mr. Partridge got to hear about this he encouraged me to write about the life and work of Heygroves, which I did. And that was the first paper I ever got published in the *British Journal of Surgery*. He was a delightful, very kind man.

Of the other characters, Roger Miles … And certain things you always remember people saying, and whenever things went wrong Roger Miles would mumble, 'Oh disaster, what a disaster.' And Bill Gammie was the other one, whenever there was a sort of … say a blood vessel had been nicked and there was, sort of, blood coming out of the wound, or out of the abdomen that shouldn't have done, most people would have panicked, but Bill Gammie would sort of mutter, 'Splendid, splendid, what fun.' And then go in and sort the problem out in a very cool, calm and collected manner, and never panic about it.

What other characters are there? Tandy, of course, you can't leave Tandy out. He was here since time immemorial and was always very welcoming. He'd entertain you with all his talking. He wouldn't stop talking. He was a nursing auxiliary down in casualty. He was great—or his family have been—tremendous benefactors to the Hospital. The Goldsmith Centre is called such because of Tandy's parents—Tandy's father—Tandy Goldsmith. Tandy was one of those people that, when you actually sit down and work out what he did for the Hospital, in numerical terms it's very little, but he was one of those people who would leave everyone in casualty smiling, whether it be staff or patients. He was one of the real characters of the Hospital.

What other characters? I think mainly because they were Sisters and I was a houseman … Sister Gaiger and Sister Monks were very, or just very helpful to me. I can't remember any, sort of, particularly dreadful stories to tell about them! I remember one, though. I think it was Sister Monks … I had had a dreadful night on call. I was absolutely knackered. I climbed back into bed at, sort of, five in the morning, and then someone rang up saying a man was in retention, where he couldn't pass his urine. It was one of the male nurses. And he said, 'Would you like me to put a catheter in for you?' And so I said, 'Oh, wonderful.' And I went back to sleep again. He wasn't in retention, though, so the catheter had gone in totally unnecessarily and Sister Monks found out about this the following day and I got, sort of, dragged into her office and torn apart for being so bloody lazy and get out of bed and see my patients in the future.

I remember John Addison. He never liked going up to the geriatric wards or the Willowmead block up there and going past all the little old ladies, many of whom were confused, having had their broken hips. He used to just sort of walk in and walk straight down the ward, and he had to say, 'That's Mrs. Smith, left fractured neck of femur. Mrs. Jones, right fractured neck of femur.' And one old lady stuck her hand up and stopped him and shouted out at him, 'Who are you?' And he came back and said, 'I'm Mr. Addison your consultant orthopaedic surgeon.' And it's terrible really in retrospect, but she then said, 'And what are you going to do?' And he replied, 'We're going to cut your head off dear, don't worry, you'll be all right.' And he walked straight on. And she just said, 'Thank you very much.' It was awful. There's no way he could do that these days. So when you ask how things have changed, that's certainly changed. But sadly those characters can't exist in hospitals these days.

Dame Alison Munro with Bill Gammie visiting patients in the mid-'80s.

By the time I became a consultant, St Richard's was still a very friendly hospital. It still had a very good reputation from the teaching point of view, so juniors were keen to come down here. I think the thing I found most difficult was suddenly being known as Mr. Allen rather than David, because as a junior doctor you're just your Christian name. I mean as a junior doctor all the nurses, everyone calls you by your Christian name and then suddenly you become a consultant and everybody calls you Mr. Allen and won't call you David. I think that was quite an interesting change. I also missed out on all the mess gossip, because you know, every morning you used to come in and find a new bit of gossip, as inevitably happens if you've got lots of young people together. But no, I mean, I think at that stage the Goldsmith Centre was still the same as when I was here as a locum and it hadn't moved to the brand new Goldsmith Centre. And there was still again a very active mess and a very active social life. But I couldn't be part of it in the same way as I was as a junior doctor. I was separated from it.

In 1977, the mess then was in the corridor just next door to the surgical wards. So as you turned left into Douglas Martin and Dixon there was a little door on your right which took you into a smallish room there, which was the Hospital mess. I have memories of a chap who was a staff grade anaesthetist who used to smoke the most revolting tobacco in his pipe, and he always used to be sitting in the corner smoking his pipe. We always used to go to the mess for tea after Roger Miles's ward rounds and sit and prepare the list. And it was then my job to rush up to theatre to deliver the list. Often that was very late, particularly if there was a test match on because Roger loved getting test match results and watching that at the end of his ward rounds.

I'm sure it wasn't less hurried than now, but it seemed to me there was more time for, sort of, sitting and having cups of tea with the boss, or cups of tea on the ward which there never seems to be time for these days. There were more nurses around. Nurses, sort of, sitting chatting to patients, having cups of tea and so on and the poor nurses just don't have time for that these days.

The mess life was good. We used to have a club called the Lotus Eaters, which was ... We were all on one in two rotas then, so every other night we were on call. And the Lotus Eaters used to meet on two consecutive nights so the whole mess was able to go out and eat. It was always the job of the people on the first night to make sure that they made such a mess in the restaurant so that the second lot weren't allowed back in there. It was fairly badly behaved, I'm afraid. It was great fun, yes, yes. But we used to do that once a month and go out and do that. In Chichester and around. There was also a big map, an ordnance survey map in the mess with all the local pubs marked on it. And whether they did good beer or good food or whatever.

I think the mess concept originated from doctors living in. Often you lived in the place for a whole year and never left the place and you often had someone actually looking after ... Sort of a 'women what does' sort of thing. Cooking bacon and eggs for the docs in the morning. That then stopped, but the mess concept carried on and it was just a place to sit if you were on duty but not busy, and so on. There were mess parties every few weeks and the nurses and porters and everyone used to come

Maureen Ward—Press Officer, Appeals Secretary and Editor, St Richard's Times, *1995-present.*

along to that. Frank and Chris from X-ray, who are still working in X-ray at the moment, they were always great followers of the mess parties, and they used to come along to that a lot.

We did a series of Christmas pantomimes. I did two, I think. One I watched when I was a student, that would have been December '77. And then I was very much involved in the one in December '78. And yes, they were a great tradition. At that time they were held over at the Royal West Sussex and there was a big, sort of, hall over there and it was *Sleeping Beauty* we did. We all dressed up and did, sort of, character assassinations of all the bosses. And one of the young nurses injured her finger while doing an operation, so she then collapsed and fell asleep. And there was the wicked witch, May Morose, which was very unkind because that was May Burrows and she was actually a sweetie. But she was someone all the housemen feared because she organised us all. So she had the mick taken out of her.

There was a chap called Lynn Evans who's one of the gynaecologists here, who has sadly died, but he had a reputation for a fairly lucrative private practice, and so he came on as Goldfinger. And yes we had great fun doing that. We still do those but not in quite the same way. Again, you see, I think we were all on duty every other night. We probably weren't chasing round quite as busy when we were on duty. I think one's whole social life as a houseman and registrar centred round the hospital at that stage, and so it was very easy to get 25-odd people together to rehearse and practise on a regular basis. It doesn't happen to the same extent now. They tend to be little skits that are put together with little groups that happen to, sort of, get on well together. And so they don't have the pantomimes and so on that we put on. They were rude and smutty but never, sort of, filthy. And never being unpleasant about people. Taking the mick, rather. And all the consultants came along, usually with their wives and often with their families. They were always put in the front row, and very often dragged up on stage to do bits and pieces. Certainly the year we did it I remember the then very young Rob Simpson, Ian Morrison—and who else was it?—John Gibson, that's right, all got up on the stage and sang a version of the 'Mayor of Bayswater'. They all joined in. It was lovely.

Bud Robinson

Well, you've lost all the camaraderie, because the nucleus of the hospital was this, I suppose, sexual orientation really, particularly of the Teaching Hospital; you've got a lot of young doctors. The nurses were out to meet some of these. A teaching hospital was the place where you captured a mate with good potential. Now, though, there are so many female medical students. I've got a daughter who's a consultant. I've got a son who is qualified. I've got six, and the two end ones are doctors. My son's never been out with a nurse. He's been out with loads of doctors. My daughter went out with doctors, male doctors, all her medical school life. I'm just trying to think if she ever went—prior to school, prior to going to medical school they weren't all medical, but since she went to medical school, every boyfriend has been medical. So nowadays it's completely different. My wife's not medical at all. So there has been a tremendous change simply because the structure of female/male medical side has changed. Of course, you now get male nurses as well helping change it.

Marjorie Semmens and Bud Robinson at Marjorie's Retirement Party, October 1992.

Robert Lapraik

There is still a Christmas show, actually, which is done by the doctors and that's extremely popular. They really do it, I suppose, for the doctors to enjoy. But I mean a cross-section of all staff attend and it is extremely good, a very enjoyable evening.

Bud Robinson

Equally, of course, the Gods have gone, relatively speaking. Who now wants to go to see a pantomime that picks at someone you hardly recognise [laughs]. It's not quite the same thing, is it?

Christopher Bateman

They intermittently resuscitate social events but they go away again. I think that's a feature of size; the place has got too big, too many staff. The other thing is that very few of the junior staff now have St Richard's as home. They are all working; nipping in in the mornings, grumbling about they can't find anywhere to park their cars and going home in the evenings. Whereas in the early days, a lot of people used to live in; it used to be their home while they were junior doctors, so the atmosphere's different and the attitudes are different, so that has changed, yes. They had a couple of cricket matches this year, though; sometimes it just depends on the enthusiasm of the people who are around.

Robert Lapraik

I think that one of the knock-on effects of the pressures on the hospital, though, is that the social events that probably used to take place have tended to die out. I think that is a pity. We've had some successful quiz nights and things. And I think there is a lot of benefit to be derived from these events. And it's one of my, sort of, unwritten objectives really to try and encourage those to take off more. I think it's a pity they've died out, but I think people feel more and more now that they are working really hard when they're at work, the pressure is on. They may be even working more than their shift. I think that quite often happens with nursing staff, and it certainly happens with other staff elsewhere. And I think there is just an edge now that the good will will disappear if we continue to press the way we are pressing, for more efficiency, for a greater throughput. The risk is that we lose out and people aren't supportive of functions. I actually think that the time is right now to try and re-introduce it, that side of the Hospital. People need to know, ideally, the people they are dealing with on the telephone. If you know the person on the other end of the phone, it's much easier to do business with them. And it's much easier for those communications across the hospital to take place than if you're just dealing with someone that you don't know and is just a voice on the other end of the phone. So I think that's quite important.

Paddy Whiteside with Robert Lapraik, Sam and Tom Lapraik on the Royal Military Police March, 1993.

REFLECTIONS
THEN, NOW AND THE FUTURE (1994 AND BEYOND)

❝ I was very happy completely throughout my career at St Richard's Hospital. It is very fortunate for any of us to work in a job you love and also to work in a job where you feel you are doing some good for some people or for society. This has been my good fortune. ❞   *(Paddy Whiteside, Consultant Physician)*

A cross-section of the interviewees comment on the NHS, St Richard's and the time they have spent at the hospital. Most recall it as a happy time and that the hospital was a community of spirits for them, as well as a means of livelihood. No matter what changes took place in management structures, technology or general ways of conducting business, most reflect that it was the people that meant something to them; that no matter how difficult it was at times to achieve what they wanted, they were comforted by knowing that they were doing good for some people and this helped alleviate many of the stresses they were forced to deal with on a daily basis.

Eric Skilton

St Richard's stands out to me in the war years, because of the people I met, the sort of spirit of everybody wanting to do something or help somebody, no matter what hour of the day. That's one of my very vivid memories of St Richard's and everybody was so good to me personally because I was only a youngster and I was thrown in at the deep end.

Jean Monks

Everybody knew each other. Everybody knew about each other. You couldn't walk down the corridor and not know who everybody was. Douglas Martin was the Surgeon Superintendent, and he was an extremely able surgeon as well as an able administrator, because he was in charge of the Hospital as well as being a surgeon. And to go back was really like going home.

Paddy Whiteside

The main changes occurred on the surgical side, but there was also a great increase in medical staffing. Gradually, over the years, and including up-to-date, there was an addition of various specialities; for instance, a geriatrician was appointed to cover the older people. A rheumatologist and a neurologist both came and shared duties. They were on the staff of the Worthing Hospital as well as of the Chichester Hospital. There was a great improvement in pathology with the appointment of a chemical pathologist and a haematologist, also a morbid anatomist, who covered all the post-mortems and police work. Dermatology and radiology also improved. Similar changes occurred also on the surgical side: the obvious changes would be the appointment of orthopaedic surgeons and gynaecologists.

These changes were slow, of course, and progressive, and they were also due to a great extent to the tremendous expansion of medicine, so that there were a large number of new specialities being defined. It's difficult to look back on 1948 when we had one physician with a junior at St Richard's and two part-time GPs, well-trained physicians at the Royal West Sussex Hospital. Now, for example, there are 15 consultants in medicine and paediatrics, and five visiting specialists.

There is a great tendency to develop, what we call, protective medicine. You wouldn't want to take a risk with a patient nowadays which we would have taken in the past. And I'm talking about risks for the patient's benefit where we might have been able to cure it with a certain treatment and where you wouldn't dare to use that nowadays because the chances of it succeeding are small.

The increase in staff, the increase in specialisation and the change in attitude in the patients: it's all changed. It is now the patient's right to have this or that, rather than them being grateful for anything they received. This reflects a change in society generally, I think. People expect more of their National Health Service.

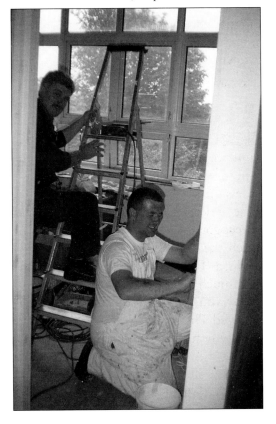

Maintenance men at work, early 1990s.

Donald Russell

The major changes that took place and I think the most interesting changes that took place, one can probably look at them in, I think primarily in two ways. There's the development of St Richard's Hospital, which as an Engineer and looking at the interface in between new buildings that go up, the commissioning of the services in those buildings and fire alarms, for example, and the interfacing of those with the existing, some of which is very old technology, it is very, very interesting. To do it properly, to document it properly and to commission it properly requires quite a lot of time. There are those sort of changes.

The other changes, which weren't so well received on all occasions, were the changes in the structure of the health service. We saw the changes from the old Group HMC, to the Districts and then we went from Districts to Area for about six or seven years and then the old Areas weren't thought to be working correctly so then we went back to Districts and latterly we've come down to full circle back to local autonomy. Now each of these changes haven't gone without a lot of trepidations for staff involved, either moving base or moving location.

Shirley Roberts

I used to get quite upset when I found that when various plans were made for this change, or that change, because things were costing too much, that tender loving care was never accounted for when they had any considerations for nursing. There was no time for that. Time and motion studies, which were quite popular in the late '60s and early '70s, included no way of measuring tender loving care. I mean at night time, particularly, when the patient is at their most vulnerable, the nurses needed to sit and talk and listen and hold their hand and make them a cup of tea, but you couldn't measure that in the new management style. Whenever they were talking about anything else, as the '70s came out, very rarely was the patient's name ever mentioned. The patient very rarely came into it. Nursing has gone back on that now and they involve the patient very much in their care and rightly so. The patient, I believe, now is told a lot more and can ask more questions than ever they did, and that's good.

Bud Robinson

There was a big change, I suppose, in 1982, when the new health structure came in, and the '80s with Mrs. Thatcher. That was a massive shake-up. It had been running along more or less the same. I think medicine as a whole had run along more or less the same. I mean my medical education at Cambridge and Guy's would be the same as somebody 25, 50, 75 years before. Twenty-five years after me, it would be unrecognisable. So it's tied up a lot with technology, because all hospitals were very much the same. You could get just as good treatment in Chichester, as Lincoln, as Guy's, as Thomas's, you know. You relied on the skill and brains of your doctor, and how much he took an interest in you and so on, and kept up to date as far as he could. Today you go where the machines are. The structure of the Health Service in 1982 changed. The region lost a lot of its power. Area Health Authority disappeared and the local system was very much more important. Since then, its fragmented even more for us, and those in general practice, fund holders and Trusts, and non-fund holders and so on. The political side, plus the dramatic development of technology, plus the fact that those in hospitals are not as rigidly hierarchical as they were before, particularly males and the senior doctors, has all changed. The whole thing is now Christmas pudding.

Of course, everybody is fighting each other now. If I wanted something I got my colleagues at a meeting to agree and it was implemented. Consultants have lost a lot of authority. There is a structure of committees now that things have to go through and be approved at various levels. You're much more accountable. You can't do it on gut feeling any more, 'I like this; I want to do this.' It's got to be costed and all sorts and on-going costs and the implications of all this to the structure and finances of the hospital. So all that's changed. I think I've had the good times, when I was a semi-God. [laughs] Had a very good time.

It's a funny thing though; it's all mixed up now. It isn't just that you get away from the patients because individually you're still intensely interested, even though other things are happening. But the whole excitement of being a doctor has gone, I think, to some people. I mean some of them are mentally retired. My houseman or juniors used to be mentally retired when they used to come and see me. I mean the idea that the educational system that I'd been involved with all my years, tremendously involved, is educating young doctors! The enthusiasm disappeared like that. Now if you say, 'This [lecture or talk] is going on at this place.' They'll say, 'Oh, but how do we get there?' And I say, 'Well, there's a train, you can go from so-and-so to so-and-so.' And they'll say, 'Yeah, it's a ten minute walk to the station, you know.' Oh, you begin to despair.

Bill Gammie

I think one of the things I've often reflected on, and one finds as one gets older that one tends to have great difficulty in remembering people's names. But I know, since I've retired, one sees lots of familiar faces when one is walking around the streets of Chichester and around in West Sussex. And one knows exactly what one has treated them for but one cannot for the life of you remember exactly their names. This is always fascinating in many ways. It's always very satisfying, too. And one of the advantages we have over our colleagues, those who work in big teaching hospitals or referral centres, is that we actually live amongst the patients that we've treated. You do get the follow-up in a far more pertinent way. You are frequently meeting these people in the course of normal living in your own environment. And I have found that has always been very much more satisfactory.

Paddy Whiteside

The two things that I notice is that nowadays very nearly as many women are trained as men. Also, when junior staff came to the hospital, in the past, they were all resident, but nowadays they are all married and live out and because of this they are less frequently available when there is either an emergency or something very interesting for them to see. I think this has reduced their opportunity of seeing interesting patients and of learning, and here again it is an individual thing rather than a general thing. There are a small number of doctors who will look at their watch and say, 'Six o'clock, I must be off.' In the past everybody worked until the work was finished. I think it's not just in medicine, though, I think it's general in the community.

Eric Lock

Purely and simply the satisfaction of being able to say, 'Well, and you know I started that shop and it's as a result of that that we've been able to do this, that and the other.' And it provides me with an interest. Of course, until my wife got beyond she used to do an afternoon a week in the shop and that sort of thing so it was personal satisfaction of doing something, which I think is a worthwhile job. One could say, as people sort of suggested, well the State provides a National Health Service but I've been in it for sufficiently long to know that there was a hell of a lot the State didn't do and couldn't do, because there still needs to be a personal element. The personal element of the trolley shop, particularly for the long-stay patients; they think it is jolly useful.

Heather Jeremy

Probably sanity. It kept me occupied mentally and physically and I loved every minute of it. I used to get very tired sometimes, but it's something you can get over. It was just something I loved doing, meeting people and actually finding I could organise things on my own as it were [laugh].

Eric Lock

I think that I feel that the organisation has become more impersonal than it used to be when there was Hospital Secretary, basically, at the head, and a Matron; it was a much more friendly organisation.

Christopher Bateman

No, I'd had enough. It becomes repetitive after a time. I'd done it 20 years and you find yourself, you've seen everything and you've done everything and you get to the stage where you start cutting corners and then you suddenly realise that your standards are going to drop and so you have to try harder and harder to keep up your standards. So I thought I'd had enough of it and I still had enough energy to go and do something else. I think we're going to find, either consultants move jobs, in a way that they don't now, or your going to get, as the country gradually gets wealthier and wealthier, you're going to get more and more consultants retiring in their early 50s because they've done eighteen, twenty years in their job and have had enough of it.

Robert Lapraik

Since 1994, it has been extremely busy and interesting because having become a Trust, where, incidentally, we had to demonstrate the viability of the Hospital, we also had to demonstrate that we could operate the Hospital on a sound financial footing. But the background was that Chichester Health Authority was recognised as being under-resourced for the population that it serves. The major driver there is the

The Trust Board, 1994.

fact that the local population is older than the average. We've got 25 per cent of the population [aged] 65 or older. When people are old, they inevitably need more health care. They need, particularly, more hospital stays and more hospital treatment. That was recognised nationally, under what they call the capitation formula, which weights the raw population for a combination of age and social deprivation factors. And really it is only now and in, sort of, late 1996 that the funding of the local population has really been up to the level that was deemed to be fair—it's taken a long time to get there. The purchaser is only able to buy a limited contract of services. It means there is an awful lot of pressure on the providers. Because you can't stop people coming through the door in an emergency, or when they're ill. And there's been a lot of national pressure to bring the waiting list down. So, really the two things have compounded to mean that there has been a lot of work going on at the Hospital: first of all to handle the rising number of emergency admissions that have been coming through the doors of all hospitals across the country, not just St Richard's; and secondly: the government edicts that the waiting list will come down first of all to 18 months and most recently to 12 months. That's meant an awful lot of work and the Hospital staff are under a lot of pressure, but equally it's meant a lot of financial pressure because, really, the resources haven't been there until recently to achieve that.

Christopher Bateman

I don't think there really has been a watershed for the Hospital. I think we are about to have one. I think the new building will lead to far more significant change in the way the hospital works and the standard of practice and what they do at the hospital than anything that's happened before in my lifetime, or my working lifetime. Basically, we'll go from a hospital with no single rooms to a hospital with 25 per cent single rooms and the scope for improving the types of work and the quality of the work and everything is going to be enormous. There's only going to be a small private wing, but its not that its just that. Take haematology, we could never put our patients where we wanted because there weren't enough single rooms and if they're going to be susceptible to infections then they need single rooms. Suddenly, that problem's going to completely disappear, so people can be treated properly. Those who should have been in single rooms will not now be treated in open wards; that's just a sort of parochial example. I mean to work in a hospital where, in this day and age, where you have two 20-bedded wards with one bathroom between them, which is what there is at the moment on South Block, is totally unacceptable. The new hospital will improve morale. It will improve the quality of the staff we attract; it will mean the good staff that we've got will stay rather than moving on. All sorts of spin-offs are going to come.

'High Hopes'—launching the Patients' Charter in 1993.

SELECTED BIBLIOGRAPHY

DHSS, *Second Report of the Joint Working Party on the Organisation of Medical Work in Hospitals* (Cogwheel 11), HMSO, 1972

DHSS, *The Functions of the District General Hospital*, HMSO, 1969

DHSS, *The Future Structure of the NHS*, DHSS, 1971

Gammie, William F.P., DL, FRCS, 'The Hospitals of Chichester', unpublished paper, and private correspondence, nd

Ham, Christopher, *Health Policy in Britain: The Politics and Organisation of the National Health Service*, Macmillan, 1994

Levitt, Ruth and Wall, Andrew, *The Reorganised National Health Service*, Croom Helm, 1984

Mickerson, Jack N., MD, FRCP, 'The City of Chichester and its Contribution to British Medicine', unpublished paper, West Sussex Public Record Office, Acc.No. 8692

Ministry of Health and Scottish Home and Health Department, *Report of the Committee on Senior Nursing Staff Structure* (Salmon Report), HMSO, 1966

Ministry of Health, *The Administrative Structure of the Medical and Related Services in England and Wales*, HMSO, 1968

Ministry of Health, *First Report of the Joint Working Party on the Organisation of Medical Work in Hospitals* (Cogwheel 1), HMSO, 1967

Office of Health Economics, *The NHS Reorganisation*, OHE, 1974

Parliament, *National Health Service Bill*, HMSO, 1946, Cmnd.6761

Parliament, *Social Insurance and Allied Services*, Report by Sir William Beveridge, HMSO, 1942, Cmnd. 6404

Porter, Roy, *The Greatest Benefit to Mankind: A Medical History of Humanity from Antiquity to the Present*, Harper Collins, 1997

Report of the Committee on Local Authority and Allied Personal Social Services, Cmnd. 3703 (Seebohm Report), HMSO, 1968

Royal Commission on the National Health Service, Cmnd. 7615, HMSO, 1979

Secretary of State for Social Services and others, *Caring for People*, HMSO, 1989

Secretary of State for Social Services and others, *Promoting Better Health*, HMSO, 1987

Secretary of State for Social Services and others, *Working for Patients*, HMSO, 1989

Spurgeon, Peter and Barwell, Frederick, *Implementing Change: A Guide for General Managers*, Chapman and Hall, 1991

Spurgeon, Peter (ed.), *The New Face of the NHS*, Longman, 1993

Thatcher, Peter, *Now Another Pharoah*, WSCC, 1988

Whiteside, John 'Paddy', MD, FRCP, 'The History of Chichester's Hospitals', unpublished paper, nd

INDEX

Note: Names in bold are the interviewees. Bold page numbers refer to illustrations.

pressure, 129, 159–60, 180; layout, 46–7;
new buildings, 65, 131–2, 181; origins, xiv–
xv, 2–3, 6–7; Trust status, 121, 130–1,
159–60, 179–80
Salmon Report on nursing staff structures, 50,
52, 120, 133, 135, 147
Sandiford, Brian, anaesthetist, 24
Saunders, Pat, Transport Manager, 8,
18–19, 43–4, 67, 83–4, 109–10, 112–13, **113**
Second World War, 2–3, 7–9; bombing
casualties, 10–11; military casualties, 8–9,
16–17, 21; prisoners of war, 9, 18
**Semmens, Marjorie, Consultant
Paediatrician**, 46, 47–8, 57–8, 79–80, 96,
100–1, 107, **126**, **173**; developments in
paediatrics, 149–51, 158–9, 162–4; social
life, 116
Shepherd, Chris, **138**
Shippam, Miss Everell, gynaecologist, 24, 45, 48
Shippam Ward, **150**
Simson, Jay, surgeon, 143
Skilton, Eric, Office Administrator, 5, 8–9,
15–18, 23, 39–40, 175; admissions, discharges
and burials, 66; Graylingwell Christmas, 34;
on nurses' home, 45; on staff, 62
social life, 27, 32–3, 105, 116–18, 171–4; sports,
32, 113–14, **114**, 116–17, 118
Sparrow, Mrs., Matron, 135
specialisation, 22, 70–1, 90–1, 134–5, 137, 154–5
staff, xv–xvi, 29–30, 79; Houseman, 141;
relations between, 27–30, 104–6, 110–12,
167; senior medical, 45–6, 56, 57–8, 67–9,
77–9, 112; shortages, 20–1, *see also* Matron;
nurses
sterilisation, 93–5, 98; early facilities, 12, 19, 21,
76–7; path lab procedures, 88–90
Stroud, Sir Eric, 128
Superintendent's House, **6**

Tea Bar, 50, 80–1, 131
technology: advances in, 85–90, 98–100, 139,
154–6; early equipment, 23–5; scanners,
120, **128**, 156, **157**, 159; ultrasound, 156
transport, 83–4
Trust Board, **180**
tuberculosis, 63–4, 86, 90

waiting lists, 78–9, 83
Walden, Miss, 41
Wallace, Dr. Edgar, 57
Wallace, Fred, electrician, 110
Ward, Maureen, **172**
wards, 43, 44, **48**
Weeks, Reg, 40
West Sussex Area Health Authority, 120
West Sussex County Council, and St Richard's,
4–5, 20, 36
West Sussex Health Authority, 55
Weston, Garfield, Lesley Goldsmith Centre, 125
Whiteside, Paddy, Consultant Cardiologist,
2, 4–5, 20–1, 22, **33**, 82, 112, **115**, 125, **174**;
on changes, 175–6, 178; Coronary Care
Unit, 90–2; on Medical Centre, 52;
relations with RWSH, 39; Social Club, 118;
on staff accommodation, 46; on technology,
23–5, 86, 87, 161
Whitney, Anne, Chief Nursing Officer, 50
Williams, Mr., surgeon, 95
Willowmead (EMS huts), 6, 7, **17**, **18**, 41, 68,
131; enclosed, 41
Wilson, Donald, rheumatologist, 45, 46
Winkler, Dr. John, 20, 29

X-ray machines, 23, 86, **160**

Zachary Merton Maternity Hospital,
Rustington, 2, 96